The Making of Men

The Making of Men

By

J.W. COOMBES, B.A., A.M.S.T.

WITH THIRTY-SEVEN ILLUSTRATIONS

GYAN

Published by

Gyan Publishing House
5, Ansari Road
Daryaganj, New Delhi-110002
Phone: 011-47034999, 9811692060
E-mail: books@gyanbooks.com

Distribution Network
gyanbooks.com
India, USA, Canada, UK, Australia, France

ISBN : 978-81-212-6394-8 (PB)
First Published, 1920

2nd Impression 2022

Printed at: Gyan Press, Delhi.

THE MAKING OF MEN
Author: J.W. Coombes

Mekala Poligadu

This new admission is shown in the illustration, escorted to the school by two stalwart guardians of the peace, with fixed bayonets. He belongs to a Pamulavadu, or criminal class, which is a sect of the Jogi caste. The boy is fifteen years of age, with both parents living (the father being blind), and earned his livelihood by begging. He is an old offender, with two previous convictions. He was sent to the school for theft of a silver necklace, worth Rs. 6, from the neck of a girl aged six years. He did this on market day, and was instigated to it by another associate.

THE MAKING OF MEN

BY

J. W. COOMBES, B.A., A.M.S.T.

WITH THIRTY-SEVEN ILLUSTRATIONS

1920

CONTENTS

LIST OF ILLUSTRATIONS

PREFATORY NOTE

It has been remarked that one of the present day cults of the child is the fact that whereas school stories were formerly written to be read by school boys, they are now written to be read by grown up persons. That classic book "Tom Brown" describes to us the real school boy human nature—the matter-of-fact and extremely reticent individual—while Stalky and Co. brings out the salient features of modern school life. It has also been remarked that for the masses in England who are taught in Board Schools, no book of an ideal nature exists and the true ideal of a Board School boy has yet to be created.

In India there is a singular deficiency of literature depicting school life anywhere, the notable exception being that relating to the Shantiniketan, the Bolpur School, established by the poet—Rabindranath Tagore. With such a dearth of books on the psychology of the normal Indian child, it is no wonder if the field of research relating to the juvenile criminal should be deserted. The scene of my labours for the past 15 years has been confined to the juvenile institution at Chingleput, and I am a debtor therefore both to the boys and to the State to the extent of making known my experience and the principles which have guided me in my work. It is almost impossible to detach one's personality from a work of this kind, and reminiscences therefore of a personal character have been included. I leave the practical effect of this book for social workers and the general public to determine.

The treatment of the young differs to some extent in various detention schools from one another, and the time has apparently arrived for the appointment of an Inspector-General of Reformatories, or a central authority in India who would discover the most effective methods of work and apply them to the advantage of the pupils. At present a vast amount of experience is being lost, and the problems already solved are re-opened, as though some fresh discovery were in sight, with the result that retrograde steps are taken. New workers come on the scene who have to be taught the work all over again, and continuity of progress thus becomes unattainable.

The object of this book, therefore, is threefold:—(1) To show what Government is doing for the country in this direction, (2) to put on record a few notes gathered in the course of my experience with juvenile criminals, which may be of use to those engaged in the study of juvenile criminality, and (3) to furnish information for a continuity of policy to my successors in office, especially during a transition period, which is often a period of mischief and unrest.

INTRODUCTION

I can think of no better way of introducing the reader to my work than to reproduce below the observations of a sympathetic visitor, who recorded his first impressions of the Chingleput Reformatory in the columns of the *Madras Mail*.

" Chingleput has seen many stirring times. The district abounds in historic incident. Numbers of events, which in their day were of the utmost moment, are on record, while others of no less thrilling import to the folk of the time, have been forgotten. The tide of war has often surged over the country side, and there have been long eras of peace. Weaker races have gone down before the invader, who has established himself, and imposed his rule, until a stronger than he turned him out. Time was when temples and sculptured figures were liberally displayed on every side. To please his wife, the legend runs, the great lord of the place built the five-storeyed Ther Mahal, which is such a conspicuous feature of the landscape. When, at Conjeeveram, thirty or more miles away to the north-westward, the great drums throbbed out their call to worship, others, at appropriate intervals, took up the summons and rolled it on to the Rajah's Palace at Chingleput. Then the Ranee and her ladies hastened to the Ther Mahal and sped swiftly up the steps which seem to have been designed for children's feet, so diminutive is their tread. The topmost storey gained, and emerging from the narrow parallel stairway to the roof, the ardent eye of devotion seemed able to discern the golden apices of the sacred fane and the Ranee joined her prayers in the rites which were being celebrated so far away. Those were peaceful times, but they could not last for ever and the reign of the Rajahs of the sixteenth century was overthrown by invasion from the north. The new-comers, in their hatred for figured things tore down and destroyed, and built the fort, using much of the wonderful sculpture in wall, ramparts and bastions. But the solidly built stone Ther Mahal was too enduring to be utterly broken up and exists unto this day. The era of the Muhammadan passed and more strangers came. This time from the distant West—men of another type and mode of thought. First one nation and then another seized the old Fort and dominated the district, and so time passed on. Chingleput is perhaps not so important now as it was in the days which are gone. Other times brought other manners, and the Fort's storied memories were desecrated. The home of conquerors and kings, fair ladies and religion was degraded to the uses of a common jail. Then another turn of fortune's wheel. For the last thirty years, the morning sun, when he gilds the eastern hill tops, floods with glory the shimmering surface of the peaceful lake and clothes anew with dazzling splendour the snowy walls and terraces of the dead Ranee's Ther Mahal, also illuminates as beautiful and romantic a story as any century can tell. It is a tale that is still in the telling, for it is the living testimony of a wise and skilfully directed effort to give the equipment of the good citizen to the children who have had no fair start in life, no chance, no opportunities, no knowledge of right and wrong, or the manners which make men. It is the successful attempt to save the little unfortunates, who, for want of light and leading have taken the only step possible to them, the first on the descent to Avernus, the tiny Ishmaelites whose hand is against every man, even as every man's hand is against them. It is the story of

"THE SQUARE DEAL."

"I don't go much on religion,
I never ain't had no show;
But I've got a middlin' tight grip, sir,
On the handful o' things I know"

And I think that saving a little child,
And bringing him to his own
Is a derned sight better business
Than loafing around the Throne."

The tender flush of dawn was suffusing the darkness and the stars were one by one beginning to withdraw from their vigilant watch o'er the sleeping earth at the advance of the day relief of the sun, when reveille rang out as shrilly clear as ever it did in military camp. The light came on apace and soon the neat buildings, trim walks, ordered squares, woke to the activities of day under the shade of stately sacred Bo, coconut palm, and rain tree, whose topmost leaves already quivered in the light morning air.

It was not long before the Superintendent of the Reformatory was making his rounds, inspecting the spotlessly clean dormitories with their long rows of swinging hammocks—the blankets were already out on the parade grounds airing. There is no available secret hiding place at Chingleput Fort for the pests about which railway travellers are so vocal. The only cots are in the hospital, where some six or seven boys were inmates—detained by nothing more serious than slight ailments, for they were all erect, alert, and smiling as they smartly saluted the Superintendent, who in brief sentences described his system. It is military discipline, rudimentary education, a healthful mixture of work, which will make a skilled craftsman, and games which fit lads, better than anything else can, to give a fair showing in the business of good citizens.

The weavers' house, with its complicated-looking looms—none driven by power, other than the boys' strong arms—was inspected. Then were visited in turn the smithy and its equipment of European and Indian anvils, the metal workers' shop, the saw-pit, where every year seven or eight tons of imported teak are sawn up for use in the carpenters' and the furniture-making shops. Next the miniature brick works where the clay is moulded into regulation form and sun dried—the school cannot yet boast a kiln. Properly burnt bricks of orthodox size are used to teach the bricklaying art in walls, pillars, etc. Everywhere the prevailing note is efficiency and thoroughness.

Sunday is an off-day at Chingleput, and yet for all that it is a busy one. The lads do their washing and mending and little odd jobs of their own and in reality it is a very full day, although duties are light. The boys were all about the grounds. Without exception their happy alertness and well set up frames made them good to look upon. The secret of it all is that they are not driven to their tasks. A healthy rivalry is encouraged. The lads are not divided into Houses. The respective trades are their divisions. The weavers play football and hockey matches with the carpenters, the smiths, and the masons. Every trade has its garden and the rivalry in gardening is tremendous; it ranks amongst the games. Challenge shields are provided as trophies to be won by the best trades at football, hockey, etc., and gardening. It is a red-letter day and a proud trade when a shield is won. It is forthwith hung up in the trade house where it remains until the holders are defeated. As often as possible teams are selected to play the school, and the school sometimes selects its best players to meet visiting teams on the fine playing field. Each lad at Chingleput is imbued with the high desire of trying to be worthy of his membership of the best squad of the best trade division of the best school in all India, and to maintain this ideal both at work and play.

The lads have their own monitors and annually elect of their number the one whom they regard as worthy to wear the medal as the best boy in the school. Strange as it may appear, these lads, few of whom have ever known home life, but like Topsy, have "just growed," whose only commandment, before they joined the school, was the eleventh, by whom dexterous thievery was once regarded as the supreme virtue, and plausible lying an accomplishment to be greatly desired, many of whom (alas! the sorrow of it) are at Chingleput for graver, darker, crimes than petty theft, are being taught that here they are trusted. A sense of honour is being instilled into them and with a wonderful result. The test of all reformatory work is the extent and permanence of the reform effected. The ordeal comes when the boys go back to their home towns and villages. At one time reconvictions were as high as 45 per cent., but that figure has gradually dwindled. At last it was only fifteen and now, marvellous to say, it has been for some years just *one per cent.*, a great achievement and one of which Mr Coombes, the Superintendent, and the Government of

Madras may well be proud. It means that the lads have not only been thoroughly trained in their trades, but that they have been animated with a sense of responsibility, a desire to uphold the honour of the school, and a determination to play the game of life as strenuously and as sportingly as ever they played at soccer or hockey. Such a result can only have been obtained by careful, anxious, nay, loving thought, and before half a dozen words have been exchanged with the Superintendent one feels that here is an enthusiast and a man who loves his work and loves his boys; one who has made this work a lifelong study, and has not only read all that has been written thereon, but has travelled the whole world round in search of ideas as to how best to save the potential criminal and direct his path upward, so that he may become a useful and respected member of society. With such a man at the head of the institution, one whose interest in each lad is so profound that he makes a living study of each boyish temperament, is it after all a wonder that these one-time pitiful waifs of the cities and the off-scourings of the villages, lads of the criminal classes, call the Superintendent Father and regard him with an affection they never bestowed upon their natural parents?

The Pets, the Museum, the Sculptures

A visit to the pets followed. They were well-fed monkeys, guinea fowl and pigeons, and at that moment some of the lads were watching the flights of their favourite birds from the summit of the Ther Mahal. After this it is not surprising to hear that there is a school museum wherein are duly preserved the specimens and natural objects picked up about the Fort, in Sunday afternoon walks, or during annual campings at Seven Pagodas, or other seaside locality. Here are also drawings, and samples of work done, and quite a library of books in Telugu, Tamil and Hindustani. There is no attempt to teach English to the lads at Chingleput, unless they desire to learn it. Instruction is imparted in the boys' own tongue by the masters, notable among whom is Mr Antonsiwami Pilai, poet, violinist, scholar, and earnest lieutenant of the Superintendent. A noticeable feature in the grounds is the number of trees which have been planted by those who have been to see the school, each being labelled with the name of the honoured visitor, and securely fenced, carefully watered and otherwise tended. During building work which has been done, many of the pieces of sculpture which three or four hundred years ago formed such a conspicuous feature of the Rajah's court, have been discovered and they have all been set up in appropriate places and some of the figures, probably stone portraits of people who bulked largely in the local annals of that distant day, are in a capital state of preservation—notably one of a Rajah in the attitude af prayer, strangely reminiscent of the crusaders' effigies so frequent in old European churches.

A walk round the ramparts, a peep into the Band room and a

cursory survey of the shining rows of brass instruments, and then it was time for Church. The service is held in a pleasant school house which has been fitted up as a Chapel. On the walls hang mottoes in English, Tamil, and Telugu. A new one is hung every year. That over the altar seemed to be the motive which governs everything in this wonderful school—" Whatsoever thy hand findeth to do, do it with all thy might.—1907." The success of the last twelve years lies in its application. Another was " Do unto others as ye would that men should do unto you." And the congregation? Seven adults—some members of the staff—and ten or twelve boys who are entered in the school books as Protestants. There is no attempt at proselytising here. The Hindu lads have their shrine, where they are encouraged to offer their devotions, and Hindu gentlemen of the district, principally Vakils, are invited to give them addresses on their faith, and encourage them in good living. The Muhammadans too have their little Mosque. The boys of that other great branch of Christendom have their neatly kept Oratory of St. Aloysius in the Ther Mahal, where, at times, a good Father says Mass for them, and where they daily offer supplication. The Anglicans get a quarterly visit from a clergyman. But this Sunday morning the Superintendent, with all becoming reverence, conducted the little service, and the Bandmaster read one of the lessons. The old familiar hymns were sung and then a short homily, the benediction said, and the simple act of worship was over.

While looking round the room one of the lads, with evident pride, pulled aside a couple of curtains and thus revealed two panels with long lists of names of the boys from this school who have been serving in the Great War. The large majority, nearly a hundred, were combatants, and the remainder, some fifty or sixty, were in the Labour and Porter Corps—and they have all done well. The Roll of Honour has not yet been compiled, it will be some day, but these names, even as they stand, redound to the credit of Chingleput Reformatory School, and the lads have every right to be proud of them. After breakfast there was another interesting event. The whole school was assembled and rose to attention as the Superintendent entered the long narrow room. A Tamil school song was sung and then the Superintendent gave the heads of a short address upon " Duty," which were elaborated by two school masters in Telugu and Tamil. The boys were invited to answer questions, and several did so with readiness. And the lesson was driven home, that, even as Nelson, at Trafalgar, expected every sailor to do his duty, so the Chingleput School expects all its boys to do theirs, not only in school, at work and at play, but when they leave it and school days are over. It was a striking sight, nearly 250 smiling faced, snowy uniformed lads, each sporting in his cap the badge of his trade. In addition many of them wore bright metal badges and medals, telling of years of faultless welldoing. As only the Tamil boys had sung, by special desire, the Telugu lads were asked for an example of their tunefulness. The request was complied with with great heartiness and the youthful performer on the Indian harmonium joined in the Telugu song with as much zest as he had sung the Tamil.

But there was a sad heart there that Sunday morning. A rather bigger boy came forward and with a few words, only half audible through suppressed emotion, garlanded the Superintendent to the accompaniment of much applause. It was explained that this was his last day in the school and on the morrow he was to go out into the world and leave the home of so many happy years, to ply his trade and face the temptations of the city on his own account. There were a few sympathetic and encouraging words from the Superintendent, much clapping of hands and the whole school broke into a farewell song. The lad was evidently greatly touched by the little ceremony. He will carry its recollection, with other memories, into his new life in Madura. He may not find his task an easy one, but his Superintendent, and the boys he leaves behind him, all believe that he will quit himself as a man made by Chingleput.

The lads had their dinner, a most substantial one, under the trees and then there was one other event. About 3 o'clock the bugles rang out again and the Superintendent went to the parade ground. The school—not a specially selected platoon or company—was drawn up as a battalion in column. A retired Indian officer, Jamadar Parasurama Naicker, was in charge of the parade and the Monitors, carrying little Union Jacks, were in command of companies. Then followed half an hour of brisk drill, admirably carried out in quick time and sometimes at the double. The Jamadar, like every one else at Chingleput, has his heart in his job, and he handled that battalion as only a tried soldier could. And the lads were up to their work. The company officers knew theirs. It is true there were little irregularities now and again, but then it must be always remembered there were many newcomers in the ranks and it was *the school* at drill. All the while the brass band played in approved regimental style. The display finished with dumb-bell exercises, and the parade was dismissed. The band played several more airs and the rest of the lads gathered round, as if they had never heard a band before, and curiously enough they all seemed to be beating time with their toes!

Half an hour later the school marched " with martial trumpets braying, and drums that throb and roll, and the music they were playing was a song that wakes the soul." The companies went by in column of fours, each monitor captain smartly saluting and the lads with eyes bright, and heads high, swung past for their Sunday afternoon " walk " outside the Fort. " And many a lad rejoices to know his duty plain . . . . . for e'en though death may win him, one thing will never die—the soul that wakes within him; as the band goes by." A mile or two from the Fort and a halt was called and the boys dispersed for a little while, until recalled by the bugles to return *home*—and not a lad was missing, for the Chingleput boys love their school. It is only the new-comers who sometimes run away.

The lads, when they arrive at the school, are more often than not under-fed, undeveloped little creatures, whose struggle against adverse circumstances has made them prematurely careworn and anxious. One of the first tasks is to teach them "how to smile." Good food, kindly sympathetic treatment, and the first six months in open air occupations work wonders in them. The precious possession of happy boyhood is restored to them: mind and body are healthfully occupied, with marvellous results in appearance and physical well being. The dry records of the periodical weighing tell a wonderful story to one who can appreciate figures.

. . . .

Once more *reveille*. In the grey dawn numbers of people are waiting for the mail train. It is late this morning, not an uncommon occurrence on Indian lines. But at last it comes fussing along into the station. On the off side, where he is not likely to be disturbed by unfeeling officials, nor harried by his natural enemy, the policeman, stands a little figure, naked save for the merest wisp of filthy rag about his loins, a dusty, dirty tiny lad with tousled elf-locks falling to his shoulders, lustrous bright eyes and a graceful pose, his little hands are held beseechingly to the travellers as he shrilly utters unintelligible words. No one is sympathetic, no one heeds his artless prayer. The whistle shrieks, the engine backs as it makes up its mind to get under way again. The forlorn little face breaks into a sunny smile. Accustomed to disappointment he bears no ill-will and gaily waves a shred of rag as the mail steams out. Poor little waif! What is his future? What is he to become? No career but crime lies before him! unless, unless, he gains admission to Chingleput School. God grant that the offence, whatever it is which sends him there, may be a very trivial one, nothing which will leave a dark stain of bitter regret upon his yet unsmirched soul. But there is no other way, "the pity o' it." If he is to have a chance to be a decent man and a good citizen he must commit a crime!! We are taught that it is wrong to sin that good may come! Alas, that our philanthropy should be so poor, our love for the children so pinchbeck, that millions such as this little lad, by the very conditions of birth and environment, are doomed to careers of crime and to become pests of society—if they are not "so fortunate" as to be caught early. Poor little chap, yours and the salvation of countless others, is the problem which awaits solution at the hands of a civilisation which professes love and admiration of Him who said: "Whoso shall receive one such little child, in my Name, receiveth Me."

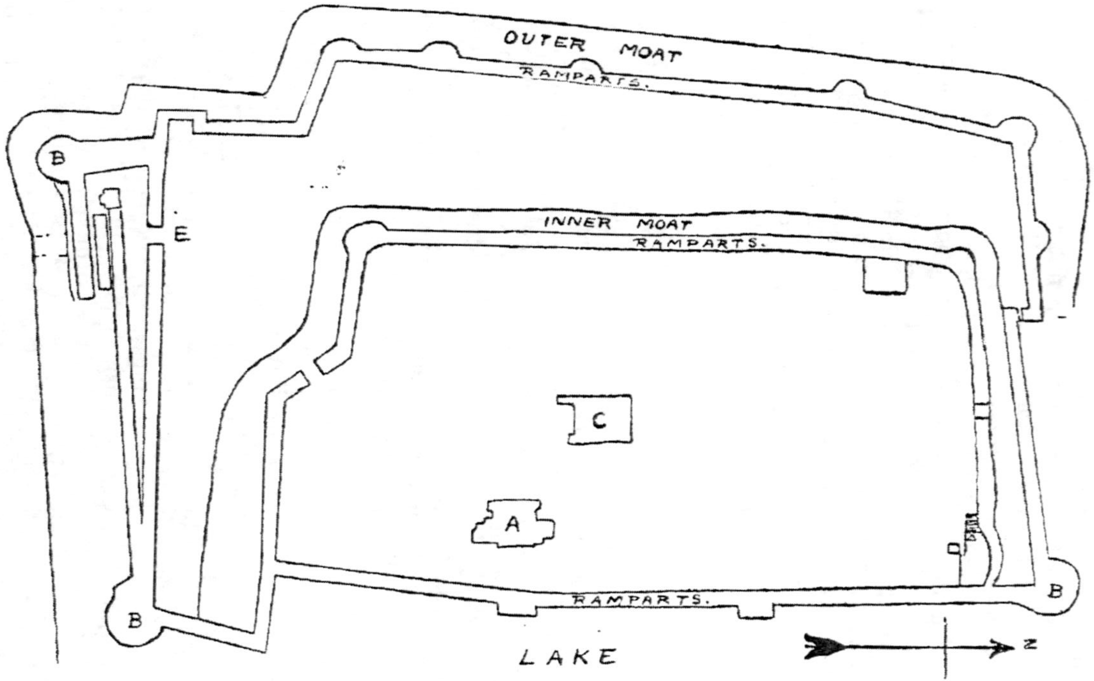

THE ANCIENT FORT OF CHINGLEPUT

A. SUPERINTENDENT'S HOUSE. C. THER MAHAL.

B. BASTIONS. E. ENTRANCE.

THE MAKING OF MEN

CHAPTER I

TREATMENT OF THE JUVENILE OFFENDER

It would be interesting to ascertain what treatment was meted out to young offenders in the time of the old Rajahs, and what was the Hindu ideal of justice in such cases. We do get glimpses of the state of things from stories current in the folk-lore of the people, but as far as I am aware no systematic search has been made for the laws—if any such existed—relating to minors. A few current stories which I reproduce throw a side light on the subject:—

(1) The people of a certain village used to go regularly to market, carrying their baskets of produce upon their heads. A man of the village also went to market carrying his little son sitting upon his shoulder. In the crowd, the little son was able to help himself as he pleased from the baskets of his neighbours. The man was, no doubt, surprised to find his son with a bunch of plantains, but instead of correcting him he told him that he was a very clever boy, and shared the plantains. From small beginnings this led to greater things until at last the boy was caught and brought before the Magistrate. The boy was asked what explanation he had to give of the facts appearing against him in evidence, and he told the Magistrate that he had always been taught by his father that what he did was right and clever. The Magistrate therefore sent the father to jail and released the boy on promise of future good behaviour.

(2) The following story illustrates the trial by villagers who formed the Court in the case of theft committed by a boy. A boy happened to be born on a new moon day.

The superstition runs that he will become a thief by profession. The parents were a little anxious on that account, and they spent many a sad hour thinking about it. The child grew to be a youth and began to attend school, and one day he asked his parents why they always wore a melancholy face. The parents at first hesitated to tell him the reason but subsequently spoke thus: "My son, it is decreed by fate that one born on a new moon day, like you, should turn out a thief by profession." The suggestion gave the boy food for reflection, and his thoughts during the night ran in that direction. To fulfil his destiny, he hoped to try the experiment on a certain new moon night. He entered a rich man's house by the backyard to thieve, but as it was past midnight he wished to hasten home and found some chaff in a heap. "My grandmother at home will feel comfortable during the winter nights if I take this chaff for her fireplace," said he, and having gathered some, he tied it in his waist cloth and returned home before daybreak. In his over anxiety he took more than his cloth would hold, and wisps of chaff marked the ground between his house and that of the owner. Next morning the theft was traced to his house and he was arrested as the thief. The villagers found him guilty for taking a false step so early in life, but he put the blame on his parents for allowing his mind to be predisposed towards the act, and the parents having confessed their guilt in the matter, the boy was forgiven, The boy, to the delight of all, turned over a new leaf and rose to a high position in life.

(3) This story points to the provision in ancient law for appeal or revision. The King alone had power to revise a judgment, and in the case of the juvenile, mercy prevailed over retribution, for the Hindu Shastras are careful to extol mercy as higher than punishment, and mild punishment as more efficacious than severity of punishment. A child lost its father early in life and was brought up by the widowed mother. In her fondness for the child the mother overlooked many of his early faults. The child grew to be a turbulent youth, and trusting to his mother's

ready forgiveness, he was tempted to go astray. He first started by stealing a pencil, a pen, a slate or a book. The mother would admonish him gently, but turning a deaf ear to her every advice he rushed headlong in his criminal career. From pilferings and petty thefts he became a robber-in-chief, and with the help of a small band he waylaid travellers and looted houses by night. He did not enjoy his mad pursuit very long, for he was ordered to be hanged for many a cruel murder committed at night. When about to be executed, he besought of the executioner as a last request that he might be allowed to speak to the mother, and this was granted. He approached his mother and tore off her ear, reproaching her thus: "If early in life you had chastised me for stealing a pencil or a slate at school I should not have come to the gallows."

The executioner brought the matter to the notice of the Governor, who showed mercy to the juvenile, and forgave him. He thereafter grew to be a great and good man, and was noted for his many benefactions.

A recent case, however, happened in Malabar where a father cut off the little finger of his child because he misappropriated some money with which he was entrusted. This was the practice, I was told, in ancient Malabar, and it certainly errs on the side of cruelty.

Those were supposed to be the good old times. But what happened in the not-so-good old times may be gathered from the remarks made by an Anglo-Indian Judge at the Silver Jubilee Anniversary of the school in the year 1912. When he went into a Moffusil sub-jail he found a little girl of 10 or 12, who had just been sentenced to five days' imprisonment for stealing plantains. He obtained from her a petition of appeal to himself, sent for her parents and let her out on bail. He did not remember what he did with her, but he was certain she did not go back to jail, and unfortunately he could not put her father in jail instead. He remembered also some years ago an incident in the Bellary District. That district was much worried from its geographical positiion, having Hyderabad State on the north, Mysore State on the south, and Bombay on the west. When criminal gangs find the climate of any one of these States growing too hot for them they migrate to a cooler climate, and incidentally pass through Bellary. They generally meet with much attention, and are provided with escorts. On one occasion he found that they had been provided with accommodation in one of "His Majesty's rest houses," men, women and children. He did not like having all the children in the jail, and so he turned them all out, with a sufficient number of females to look after them. The presumption is that in the not-so-good old times the children went to jail. What became then of them in jail? They associated with criminals, and instead of being reformed they learned new methods of theft from their elders and became confirmed criminals. Contrast this with the present treatment of the boys. The Hindu Law vests the guardianship of minors in the sovereign as parent of the State. The natural parents are mere delegates. If these delegates are found to be unfit, because they tell their sons they are clever boys when they purloin plantains from a neighbour's basket, the boys are removed from their guardianship. His Majesty the King Emperor resumes his authority as guardian through the Local Government, and sends the boy to the school, and the reformatory is the school to which he is sent. It cannot be too strongly emphasised that the reformatory is a school and not a jail. The first thing the boy is taught when he goes there is to forget the reason why he came, and to forget his past and his evil practices. He has to look forward to a new future and be equipped for the battle of life.

These schools, however, were the outcome of earlier arrangements, under which juvenile offenders were kept in separate wards in jails, and where some endeavour was made to give them an industrial training. With a growth of this nature it was perhaps excusable that the mistake of placing these schools under the control of the Jail Department instead of under the Educational Department should have been made, but it was fatal.

The Madras Government, with commendable foresight, brought the Madras School, which was for a few months fostered by the Inspector-General of Jails under the management of the Education Department, and at a station where there was no prison. At the suggestion of Lord George Hamilton, the then Secretary of State for India, the Government of India called for a report on the working of the system in the Madras Presidency, with a view to its being followed in other provinces, as it was patent that the work of reformation could not be carried on with any hope of success in a school which was associated in the minds of the boys themselves and in public estimation with the idea of a prison. The views then expressed on the subject of the proposed transfer are old-fashioned enough to raise a smile, and show a lack of appreciation for new methods of work and a disinclination for experiment. An Inspector-General of Prisons wrote:—"I cannot say that I think there would be any better results if the schools were placed under the Education Department. These schools must be run to a certain extent on prison lines. The inmates are criminals and cannot be treated as ordinary school boys, and it may be presumed that the Prison Department would be better able to control such places than a department which in no way concerns itself with the management of criminals." How utterly opposed to reform was the root idea contained in these lines that a juvenile offender was a criminal. A Director of Public Instruction had even stated that to remove the reformatory to a place where there was no prison would be presumably to throw the responsibility for its successful working upon the Educational Department—a Department which had not the expert knowledge which the Jail Department possessed, and which seemed to be essential in dealing with criminals whether old or young. The obvious answer to this was that the Jail Department never did profess to have exclusive expert knowledge in the work of reforming criminals.

A Superintendent of a jail was of opinion that for the class of boys confined in the reformatories, who were mostly thieves by habit, and many of whom were violent in temper and when in a passion really dangerous, no discipline short of that now enforced would be sufficient, while the discipline would be likely to grow slack under the administration of educational officers. The expression of such an opinion passes condemnatory judgment upon itself, for if a schoolmaster of the right stamp cannot maintain discipline, it is questionable whether the training of an officer in any other department is likely to produce a better disciplinarian. Leaving the question of strict discipline alone, the accessories of the Education Department are more conducive to moral reformation than the Judicial Department, the function of which is rather the detection and punishment of crime. And this aspect of the question had so forcibly appealed to the Secretary of State for India that in spite of the fact that the Governments of Bombay, of Bengal and of Burma, and the Chief Commissioner of the Central Provinces, were not inclined to accept the proposal of the transfer of the management of their reformatories to the Education Department, Lord George Hamilton affirmed that he would be glad to see the Madras system adopted in other provinces, as reformatories should be mainly schools for the education and reform of boys, and not jails for their punishment by long periods of incarceration.

The Government of India accordingly, after making a careful examination of the system of management and training followed in the different schools and of its results, resolved upon the transfer of all the schools to the Educational Department, on the ground that the Department which has experience of the training of youth is likely to be more successful in the management of such institutions than the Department which deals with the punishment of criminals.

Apart from these considerations, there are several important advantages to be derived from emphasizing the school aspect of the reformatories. National sympathy on the part of the Indian would be more readily enlisted on their behalf, and make it easier for the boys to obtain employment, the school itself being able to assist them to a greater degree; while the boys, feeling less shame at having been connected with the school, are readier to accept its help and keep up communication with it, and thus enable the authorities to keep a watch over them after they leave, for at least a period of three years. In all these aspects of the question, the Chingleput Reformatory School has always been held up as a pattern.

The orderly appearance of the boys even at that time struck one forcibly at a first visit—a fact which called for remark by the Honourable Mr Cardew, a former Inspector-General of Prisons, when he drew a comparison between this institution and that at Alipore, then under the Jail Department. Writing with the knowledge of after events, it is now freely admitted that Madras adopted the correct course to follow. The administration is such that the 'Old Boys' are not ashamed of their connection with the school. They visit the school to recall old memories and give expression to feelings of pleasure. It is no unusual sight to find an ex-pupil in the full uniform of a bandsman of a native regiment knock for admission, spend the day at the reformatory, take his old place in the school band, join in the boys' sports, and before leaving ask the Deputy Superintendent, as a special favour, to take his photograph, to the amusement and delight of the whole school. The practical outcome of this feeling is, that it makes it easier for the authorities to keep a watch over ex-pupils, whose whereabouts would, perhaps, be otherwise unknown.

The Government of India rightly pointed out, too, that the system adopted for the moral and industrial training of the boys and their schooling was much better in Madras than that followed in any other province, and that the main object of fitting them for a useful life was kept steadily in view. Here strict discipline is maintained without difficulty, but it differs in character from the discipline enforced in a jail, and tends to teach the boys self-reliance and self-respect. These are the facts that clinched the whole matter in the face of great opposition to the proposal of the transfer. A Jail is a jail and a School is a school, and no sitting on the fence or jack-in-the-box attitude can ever help the cause of reformation. Compromise is an effective method to be adopted where adults and men fixed in habits and bent upon carrying out their desires are the materials to be dealt with, but in the case of juveniles with a plastic surface for fixing impressions, the attitude of suspicion should find no place, and the inmates being boys must be treated as boys, with an environment conducive to physical and moral well-being.

There is still plenty of up-hill work to be done in trying to educate the public, and even officials in authority, in the fact that the reformatory is a school. The attitude which some people take up towards the institution and its inmates may be gauged from a typical passage-at-arms between a Superintendent and a Justice of the Peace. A Magistrate sent a boy to the school, and in his detention order stated his age to be "over 10 years—viz. about 15 years." In the High Court of Judicature the order was pronounced to be irregular in form, as the Lower Court did not state whether the prisoner was under the age of 15 years. Accordingly a warrant followed, summoning the boy to appear again in order that the Court might record evidence as to age and revise the previous order. The boy was sent in charge of a peon of the school, who seemed to have availed himself of the hospitality of an ex-reformatory boy and stayed in his house for the night, his presence being required on the following morning at the Court House.

Here was a golden opportunity for the lad who evidently had enough of school discipline, to fight shy of it. He had roamed about to his heart's content in the open country as one of nature's free-born children, and he was not going to be cooped up again within the walls of the school. No sooner did he sniff the air of possible liberty than the thought of escape gripped him. He was helped, though unintentionally, in his proposed adventure by the maudlin peon. Steeped in the traditions of proper and decent educational up-bringing, the peon thought it did no credit to the noble Department to which he belonged that suspicious looks much less fetters should be allowed to embarrass the urchin in his future rising to respectability, he having become enrolled a pupil of the school. He was right in his view, only that he made the mistake of not exercising care and watchfulness under the disguised garb of decency, particularly as the youth was a "freshman." It happened that while he was jotting down the details of expenses, the lad made himself scarce, relieving, at the same time, the peon of four rupees which he had placed by his side.

The Magistrate waxed warm over the breach of the law of custody, and in his letter reporting the escape he stated that the 'boy convict' had been allowed to escape, and that the peon was sent in custody (what an indignity to a peon of a time-honoured and respected Department) to the Inspector of Police for investigation, and report if any offence under section 225—A, I.P.C. could be made out against him. Gratuitously he pointed out to the Superintendent of the school that the juvenile should not have been entrusted to a peon but to a proper police guard (Oh, horror !), under the rules framed under the Prisoners' Testimony Act III. of 1900. The Superintendent pointed out that the youth was not a 'boy convict' but a pupil of the school, and as such he was sent in charge of a school peon. The Magistrate of course took up the challenge, and in a further note remarked that he did not agree that juvenile prisoners committed to the Superintendent's custody became pupils in the ordinary sense of the term. In his opinion they were to be deemed prisoners in a special prison. He, however, did not press the point, but preferred to take his stand behind section 34 of the Prisoners' Testimony Act III. of 1900 applicable to reformatory schools and to detention therein, and according to the rules framed under the Act he was of opinion that the boy should have been escorted by two police constables. The despatch, therefore, of the juvenile under the custody of a school peon was contrary to law. But at the same time he admitted a doubt as to how far the peon was legally bound to hold the "prisoner" in custody. In the end, the peon was departmentally punished and the police charge against him was withdrawn.

The juvenile was captured shortly after, and being guilty of the offence of having escaped from lawful custody, he was convicted by the second-class Magistrate and sentenced to six months' rigorous imprisonment, and as the District Medical Officer stated that he was then above 15 years of age, and as it could not be possibly proved that the boy was less than 15 years, he was entitled, in the language of the Court, 'to the benefit of the doubt' and he was therefore sent to fulfil the remaining period of his sentence in jail. It was indeed a poor sort of 'benefit' for the lad—a short sentence in jail in lieu of a three years' industrial training in a reformatory school!

For future guidance the Government of Madras was pleased to pass an order that as they considered it undesirable to send boys from the reformatory school in charge of police constables, the present practice of sending them in the custody of peons would be allowed to continue. The particular question has now been laid to rest, but how far the main principle has been understood of keeping the juvenile away from the police and from unfriendly treatment, and if understood, to what degree it is acted upon, cannot be answered satisfactorily.

It is not unnatural, however, to expect that in time there will be a growing trend of opinion in the direction of placing a diminishing amount of reliance upon the police, and those who administer the criminal law for the reform of the delinquent, and the success of the Chingleput School under the education authorities ought to hasten the process of entirely eradicating the antagonistic tendency of viewing the school as a special prison, or as a hybrid institution to be shuttle-cocked between the Educational and Judicial Departments.

The passing of the Reformatory Schools Act in 1876, which led to the establishment in India of the first seven reformatory schools, marked an important stage in the history of the treatment of juvenile delinquency in this country. The child then came to be viewed as an offspring of the State, to be cared for by it, and not as an enemy to be punished by it. The Reformatory Act recognised that the criminal career of a child was not of his own making but was the result of conditions over which he had no control. Reformatory schools were therefore established to provide a suitable atmosphere for moral growth as well as the means of giving youthful offenders an industrial training.

Prior to this, the position of the juvenile offender differed very little from that of the adult criminal. Under twelve or thirteen, a boy was charged by the police, either alone or in conjunction with accomplices, for a criminal offence. He was put up before a magistrate, and was remanded to a sub-jail till the case was tried. Here he associated with older criminals, and in many cases was probably made one degree worse. If the boy were found guilty, he was transferred to a central jail where he herded with other prisoners of varying degrees of criminality. Being a first offender, his detention was of short duration—too short for any manual training, but quite sufficient to have any sense of decency knocked out. By familiarity with hardened criminals, his first feelings of shame and disgrace were blunted. The punishment intended to remedy matters failed, and the road to a criminal career widened. The first step towards the amelioration of the juvenile was taken when separate accommodation was provided for them in jails, and an attempt was made to give them an industrial training for a period which was subsequently found to be too short to be successful.

Hence the introduction of a reformatory scheme engaged the attention of the legislature about the year 1861, and in the codes of criminal procedure passed respectively in 1861 and 1872, the legislature kept in view the necessity of enabling Courts and Magistrates to send juvenile offenders to reformatories. In 1867, the Government of the Madras Presidency made a forcible representation on the subject, and the Government of India, in passsing Orders, described as insuperable the difficulty of establishing an effectual reformatory scheme in the absence of direct religious teaching. In 1875, the Government of India came to the conclusion that it was undesirable to postpone resort to legislation on the subject, and in the Supplement to the *Fort St George Gazette*, dated 17/8/1875, a statement of the policy of the Supreme Government on the Reformatory Schools Act was published. Briefly put, it was to establish in British India institutions, which as regards males might serve the combined purposes of the reformatory schools and the industrial schools so successfully carried on in England, under 29 and 30 Vic. cc. 117, 118.

The peculiar circumstances of India rendered it inexpedient to bring girls within the scope of the law. Local Governments were empowered to establish reformatory schools (which were defined so as to include schools in which industrial training was provided), or to use as reformatory schools, schools kept by persons willing to obey such rules as Government might prescribe. Three classes of boys were liable to be sent to reformatory schools: (*a*) boys under fourteen, convicted of offences punishable with transportation or imprisonment, but not sentenced; (*b*) boys under twelve sentenced to imprisonment; and (*c*) boys under fourteen who associated with thieves, vagrants, etc., or were without visible means of subsistence. The minimum time of detention in a reformatory school was two years, the maximum seven years. But no boy was to be detained after he attained the age of sixteen.

As to the expenses of these schools, municipalities were empowered to apply municipal funds for their establishment and maintenance, and Magistrates of the first class were empowered to order the parents of youthful offenders to contribute a moderate monthly sum to their support.

Provision was also made for the control and management of the schools. There was a Board of Control, and two at least of the Managers were to be natives of India. They had power to license youthful offenders to employers of labour, to cancel such licenses at the employer's request, and to apprentice youthful offenders.

In the following year, the Reformatory Schools Act V. of 1876 was passed by the Governor-General of India in Council, and the first school was opened at Alipore, near Calcutta, on the 20th February 1878, but it was only after several years that an Order of the Madras Government, dated 5th May 1882, No. 320, Judicial Department referred to a Committee the general question whether it was necessary or desirable to bring the Act into force in this Presidency.

The objections to the reformatory system involving

matters of principle were—(1) that which may be called the religious difficulty; (2) the removal of juveniles from their homes and friends. The first objection, if valid, was equally valid against the whole system of State Education in India. While the Government adhered to the principle that no creed should be taught in schools conducted on the principle of religious neutrality, it not only allowed but directed the great truths of religion and morality common to all mankind to be taught in schools. Apart from religious instruction, much might be effected by moral influence and example, and by teaching habits of obedience, regularity and industry.

The Committee therefore came to the conclusion that the Government should not be deterred from establishing a reformatory merely on the score of religious difficulty. The second objection was that where the distance was great and the climate different, the removal to a central reformatory to Madras would practically be adding transportation to imprisonment. One great object in the reformatory system must be to remove children from the influences of bad associates and surroundings, and even of their parents, where the example of those parents was evil. The State stepped in when the parents forfeited all claim to consideration by neglect of their duties, or by having encouraged their children to crime. The hope was, however, expressed that in time reformatories might be established at different centres. The Committee quoted the opinion of the late Miss Carpenter as to the kind of institutions that were needed. "In the first place there should be nothing of the jail element in reformatory schools, except the element of detention, and that was not to be effected by walls, bolts or bars, but only by means of moral discipline.

"These schools are not to be in any way like prisons."

The Committee was also of opinion that in the selection of the teachers recruitment should be made from the lower castes, and perhaps for choice, Indian Christians. The great majority of the boys being of the lower castes and classes, teachers of the class suggested would find it more easy to sympathise with the boys they would have to deal with and take more real interest in the attempt to raise the moral tone of the pupils than would perhaps be possible for teachers of the higher castes. The attitude of the Madras Government was still further strengthened by the judicial pronouncements of the late Judge Kernan. Times without number he pressed upon this point, because juveniles in those days were committed to the Sessions as the Magistracy had not jurisdiction to try certain offences in which they were concerned. The result was that on conviction they were huddled together with those hardened in crime, and consequently when their terms of imprisonment expired they pursued the calling of those with whom they were associated in prison. No handicraft was taught, no discipline maintained, and no lessons inculcated to make them better citizens when they grew up.

With this report of the Committee before them, the Madras Government passed Orders that the Reformatory Schools Act should be applied to this Presidency, and a school was declared open within the fort at Chingleput on the 15th October 1887 with accommodation for 86 pupils. The buildings occupied belonged to the late district jail, and recourse was had to the "patch and alter" policy—an absolute mistake—because the buildings conformed very badly with the type requisite for a juvenile reformatory, and being radically unsuited for the function expected, it would have been wiser and more economical in the end to have chosen a good site with plenty of arable land, and constructed there a suitable class of buildings.

The assistant-surgeon of the station was the first Superintendent, sub. *pro tem.* He was assisted by a staff of two masters and three peons. A clerk, a hospital assistant and two additional peons were subsequently appointed. The first batch of twenty pupils was received by transfer from the penitentiary at Madras, and at the end of the year the number rose to forty-two, when the District Surgeon assumed charge of the school as its permanent Superintendent. In June 1888, Mr Lewis, an officer of the Educational Department was appointed Deputy Superintendent, when carpentry and gardening, started on 1st March 1888, were the only trades taught. The tailoring class was formed on the 22nd June, and the blacksmith class on 14th July of the same year.

On the 1st October, the school was brought under the Educational Department, effected under G.O., dated 28th August, 1888, No. 1808, and Mr H. B. Grigg, I.C.S., the Director of Public Instruction, took charge of the school, when the strength stood at seventy-two. He did a great deal for the school, and took a personal interest in all its detailed working, and it is to his sagacity and sound policy that the institution owed much of its initial success. The introduction of the rules for the regulation of the school was sanctioned in G.O., dated 10th December 1888, No. 2545. The districts from which no pupils were received were Anatapur, Bellary, Cuddapah, Kurnool, Nellore, while the Nilgiris was badly represented.

"What's in a name" is an expression as common as "Give a dog a bad name and it sticks to him." The true value of each of these sayings in their application to the present theme depends on the past associations of the place, and on whether the name given tends to help or retard the progress of the individual in his future career. The objection to any name is always heightened by its inherent meaning, and the word "reformatory" is so pregnant with it that the public is apt to overestimate it. To mention one instance, an author of a school geography in Tamil describes Chingleput as a town on the banks of the river Palar. Here, he says, is a Sub-Collector's office, a District Court, and a reformatory school for juvenile *prisoners*.

Such language surely is most objectionable in a text-book approved for use and which the pupils are asked to study. When the offending word is pointed out the only comment forthcoming is that the use of the book, otherwise satisfactory as a text-book, should not be discontinued in the school, that the mistake might be pointed out to the pupils, that the opportunity might be taken of impressing upon them the distinction between a prison and the school in which they are placed, and the obligation which their more favourable treatment imposes upon them; that in this or in some similar way the mistake might be turned to good account. But the school is crowded with associations to remind its inmates at every turn of its kinship with a jail, and the problem is rather how best to get rid of these baneful traditions. Further, the boys are fairly saturated with moral lessons about their obligations without requiring the fictitious aid of a text-book to teach morality by glossing over a regrettable mistake in the translation of a word. Ordinarily, the word reformatory has come to connote a place where juveniles who have committed a criminal offence, and have been convicted in a Court by a Magistrate, are detained for reformation. The flavour of a junior jail therefore hangs about the word and, since the name has prejudicial associations because the children in the school have been convicted, it may well be changed into "Industrial."

To speak with knowledge, many a successful boy is branded in after-life by its use, and several instances can be quoted, but one typical example should suffice. A boy trained in gymnastics was appointed an Instructor in another institution, and the pupils, some of them quite little urchins, cast up to his face the fact that he graduated through the reformatory, and had it not been for the moral support of the principal in putting his foot down on such senseless remarks the lad's life would have become a burden to him. It is because the word handicaps a boy after discharge that substitutes with a euphemistic import are adopted in other countries: such as "the village," "the Catholic Protectory," "the George Junior Republic," "the little Farm," "the Philanthropic Farm School," "the Training Home," "the little Commonwealth."

In the British Isles, the chief difference between a reformatory school and an industrial school lies in the fact that a boy is "convicted" before he is sent to a reformatory, whereas he is only "committed" to an industrial school. Managers of schools find that the name reformatory stands in the way of a lad emigrating or joining the Navy. Some Government Departments, like the Post Office, will not receive a boy convicted once, and therefore the mere change of name from "Reformatory" to "Industrial" will not altogether remedy the evil. The word "convicted" also ought not to be applied to any juvenile offender.

To the superficial thinker the alteration may seem unnecessary, except in so far as our boys have to do with the educated minority in India. But the non-educated take their cue from the others and form their ideas accordingly. It is amusing to hear from their lips the many comical transformations of the English word, and is useful perhaps in illustrating Grimm's Law on the interchange of sounds. It is a hard word to pronounce in the mouth of the average Indian, for the accent falls out of a soft tongue and fixes its emphasis perversely on the first syllable of the word. It is often torture to the delicately trained ear of him who heareth. Here is a goodly array of words to confront any student of phonetics: Reforament, Repartment, Refforment, Deforment, Rifarementary. Is there to be no deliverance from such phonetic inexactitudes? A few verbal alterations in the Bill would do this, and what is infinitely more important, it would remove the difficulties that now stand in the way of our boys making a fair start in life.

It may be remarked that the Chingleput School is the only one in India that has adopted the use of the educational term "Peon" to designate the underlings who keep an eye on the boys to see that they do not go out of bounds. It has already ousted the jail term of warder from the pages of our roster. One is apt to say "yes," the idea is good, and it is the correct thing to do, as it carries out the intention to make all things conform to the school aspect of the institution. But in India one does not know what harm is going to follow even from a good intention. A Government Order which was passed to change the offending name of warder to that of peon immediately lowered the status of the men, and classed them as inferior Government servants for purposes of pension. A warder of a jail or of a reformatory is supposed to be a dignified custodian, but a peon of a school does not command the same amount of respect.

A peon is a peon, whether he be employed in a reformatory school, or in a Tahsildar's Cutcherry.

To remove the disability under which the Head Peon was suffering, the name of his office was recently altered to that of Assistant-Sergeant.

CHAPTER II

CHINGLEPUT

The health of Chingleput is generally remarkably good; this fact and the presence of land available within the fort, which is washed on one side by a lake, were the determining factors in the location of the reformatory for southern India in this town, which is conveniently situated from Madras. The existence of certain buildings formerly used as a district jail were taken advantage of and altered for the object in view, and although the school presents a picturesque appearance, it would have been better if a site had been selected away from all town life to ensure healthy surroundings.

Chingleput means the lotus or water-lily town—a significant name for a place where the surroundings are pretty, and the horizon of a pleasing outline. Tradition states that a well-known chieftain, who had lost his wife, had a dream in which he heard a voice say that he was to wander over the face of the earth and place a pot containing the bones of his wife near a river, and that wherever the pot burst and there bloomed forth a lotus flower, he was to stay in that place and become the ruler. This happened on a spot near the Palar, and Chingleput was the name given to it. The abundance of the lotus flower in the ponds and tanks around Chingleput lends colour to the origin of the name.

The fort is of Vijianagar origin, and was built after the battle of Talikota in 1565, when the power of the Vijianagar Kingdom was broken by the Muhammadan Kings of the Deccan. There is a slab embedded upside down in one of the ramparts, which relates some deed of Narasimha, who was the founder of the second Vijianagar dynasty. Tradition states that the fort was built by Timma Rajah, an offshoot of the Royal House after their flight to Chandragiri. The grant to the English of the land on which Fort St George is built was made by one of the Naicks of Chingleput, and was one of the last important acts of the Hindu Vijianagar Princes.

This fact was emphasised by the residents of this town in an address to Lord Ampthill, who in his reply said: "I do not think that there is any other place where I could have more appropriately begun my visitation of the Presidency, seeing, as you say, that it was from Chingleput that the 'British authority emanated.'" The fort dates from the 16th century, and the buildings inside show that the place must have been of some importance in those days, and it was once, with Chandragiri in North Arcot, the capital of the fallen Vijianagar kings, after their dynasty had been overthrown by the Mussulmans. And it is stated that the Vijianagar sovereigns held court alternately here and at Chandragiri, and while the authority of Sadasiva was acknowledged three years later than the fatal battle of Talikota in 1565, which ruined his family, we find that he was left captive and that usurpers were in the habit of giving grants in their own name. Thus it must have come about that one of the chiefs or deputies at Chingleput gave permission to the English, in the person of a messenger from Mr Francis Day, to erect Fort St George. While these Naicks or chiefs professed to be independent they continued to pay allegiance to the fugitive king of Vijianagar after his flight to Chandragiri, and hence it was that the Charter granted had to be confirmed by the suzerain lord and, for this purpose, Mr Francis Day seems to have gone over to Chandragiri, the ruling Vijianagar king at that time being Sri Ranga III., and not Damarla Venkatadra.

About four furlongs to the south of the fort, a pond goes by the name of Timma Rajah Kulam, and tradition speaks of a subterranean passage which connected the royal apartments within the fort with the *kulam*, where the ladies of Timma Rajah's family used to bathe in privacy. Another work attributed to him was the deepening and enlarging of the lake on the east side of the fort, so as to give it the appearance of a "little sea."

The fort is a typical Hindu structure, built after the model of Ginjee, "the modern Troy." The walls are formed of roughly dressed stone, hewn for the purpose by families of workmen who affixed their marks to the stones. It is nearly a parallelogram 400 yards by 320, and had an entrance in the shape of a Greek fret with a mantapam at the first turn, and at the next a temple dedicated to the monkey-god Anjaneya, who was a devotee to Kothandramasawmy (Rama with a bow) and to whom a temple was erected within the fort. This temple was removed in 1813, with the permission of the East India Company, and erected in the town where it stands at present. The fort defences consist of broad ditches 60 feet wide, with an outer and inner rampart 18 feet high. At the southern end the corners were strengthened by bastions. To this day, cannon balls of rounded granite are dug out of the ground, and these were evidently propelled from 9-inch mortar guns. The barrels of the blunderbuss or musket with which the Naick's troops were armed form now the bars of the windows in the buildings used at first as a District jail in 1802, and afterwards as a dormitory of the reformatory school located in 1887 within the fort.

The sovereignty of the Vijianagar house over the Carnatic having been ended about the year 1639 by the Muhammadan King of Golconda, the Chingleput District was shortly afterwards taken possession of by Mir Jumla, the General of the King of Golconda, and on the fall of Golconda in 1687, it passed with the rest of the Carnatic into the hands of the Moghul Emperors. The French acquired possession of the Chingleput fort in 1751 and it was taken by Clive in 1752. He established a battery 200 yards on the southern side and made a breach in the inner and outer ramparts. There are two places where the gun shots are still visible. During the struggle for supremacy in the Carnatic between the French and English, the latter found the fort valuable as a base for keeping stores and for harassing the rear of the army investing Madras. The first English Governor of the fort was Captain Smith, who was the founder of Freemasonry in India. In June 1758 it was temporarily evacuated after the reduction of Fort St David by the French, for the troops were required for Madras, but on the arrival of fresh troops from England, Chingleput was reoccupied the same year.

Chingleput was handed over to the English as a Jagir in 1760 by Mahomed Ali, Nawab of Arcot, for services rendered, and the grant was confirmed by the Moghul Emperor in 1763.

During the wars with Hyder, Chingleput was once taken and twice unsuccessfully besieged. On the latter occasion, it was relieved by Sir Eyre Coote in January 1781. Since then the fort has remained undisturbed in the hands of the English. The fort now is partially in ruins and undisturbed. The royal apartments, the granary, the barracks and armoury have all been razed to the ground, but two old buildings still exist.

THE RAJ MAHAL

This structure is also known as the "Ther Mahal," the word "Ther" meaning car; for the building is in the shape of a festival car attached to temples. Thimma Rajah built this "Ther Mahal" exactly in the form of the Conjeervaram car and celebrated within the Chingleput fort, on a smaller scale than that of Conjeevaram, the Brahma Voothsavam (festival) of Varada Raja Swami, one of the presiding deities of the Vishnu temple, then situated within the fort of Chingleput. On the seventh day of the festival, the car, *i.e.*, the Ther Mahal in the fort, was ornamented on the outside with flags and bunting just in the same way as the Conjeevaram car was decked, and after the decking of the building with all the usual car paraphernalia, the idol was brought from the fort temple and placed on a beautifully designed seat on the second floor of the Ther Mahal building.

The School Band playing below "Ther Mahal" (page 38)

A Bird's-eye View of the School (page 100)

CHINGLEPUT

The Mahal is the best architectural remains of the Vijianagar line of kings. It originally consisted of five storeys, built in wedding-cake form, but one of these was subsequently pulled down. The unusual height of the structure was due to the fact that the Ranees of the palace desired to worship daily at 12 o'clock facing, with its towers in sight, the temple of Conjeevaram, the religious metropolis of the south, and thus avoiding the personal discomfort to themselves of attendance at its shrine, especially on festival days. The time of the *pooja* was announced to the Ranees by beat of drums from the tops of towers erected at intervals of four miles on the road from Conjeevaram. This quaint, solid structure is composed of a series of arcades of Moorish arches, surrounding a small inner dome-shaped room without a single piece of wood in its entire construction. The roof of the dome-shaped room in the first storey is decorated with panel work, and was evidently used as a mantapam for the habitation of the household deities. The staircases were straight and were all located inside and ran parallel to and above each other from one storey to another.

The steps are extremely narrow, but they furnished sufficient foothold for the small feet of the Ranees. On a bright day the building dazzles the eye when the rays of the sun scintillate upon its limed-washed walls (once mistaken by an archæologist for marble), and on a moonlight night one can picture the little Ranees on the terrace with their garlands of oleander and jessamine, playing and singing to the accompaniment of music. It was in the Ther Mahal that permission was given in 1639 by the Chieftain of Chingleput to the messenger of Mr Francis Day to erect Fort St George, and this was confirmed by the suzerain lord, the Rajah of Chandragiri. In the last *Journal of Indian Art and Industry*, an historical tableau represents the Rajah of Chandragiri, Damarla Venkatadra, granting to Mr Francis Day the Charter which was written on a plate of gold, technically styled a palm leaf, for the founding of Madras, in the Durbar Hall of the Old Palace at Chandragiri. The price was 12,000 pagodas a year for a strip of sandbank some six miles along the bay and a mile inland.

The Charter, which was dated March 1st, 1639, unfortunately disappeared during the French occupation of Madras, and it gave the company "full power and authority to govern and dispose of the Government of Madras in order to make more full expression of our affection to the British nation and to enjoy the privilege of minting without paying any dues or duties whatsoever more than the ordinary wages to those who shall coin the monies." The Company was also exempted in perpetuity from customs duties on merchandise or provisions.

When a gubernatorial party was about to visit Chingleput some years ago, it was proposed to entertain them, and among the several suggestions put forward, the one that met with most favour was the enacting of a pageant to represent Mr Francis Day receiving from one of the Naicks of Chingleput the Charter granting him permission to build Fort St George, which local tradition says took place on the second storey of the building known as the Raj Mahal or "Ther Mahal."

The pageant would have represented the Rajah seated on a palanquin accompanied by his Court ministers and followers going in procession headed by elephants. This would be from the north side of the fort where the present District Court is situated. From the opposite side, Mr Francis Day, in doublet and hose, and wearing a cloak and a tall, broad-rimmed hat and top boots, and with a few followers carrying presents for the chief, would be represented approaching the Rajah seated under a canopy.

The other old building is the lower storey of the quarters of the Deputy Superintendent of the reformatory school. The bungalow represents in stone the three periods which make up Indian history—the Hindu period, the Muhammadan period and the English. The lower storey was first a Hindu temple for the use of the Prime Minister of the Rajah. When the fort was taken by the Muhammadans, it was partly converted into a mosque, and the Muhammadan arch and the Hindu pillar exist side by side. The English period is represented by the upper storey, from the verandah of which a picturesque view is obtained, with the lake in front and the hills forming a background. There are still frequent visitors to the fort, but the object is more or less to see the reformatory school. It is within easy reach of Madras by motor car, and occasionally an amateur artist motors up to paint the beautiful colours in the waters of the moat, which unfortunately are visible only to the eye of the artist.

CHAPTER III

PSYCHO-PHYSIOLOGICAL TREATMENT

THE Juvenile Criminal! What a contradiction in terms. How big and pregnant a subject! How fathomless the abyss of evil reaching down into the depths of human nature! Such, mayhap, is the casual remark of one who professes to be an interested observer in matters affecting the juvenile world. Scientists may theorise on the dual origin of matter, original sin, or, call the doctrine by whatever name you like, to explain the origin of evil; but we cannot shut our eyes to the fact that evil exists in the world, and that an evil tendency shows itself at a very early stage. It may be the result of heredity—defining it to be a potentiality towards good or evil—or the result of environment. Apart from theories of heredity, it is safe to assume that environments, mental and bodily, influence children. If the parents live in lowering surroundings, the reserve stock of energy and resistance becomes weaker in the children. But the main question, from a practical point of view, is how are we to grapple with the presence of evil in the child? It will be readily conceded that every normal person, old or young, is responsible for his acts. Can success then attend one's efforts by assuming that this degree of responsibility with the young must remain intact? On the other hand, are we to argue that no responsibility lies with the child, as he is the victim of his surroundings, of parental ignorance and wilful neglect; that the moral evil in him is the result of his physical or mental weakness, which may be corrected by proper treatment and the exercise of self control? The moulder of character, therefore, is at the very outset of his task confronted with the complex nature of his work.

PSYCHO-PHYSIOLOGICAL TREATMENT

For all practical purposes, it is well as a first principle to recognise that a child, on account of its immaturity, is incapable of committing a crime. When, therefore, he is brought before a Court of law, it is not with a view to determine the amount of guilt and impose the punishment prescribed, though this is necessary as a preliminary step, as to ascertain the condition of the child—whether he is delinquent, dependent or neglected, and accordingly commit him to a suitable school for remedial treatment. Take the case of a boy who needs money, breaks into a house and enters it for this purpose. He does not think about the illegality of his deed; he may of the chances of being caught. Among the criminal classes a child is asked by his parents to steal, and he does so at the bidding of his elders. Such cases must be carefully distinguished from the moral delinquent. An investigation into the amount of guilt involved is no safe guide for future treatment. My idea is that there should be a special law, special courts, selected judges and a special procedure for juveniles. The "retributive" element should be eliminated from all forms of punishment: stress should be laid only on its "preventive" and "reformative" character. The common law should presume that a child under 14 is incapable of committing crime, and should abstain from dealing with him. In certain cases where it is proved that a boy had sufficient capacity to understand the act charged against him and its consequences, and does not look to be under 15, he should be sent to a suitable adult institution where reformatory principles are in operation, though not altogether on ordinary school lines. When the question is one of limited mental capacity, and therefore of limited responsibility, special treatment is required for those defectives who can be influenced by the motive of self interest in an environment adapted to their needs. To commit juveniles of all classes to one or the same kind of institution is to retard progress in the direction of diminishing criminality. Various physical and psychological tests have been laid down from time to time to enable one to differentiate and classify the ordinary from the defective delinquent. By the use of these tests, the mentality of a child is gauged, and a fairly accurate means obtained of placing it in surroundings suitable to the right sort of educative treatment that should be meted out to it. These means alone can ensure any success being achieved in the matter of grappling with juvenile delinquency. The time has come when such terms as "criminal" and "ex-convict" when applied to juveniles should be severed from their *juxta* position. In their application to the class known as juveniles, nothing should be done to handicap them by the use of epithets suggesting, to the ordinary lay mind, walled enclosures, barred doors and gates.

Many letters were received during the course of my work from a lady, and they find a place in the book. On this subject she writes:

DEAR FRIEND,—

The coining of a catch-phrase, such as "Cavemen and the Catechism," has been the means of liberating in my mind a long train of captive thought. . . . Ideas have a way of simmering in the brain-pan—one is conscious of the process, somewhat chemical and electric in nature and combination; suddenly the whole mass becomes fused; atoms take shape, and *form* appears.

I've been thinking how you, in your life-work have been dealing with a certain *stage* rather than a condition of human evolution. To start with, I suppose we may accept the axiom that humanity in process of evolution is liable to set-backs—in other words, the scientific mind may calmly regard abnormalities in undeveloped human beings as merely throw-backs, such as occur in the process of breeding in the lower animal world?

Luther Burbank, for instance, has given his life to a patient investigation of plant-life conditions and a culture of the fittest to perfection point. He has worked miracles with the grasses of the field and the flowers of the forest, and the weeds by the road side.

From the insignificant, stunted, starved field daisy he has evolved a gorgeously beautiful flower: from the bitter crab-apple he has raised by scientific cross-breeding a magnificent seedless apple—a king among fruits. This is the romantic side of science, though all will allow its utilitarian results. But the work calls for unsleeping vigilance and the devotion of a lifetime. The wonder-worker must ever be on the alert, and is continually coming up against Nature's ruthless processes, and ever and anon his specimens revert to type and fill him with disappointment. Of a million seed sown, the greater part revert to original type, and but a few respond to culture.

How, then, shall we expect it to be different with the genus Homo?

Of course names will and must be misleading always. Confront, if it were possible, a cave man, a primitive creature, with the Catechism, and endeavour to inculcate its precepts. At no mental point could possible contact ever be struck!

For this lack of response would it be fair to call the cave-man criminal, in root and branch and tendency? To regard him as *low* and bestial and beneath regard? By no means. On the contrary, he is a factor to be reckoned with, for—of such stuff are *we* made. Such our manifold nature, so rooted in antiquity are our tendencies and our instincts! Now, then, when we are face to face with this "low" type of mankind, this reversion to type, this throwback on Nature, this abnormality—how are we to regard him?

In no other way than calmly, philosophically, and from a scientific standpoint.

To meet this emergency with punitive measures—with the cat-o'-nine-tails, with bolts and bars, and a brutalising outfit—is but to brand our civilisation with the quality of brutishness that in mediæval times burnt at a stake poor, repulsive, ignorant old women!

You were qualified by some strange mental equipment (shall we say spiritual instead of mental) to seize upon that urgent moment which always *has its man*. Happy the moment and happy the man when they mutually find each other. Your work in the reformatory speaks of the outcome of this "finding."

Humanity in progress has received a momentum—an impetus onward—and what *now* has to guarded against is a mere mechanical continuation of your work during future years when the prophet's fire will peradventure have died down and but cold ashes remain upon the Altar!

This kind of thing "goeth not forth but by fasting and prayer," *i.e.*, the prophet must spend and be spent in order that he may fuse the work by living, miraculous fire from heaven.

Is the theme worthy of such high inspiration? St Chrysostom's saying in reference to the Shekinah—"Ark of Testimony," visible Revelation of God, among the Hebrews, must be recalled.

"The true Shekinah is Man."

Carlyle quotes the devout Novalis thus: "There is but one Temple in the Universe and that is the Body of Man. Nothing is holier than that high form. We touch Heaven when we lay our hand on a human body."

This is more than a mere flourish of rhetoric! He goes on to say: "If well medicated, it will turn out to be a scientific fact; the expression, in such words as can be had, of the actual truth of the things." "*We* are the miracle of miracles, the great inscrutable mystery of God."

Greater work, therefore, cannot be than to take the specimens, dwarfed and starved and twisted and stunted that occur, and with loving hands heal and mend and bind up and graft upon, and to perform the wonders of mind-surgery upon such wondrous plasticine!

The greatness of the opportunity lies in the fact that they are delivered over to you *young* to deal with.

Child nature, boy-forms, retarded intelligences to gently unfold, suspended spiritual animation to resuscitate, joy-less lives to irradiate, loveless hearts to animate if only to a dog-like devotion, unsmiling lips to provoke to mirth. Aimless existence to interest.

What a work—what a miracle to attempt!

Down in the human heart, crushed by the tempter,
Feelings lie buried which grace can restore.
Touched by a loving hand, wakened by kindness,
Chords that were broken may vibrate once more.

Success is yours so far—and your work its own reward.

Your faithfully. I mean sincerely.

To revert to my views. Studying the raw material, working with it, playing with it and talking to it can alone secure the first stirring of a new and quickened spirit. And first of all, the boy as soon as he arrives must be taught to smile, and for this object to be attained he must be taught to play.

I remember when I first came to the school the boys were accustomed to huddle together in groups, doing nothing after work-hours except to wait patiently either for the feeding-time to come, or for the hour to be locked in. There was no running, no shouting and no kicking up of the heels. To secure these activities the place was made as homely as possible, with no barrack-room dormitories or plain walls. Little gardens and bright spots dotted over the grounds, airy dormitories with dados and friezes, school and hospital walls decorated with pictures, and workshops with free egress and ingress all bring freshness and coolness into the place. It is for this reason that boys are allowed to have their meals served under the shade of widespread banyan trees with grass mounds ornamenting their stately trunks. At the fruit-bearing season, it is true, the crows do prove a nuisance, but a timely shot at them with the bow scares them away. The *al fresco* dining-saloon lends itself to a feeling of constant picnicking at meal time. The clean Cuddapah slabbed seats washed, every day, leave no trace or smell of food, while the tin plates of the boys are raised off the ground on to narrow cemented walls serving as racks. During the rains the food is distributed in one of the workshop verandahs, but such days can be counted on one's fingers.

If possible, each of the big boys should have a box in which he may keep his belongings to interest him in his leisure moments and to teach him what the word property connotes. Every youngster delights to turn over and look at his things a thousand times and to arrange and rearrange them. Pets about the place ought to be encouraged to stimulate love in the pupils and kindness towards dumb animals. The daily round of school-life should not be too monotonous. An occasional hockey match between the staff and the pupils is a source of amusement, the observance of the Superintendent's birthday, a friendly football match with an outside team, an excursion to the riverside, an annual camp, sports, dramas and exhibitions, etc., throw a glimmer into the place and make for a sense of freedom. All such breaks in the routine give the boys a new outlook on life and tend to shape them into normal children. Lastly, some form of self-government to create a brotherhood of discipline and control is required among the bigger boys, who should be held responsible for the good name of the school—in doing so they bring into play self-control and become responsible for their own good behaviour. Smoking, for example, can never be eradicated or minimised without the co-operation of the senior boys, who, when they are given certain privileges and duties, guard them with the tenacity of a permanent and paid official. When a boy has everything done for him without doing something in turn for the school, he becomes a machine. The privilege of serving and helping, therefore, should be made an incentive for maintaining discipline and checking irregularities.

The aim of the school is to detain a boy for a period sufficiently long to enable him to receive an industrial education, an elementary general education, and to develop him physically and morally—in short, to equip him for the battle of life. As these boys have to earn their livelihood by manual labour, the first step is to assist nature to endow a boy with a strong bodily frame, capable of standing exertion. Physical training therefore forms an important part in the general scheme. As soon as a boy is admitted into the school, he is drafted for six months into the garden class for an open-air course of training. He learns the elements of agriculture and the use of the spade, the shovel, and the mammoti; and the whole class raises water for irrigation by means of a rope and leather water-bag. This exercise helps at the very outset to develop the physique of the boys. It has the additional advantage of producing a very keen appetite, and very quickly reconciles them to the ragi diet, to which most of them are not accustomed in their own homes. Gymnastics, drill, route marching, football, hockey, and other games, as also manual training, help in the same direction.

Moral training is based on the broad principles of a morality common to all religions, and care is exercised to infuse a moral ideal into the school and to create a good public opinion among the boys. At the same time, definite religious instruction is given according to the creed of the boy, and, to prevent the boys losing the religious instinct of their forefathers, each community is provided with a religious place of worship. The Muhammadan attends the school mosque on Fridays and recites his prayers three times a day. The Hindu observes his occasional festivals, and is instructed in his religious duties by Hindu gentlemen, while the several denominations of Christians attend their respective churches. The Roman Catholics have a little Oratory of their own inside the school, the "Oratory of St Aloysius," in which Mass is said by the parish priest occasionally, and in which daily prayers may be offered. The moral lessons with which the school reading-books are interspersed are impressed on the boys by frequent references to them. For the Sunday lesson, a moral story or principle is selected, bearing on every-day work, upon which a lesson is given with the help of the blackboard. The importance of the Sunday lesson cannot be exaggerated, for it is found to be one of the most powerful means of elevating a boy's character. Singing of Tamil lyrics and of clean, high-toned songs to relieve the monotony, and the narration of interesting tales, with definite morals found necessary to correct juvenile delinquencies of the hour, lend additional interest to the lesson. A sense of loyalty to the British Raj is maintained with the aid of the Union Jack, which is hoisted on the anniversary days of the Royal Family and on other high days. It is explained to the boys that the flag stands "for justice, good government and liberty." Miniature Union Jacks are also worn by the boys on Empire Day, and, at the conclusion of every festivity or gathering, the National Anthem is either sung or played by the boys.

Much is also done to develop character and to check anti-social tendencies on the playground, and the games master, in the person of the European Sergeant, by a judicious handling and control of the boys during recreation hours, wields an additional power for good in that direction. Boys, especially of this class, in competitive games, easily lose their temper, and cannot take their defeat with a good grace. The checking of these and other undesirable qualities forms an important part of the moral scheme. Of all games, football seems to be the best adapted for a school of juvenile criminals. The pupils are carefully supervised on the playground, where, in the society of companions of equal age and pursuits, their character and disposition are checked or developed. The use of obscene words or language, a prevailing fault in native boys, is summarily checked.

Reformation is also sought by training the pupils to habits of obedience, truth speaking, regularity, industry, order, cleanliness, coupled with a judicious system of rewards and punishments. Drill is another element for moulding character, for inculcating the mechanical habits of smartness, order, physical development, and ready obedience. At the same time, it is a preliminary training for the Army.

There are other minor aids to reformatory work, such as the magic lantern, to illustrate and impress moral truths on pupils. Concerts, theatrical performances and gramophone recitals also have a civilising influence, and help to counteract the dangers of the strain of criminality in their blood. The boys themselves are able to stage a drama, and they do it most creditably.

On a Sunday afternoon, the boys headed by the bugles and drums have a walk out through the town or along the fields, and the donkey mascot, "Mike," harnessed to a coster's cart, forms an important unit in the supply and transport department for the purpose of carrying parched peas and other comestibles on route marches. At times, on a holiday evening, they have a romp on the sands of the river Palar. On several occasions they have been taken to see a circus, and on one occasion a picnic was organised to an experimental farm, but which unfortunately ended in disastrous results, by two boys eating datura seeds and nearly poisoning themselves.

A great amount of liberty has been gradually allowed to the inmates. They are sent out on errands without escort. On a holiday they go out in batches to see the sights of the town, while during Christmas they enjoy a camp at a sea-side resort, where they are as free as they can possibly be.

The general treatment adopted in reclamation is briefly this. When a boy is admitted into school, all particulars about himself and his home surroundings are recorded as a guide to future treatment. His caste and previous occupation determine what trade he should be taught, though as a rule the choice is with him. It is inadvisable that a boy should be sent for a less period than four years if he is to be taught a trade by which he may earn his bread. To operate straight away on him morally, the lower motives are first appealed to. The rewards and punishments and what constitutes a school offence are explained to him on the first day. The reward is in the shape of a good conduct badge, and if a boy does not commit an offence for a whole year, he receives, as an incentive and an encouragement, a badge in the shape of an oblong piece of copper.

These badges are worn like medals on the left breast and are prized for the money value attached to them, half of which may be spent in sweets, toys and other unforbidden articles. The prospect of immediate use of money is a great incentive to right conduct, for a boy appreciates the value of ready money a great deal more than the same amount of money locked up for future use. The portion banked in his name teaches him, however, the lesson of thrift, and provides him, when he leaves school, with the means of purchasing tools to start him in business. The greatest amount ever carried away on discharge by a boy was Rs. 100. He banked every pice of the money earned by prizes, by sports and by work, and never spent money on sweets. On the average, however, a boy can put away Rs. 5 a year, and after a stay of five years he takes with him a sum of Rs. 25 to purchase tools and other necessaries for a start in life.

On the other hand, a boy is informed that misconduct will be punished at once. The smallest offences are visited with appropriate punishment in order that the association between wrong conduct and punishment may be fixed firmly in the mind of a boy, for the children have at first to be trained to avoid wrong acts by the dread of immediate punishment. No offence is allowed to go unpunished, warnings being of no use except in a few exceptional cases. The discipline maintained is military in character, but it is necessary in dealing with a criminal population to suppress that which is undesirable in itself. At the same time, the boy has many interesting occupations to keep him away from temptation.

"One offence, one punishment," is a good rule, and immediately the punishment is administered, the boy is made to feel that no grudge is borne against him, and that he is punished for the offence and not from any personal motive. This fact is impressed upon him by making him salute the person who punished him. In some cases, refractory children are found to require medical treatment and not punishment to set them right.

The chief supervising officers stand *in loco parentis*, and by private talk and conversation with individual boys try to mould their character. They give them occasional treats, and by specific acts of kindness show them their sympathy. A personal talk acts like a charm—it brings tears of contrition to the eyes of a boy, and the roughest character is softened down by such means, particularly if a close and friendly supervision is exercised over him. At all times individual attention should be paid to each boy, and proper treatment meted out to suit individual characters.

During his stay in school, a boy is made to feel as happy as possible, but not at the expense of discipline. Nothing is done to lower him in his own eyes or in the eyes of the public. The convictions which were the cause of his detention in the school are forgotten, or are only remembered as symptomatic of character. He is called by his name rather than by the number given him on his admission—in short, he is treated as a human being. In their work, the boys are associated with individuals who are their superiors, and the masters take part in their games and watch their conduct. Excepting new-comers, no check is placed upon the movements of any boy during recreation hours.

The general education imparted to the boys is of an elementary character, and is just sufficient to enable them to keep accounts, and to read and write their own vernacular. A few boys are taught colloquial English.

The industrial training is intended to train the hand and eye, to teach the boys the use of tools and to enable them to earn a livelihood after their discharge. In their work, a sense of their abilities is aroused, and how those abilities may be used in making an honest living is demonstrated. In the present stage of India's economic condition, it is not desirable that machinery worked by power should be introduced into reformatory schools, at all events to any large extent, until the factory system develops and a demand arises for skilled artizans. A few of our boys who live in the big towns do get admission into the railway workshops, but the majority find their way back into the villages, and for these, hand labour is the best. It forms an excellent preparatory training to the handling of machinery, and a youth who is able to make things with his hands easily learns the use of machinery, and readily acquires skill in that direction. Then, with regard to hand labour: should the course be a manual training one, or should the boys work on industrial lines and turn out finished articles for sale? A medium course is, I think, the best. Take the carpentry department. The little boys would be trained to plane true, and make several joints to scale. During the latter period of their course, they would take part, under the supervision of a maistry, in the making of a saleable article. This is a safe course to pursue. The boys here are not given any task work, but during training they are kept, or ought to be kept, under strict supervision; after a time they get into the habit of work, and toil on without a sense of compulsion or even of control, and the result is spontaneous action with indications of individuality. If a reformatory boy is taught to work under these conditions, there is hope of his succeeding in life. But if he always feels control, then, on discharge, when he becomes a free agent, he goes to the bad, because he has never had the opportunity of exercising the important habit of self-control.

I approve also the plan of giving more hours to industrial work and less to general education to the outgoing boys; the little boys receiving more general education and less industrial training.

The senior boys receive six hours of industrial and two hours of general education, and the juniors three hours of industry, three hours of general education and two of gardening.

CHAPTER IV

THE COMMITTEE OF VISITORS

In an institution which is superintended by a Commissioned Officer, aided by an Educational Officer of the Provincial Service, no great advantage is gained by the appointment of a Committee of visitors provided for in section 17 (1) of the Act. The institution as it is, is a much inspected one, and official visitors are constantly in and about the place. One cannot take any exception to the existence of a committee who on the whole try to aid the work of the school, but occasionally a great deal of harm results by a member whose zeal outruns his discretion, and who wishes to show it by interfering with the discipline of the school, forgetting that only one head can keep discipline. The boys are able to detect where power lies, and if they suspect that a committee of visitors has power over the Superintendent, however slender that may be, they are not slow to take advantage of it, to the detriment of good discipline. The proper view to be taken by the committee is the one laid down in the school rules—viz., that the committee should *aid* the Superintendent in maintaining discipline and that they are an advisory body.

In all institutions the day set apart for the visit of the Committee is not usually one that a Superintendent looks forward to, and I must confess I am no exception. The meeting of the Committee, although held only once a month, at times interferes with the smooth working of the institution. One is sometimes tempted to treat the whole business as a social function, and to make a substantial tea take the place of discussion, but unfortunately the matter cannot be got over so easily, as the members are mostly Hindus—

some of them Brahmans, some non-Brahmans, and the rest Europeans. The most effective way is to guide without leading, to answer all questions politely, to furnish all information required, and gently persuade them to acquiesce in the changes one wishes to see accomplished. The Superintendent's duties and responsibilities have all been fixed by Government, and the Committee's authority has its limitations. But individual members forget this at times, and would like to make him a mere figurehead to take orders from others.

The Committee naturally then look upon themselves not as an advisory body but as part of the executive. Thus it happens at times that a member with an axe to grind suggests the introduction of an industry which perhaps for practical reasons cannot be considered for lack of proper mental equipment on the part of the boys. Any opposition on the part of the Superintendent is resented—some take it as a personal snub and feel sufficiently vexed to return to the subject periodically. If the ear of a high-placed official can be secured, the proposal is put forward anew, the opinion of the authorities being ignored. The whole old set of arguments against it has to be trotted out once more, causing a fresh wound in those tender spots that distinguish our zealous friend. Another trustee perhaps takes it into his head to probe deep into matters for the purpose of discovering a supposed scandal, and he goes round smiling with approbation on any boy smart enough to size up what his questioner wants. Accordingly, an attack is launched against the executive head whom the boy, from some fancied wrong, feels to be his natural enemy. The whole thing is without foundation and ends in a farce, the boy in the end perhaps suffering for it. Sometimes it requires a firm and steady hand. "You have to keep them in their places" is the advice given by an American.

I am afraid that plan would fail if adopted in India. Here one has to carry his Committee along with him if he is to do any real good and his proposals and suggestions are to have a hearing. At times this is possible only when they are put in a form carrying the impression that the initiative comes from them. In this way the Committee is often useful to support the Superintendent for the purpose of enlisting the sympathetic consideration of Government in any scheme of reform dear to his heart. It is prudent, therefore, to humour the Committee in all non-essential details, as they do not like to be ignored, and to use a little tact to smooth over expected opposition when a weighty matter is placed before them.

As matters stand now, their duties are of a nominal character, and if the Committee are inclined to take little interest in the school the fault is not wholly theirs. It is the system that is to blame—a system that gives power to a Committee, and at the same time holds the Superintendent responsible for the discipline and internal economy of the school can hardly work at its best. One can understand an Inspecting Officer coming round, seeing things for himself, suggesting improvements and sanctioning reforms; but how could a Superintendent and a Committee of visitors jointly look into things? A paternal form of Government reigns in the school, and this would tumble to pieces at the least shock sustained by even the slightest breath of opposition from the other quarter. Inflammable material, it must never be forgotten, is present always, and friction of any kind arising from dual control will kindle the spark necessary to send things ablaze, and the happy home suffers. So long as the Committee is composed of normal business-men, nothing terrible can happen, but who can always guarantee the composition of a Committee? One firebrand is enough to set the whole structure ablaze.

There can be no doubt that the whole institution is coloured by the character and personal influence of the *Head*. If he is harsh and unsympathetic, then failure will be writ large on all his attempts to shape character according to the individual needs of each. If, on the other hand, he is lax and indifferent, trouble will be in store. The boys are numbered to facilitate identity, but their names are memorised by the Superintendent, who thereby tightens his grip upon them. At a Sunday moral lesson or on parade it must be disconcerting to a lad who regards himself as an insignificant and unknown unit among 250 others to hear admonition and his name coupled together ringing out like chain-shot along the crowd of boys. Of course, the discipline is required to be strong, but it could be tempered with sympathy, and it is wonderful how boys begin to respond to such treatment, knowing and feeling that their best interests are being attended to and safeguarded.

A boy must be convinced that we are his friends, but also the determined enemies of his misdeeds. The Head must be a man who is blind to the paltry foibles of child nature, for if he attempts to see things through the back of his head life will certainly become a burden to him, even if it does not tend towards the loss of hope and reverence for the unfortunate lad. At the same time he must know everything that goes on in the school and be able at a distance to scent mischief that leads to bad influences and lowering of character in others. The nearest approach to active espionage permitted himself is hovering in the vicinity of the kitchen or near the latrines. He may mix freely with the boys, and unbend without discipline suffering, but he is not expected to find out by cross-examination of any boy the inner-workings of another. Self-control is necessary for the sake of example, for in the pursuance of petty details, in supervising cooks and bringing to book sweepers and peons, in investigating complaints against those who think it "funny to pile up offences," any loss of temper is so much loss of dignity, and detracts from his reputed character as one free from the ordinary weaknesses that flesh is heir to.

A sense of humour in addition will carry him through many petty worries, and help him to preserve a cheerful exterior in a more or less monotonous atmosphere. The comicalities of youth are often of an unexpected nature, and will come up to the surface even during the investigation of serious offences, and every complaint has to be gone into with the patience of a saint. To be classified as infantile offences or innocent crimes, things must be seen in their true perspective, and judged with a knowledge of the secret springs of action in youth to discover whether an offence is as serious as it looks in the abstract. And surely there is nothing like humour to balance one in arriving at a decision which would do the minimum amount of harm, when deceived by appearances. On the other hand, it helps to view with sympathy the savagery and irresponsibility that often cause petty annoyances, and in misdemeanours bordering on criminality.

One is often called upon to mete out punishment suitable to the offence, and doubts whether the form of punishment will do harm or good to the law-breaker. In such cases it is safe to remember that children are neither good nor bad, neither strong nor weak, neither moral nor immoral, but unmoral. Second thoughts are always the best for guidance. To err on the side of leniency compatible with no show of weakness or softness moulds character in the right direction rather than an easy swift form of punishment with no tact or sense of humour to give point to it. A sense of justice combined with humour and sympathy appealing to loyalty will tend to maintain a good tone in any institution, and fatherly instincts will do the rest, for the Head has to play another role and accept the title of "father." If he cares for none of this, he must ask his deputy, who resides with the boys, to inspire them with filial affection, and they will look upon him as a father for the time being, speak of him as such, and his dwelling among them is tantamount to his being the head of the family. This domestic relationship is to be encouraged, for the finer feelings of a boy can never be brought out otherwise. "That we are members of one family," should form the basis of all reformatory work. Too much care, therefore, cannot be exercised in the selection of that officer, and if there is character behind the personality, no word of advice or warning can be lost upon the boys. Even in the selection of the lower subordinates it is necessary to exercise care, particularly if they reside within the precincts of the school. They should possess plenty of human sympathy, a happy temperament, tact, firmness and patience. In fact, a special training school is required to train teachers for expert work in reformatory schools, but the number of these schools is too small to warrant such a step being taken at present. The pay also of these men should be made progressive, and sufficiently encouraging to make the work they are engaged in a life work and a life study. Free quarters should also be furnished, to make up for the isolated life the staff is obliged to lead here.

CHAPTER V

THE RAW MATERIAL

The material sent to the reformatory is sufficiently "raw" to exercise the mind of the most capable workman whose business it is to "make over" the stuff into something useful. There are ugly spots to be removed, pale listless children to be cheered up, and it looks at first sight almost impossible to bring sunshine into the hearts of so many who have lost the care and affection of parents. As the future of so many human beings lies in the hands of one individual, it is indeed a stupendous undertaking, and even culpable, for any person to take up the work expecting an easy and comfortable time. The boys, when they arrive, do not know how to play or even to smile, their health is below par, and half of them are anæmic, with skins and heads perfectly sickening to look at, while an ignorance of letters completes the sombre picture. Behind it all, is the venomous atmosphere of their surroundings that follows them into the school. Every child, therefore, has to be converted into a worthy citizen, for the future health and happiness of so many hundred beings—their future children and grand-children.

The Superintendent, therefore, must be a worker if he wishes things to move in the right direction. The skin problem is always present in the shape of a dry epidermis needing oiling, nourishing and daily tubbing. The beat of the pulse has to be quickened by games, drill and work, with the concomitant result of an appetite for food not over stimulating. A weekly inspection is necessary to see that the weaklings are brought up to specification. A boy's parentage and hereditary statistics are carefully taken and examined to get the lines along which development is to take place. But how is this to be accomplished, when individual attention cannot be given from the start and individual faces or names cannot be picked out from a composite blur of straggling limbs and solemn faces? In spite of all this, the material inspires one with hope, for boys sent here for mischief must naturally possess some brains and energy. An unusual history lies behind most of the admissions to the school, and the solution of the problem resolves itself into keeping them busy every moment, either at play or work, and teaching them things for which they have a genius, while the award of marks gives the necessary aid for maintaining discipline.

Book-learning the boys do not take to readily, but anything involving movement of hand or leg is welcomed by the newcomer who shows an interest in the mechanical, for it suits his taste. Spitting on the ground, dirtying the walls with finger-marks, dirty hands and feet, ill-kept bodies, slouching habits, idling of time, vice in any form, have all to be eradicated, and for this purpose the boys are watched closely and individually.

With the existence of an inability to read or write, with dreadful memories, improper songs stored up in the far-back corners of their brains, accustomed to language both lying and obscene, a sense of right and wrong feebly flickering, an absence of self-control, self-reliance and initiative of the right sort, optimism is required to surmount these mountains of difficulty in the juvenile world. Composed of an inherent mischievous tendency, the problem of dealing with them is as difficult as any U-boat equation. Coming as they do from the lowest dregs of the social scale, strict laws need to be enforced from the first, and it is interesting to watch how, when the moment of pressure is relaxed, a rebound is made to the old form, proving how difficult it is to eradicate at once criminal tendencies deeply planted and growing luxuriantly for many years in an unhealthy atmosphere.

The process of re-shaping is a very gradual one and a harassing one, involving the straightening out of every moral

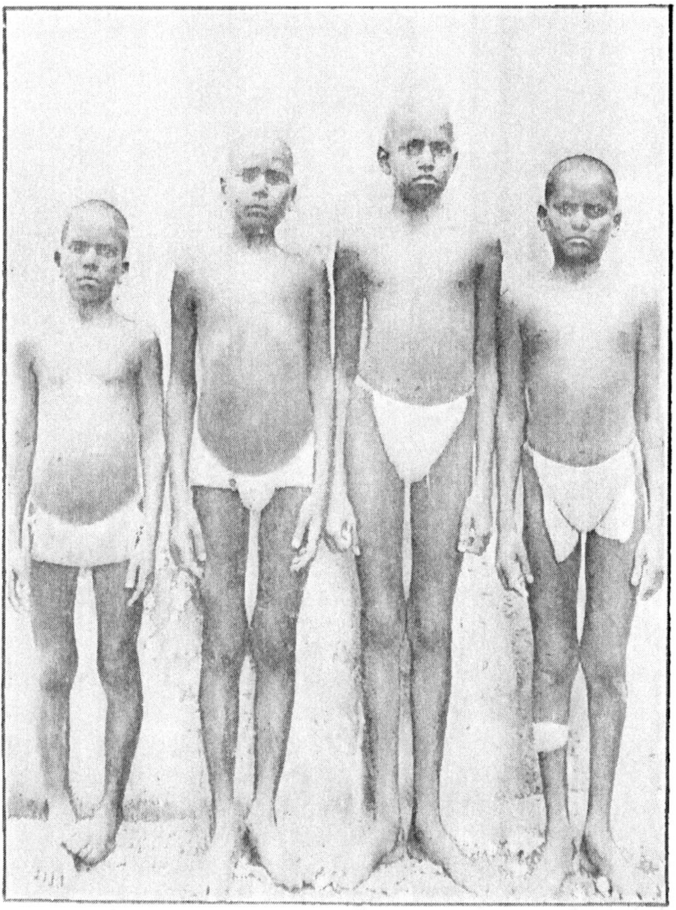

A Group of Muhammadan Counterfeiters (page 62)

fibre and fixing them in position so that they may not readily give way to the pressure of temptation. To use another metaphor, the planting is necessarily promiscuous, involving so many varieties that it is difficult always to keep away the weeds from choking the good plant. And who is sufficient for these things? The optimist, is the reply.

There are some boys in the school who ought never to have been admitted there. They are physically wrong, and to them the institution, for all practical purposes, will be nothing more than an infirmary. To take an extreme case: A boy is found on admission to be suffering from tuberculosis; his presence is a danger to his bedfellows, and, as his first need is oxygen, he is segregated. In a couple of months he visibly declines, and on the report of the Medical Officer his immediate discharge is recommended. This is easier said than done, for things move slowly in the official world. While orders are awaited, a visitor turns up at the school to see a brother, and at the end of his interview requests that he may see the sick boy, who hails from the same quarter of Bangalore as himself, to hand over some clothes, sweets and pickles sent by his mother for her son. The poor boy is anxious to taste the sugar candy and is allowed a small portion of it, but his stomach rejects it. The messenger is asked to convey to the mother the condition of her boy and his likely discharge in a few days from the school, with the request to come over and take charge of him, or in the event of her inability to do so, he was to say that a peon would escort him to his home.

After some six weeks the order is received, and as his condition is growing worse every day, a consultation is held with the Sub-Assistant Surgeon, who advises that the boy should be sent away at once. The boy brightens up on hearing that he is to go to his mother, and wishes to be sent away at once. A conveyance takes him to the railway station and he is able to walk across the platform to his compartment, while provision is made for suitable nourishment during the journey. He arrives at Bangalore early next morning and is taken to the mother's house, which he is able to find by making inquiries along the road:

On arrival there the mother, with a heart overflowing with tenderness and love, embraces him and sets before him coffee, some rice dumplings and pineapple—to one who has been living on slops for many a day. Soon the happy meeting ends in a tragic and pathetic manner. The boy is taken in a bandy at 9 o'clock to the Magistrate's Court and the mother accompanies him. His Honour arrives at 12 o'clock, but at 2 o'clock for the opening of the Court the peon finds that the boy's eyes, filled with tears, are fixed on his mother. Hurrying to the Magistrate, he reports his precarious condition, and before the letter about the discharge of the boy from the school is opened, he has quietly passed away, looking up to his mother. The question arises, why was the boy allowed to travel in the condition in which he was? On a post mortem examination being held it was found that tuberculosis of the lungs was the cause of death. The Magistrate inquired whether responsibility would be taken by the reformatory authorities for his death and the condition in which he undertook the journey. There was no question of responsibility involved here. The death of the poor boy was a matter of a few weeks, and it was wisely decided that he should rather die by the side of his mother than be left in the local hospital at the mercy of a stranger.

In the work of reclamation, some form of classification and segregation is necessary, and it is a necessity to be welcomed, for it brings about a smaller size of school, where the individual attention required to avoid manufacturing one type of product is secured. There can be no doubt about the wisdom of separating the juniors from the seniors, and if from a financial point of view this cannot be carried out, an adoption of the shift system lends a solution to the problem. A distinct advantage is obtained if the boys of both divisions are brought together for industrial work, when all are required to help and to co-operate with each other in the manufacture of articles. But as regards general education, and more particularly in respect of sleep and play, the division should be definite, for obvious reasons.

Most of the cases of fighting between the senior boys is caused by the small boys and their undesirable friendship with the bigger boys, and however strict the supervision may be over the two divisions to keep them apart during holidays and play hours, evil is at work in a number of indirect ways. Little boys are made use of to secrete contraband articles, and they give away a portion of their food to big boys who consent to wash their clothes for them. The conversation, also, of the big ones is not very edifying for the smaller ones.

The success of reformatory work, further, depends to some extent on the segregation of pupils of various degrees of criminality from each other, and there are boys who commit just one class of crime, *e.g.*, a pickpocket does not go in for stealing a Gladstone bag. By the above remark it is not meant that there should be a regular classification according to the offence of the boy, for it is quite probable that a boy sent for murder or some other heinous offence has a less baneful influence over others than a boy admitted for a minor offence, but who is found to be incorrigible. Roughly, boys of the worst type should be sent to a place where hard work and strict discipline are combined, in order that they may acquire the habits of industry, and boys who have committed only petty theft to an institution where domestic feelings and individuality are cultivated and where work is made attractive and educative. These children should receive kind and sympathetic management, and they will respond to every suggestion and advice of the teacher. In fact, liberty more or less of the type of the boarding school should be allowed. By these means, juveniles are associated together who profit best under the same treatment.

Every one will admit that boys with criminal tendencies should not be associated with those who have become habituated to crime, for not only is the discipline, the training and the incentives required for each class different, but what is more dangerous, is that the vicious are bound to contaminate and exert a bad influence over the minds of comparatively innocent ones admitted into the school for trifling offences. If we view criminality as a moral disease, then to prevent contagion we must have faith in the scientific treatment of segregation. And one bad boy is quite enough to contaminate a whole class, especially if he possesses a few heroic qualities for which he is looked up to by his schoolmates less acute than himself and weaker in physical strength. One instance of a riot in the school can be traced to this cause, and several acts of insubordination and indecency. So that not only from a moral but also from an educational point of view, differentiation, classification and segregation of juvenile criminals is essential. The creation of different types of institutions will also in the long run prove to be the most economical method, and the only sure way of reducing juvenile criminality.

Idaiyan (Shepherd) Group (page 61)

CHAPTER VI

GENERAL ROUTINE

The Superintendent sits in his office chair, at his office table, in his private room, busy with the many details of office routine, when a new inmate is announced. The little street urchin is ushered into the presence of the Superintendent by the Duffadar or Head Peon, followed by two police constables. He may salaam or he may not, if he is at his wit's end, but his previous history and temperament are soon discovered in the course of a few questions. These are necessary for the purpose of filling in the form of admission. The entry against caste is a difficult column to fill, not only because of the many sub-divisions which separate the various communities, reducible though they are to a few major ones under the basic element of occupation or trade, but the tendency of the boy, especially of the criminal class, is to take advantage of the status given him by caste and to put himself down in a class superior to his own. In a few days it is often found that he has overshot the mark of even fictitious veracity, and he receives his first warning. As for his residence, it is easy enough to discover his place in the Indian sun, for, as the country is divided into districts, these into Taluqs, and these again into so many hamlets, villages or towns, some idea as to the boy's environment is thus obtained, while particulars about his relatives reveal the fact that either he has been seriously neglected or has been encouraged to steal by his parents.

There is no necessity to question the lad about the offence which has provided for him the "Open Sesame" to the institution, for a copy of the judgment of the Court is among the papers, and the crime of which he was convicted, with the judicial sentence, age, date of detention order and period of detention are recorded. Particulars as to weight, height and health are also necessary for the purpose of watching his physical development. With these preliminaries gone through, the boy is informed that he has been sent to this school for so many years, with no undue emphasis placed on the word *school*, for he is allowed to discover for himself the homeliness of the treatment he receives, with plenty of opportunities for improvement, and compare it with the jail life he has perhaps heard about or has himself experienced for a short time prior to his admission. What is considered in the school as sins of commission are next categoried, and he is warned not to steal, not to tell a lie, not to touch tobacco, not to join bad companions, and is advised to be obedient, to learn how to read and write and to perfect himself in the elements of a trade. It is interesting to compare the boy on admission with his deportment a few weeks later. Watch him now as he is marched off to the tailor's shop to be fitted with a suit. He drags his legs along with a bewildered look, and dawdling along after a Monitor, who, by the way, is fully conscious of the role he fills in being guide to the new boy, while his surroundings slowly unfold kaleidoscopically to the little man. A good scrub and soaping is accompanied by a variety of questions shot at him by his strange schoolfellows. These questions often set him at ease, but they are begotten of a natural curiosity to get possession of the facts relating to his recent escapade and to catch a glimpse of the outside world. It is one of the doings of fate that crime should open to him the portals of an institution, which even respectable parents desire to have done on behalf of their wayward children, but have been denied in language tantamount to the inhuman suggestion that they should get their son convicted, thus placing a premium upon crime. Thus does crime indeed open out to the young delinquent advantages of a sound training, with prospects of a good after career, often denied to the respectable classes. When a newcomer takes his place for the first time in the Sunday School he is welcomed publicly in a song sung by his schoolmates.

A rough translation by one of the Hindu staff is given below :—

CHORUS

" We welcome you, new comers, to rejoice,
So that, cease your nefarious deeds outside and enjoy our family with one voice."

STANZAS

1. " This joint family, nowhere exists.
Our Father is an acquisition ; everyone insists
Fear here does not find a place.

2. " It is no use recounting our history past ;
Our father, lovely and protecting, inspires us fast ;
Let us hold his wisdom fast.

3. " As long as we live here pleasant time we have.
The Chingleput Reformatory our interests will save,
If we abide by its teachings in right earnest.

4. " Work hard at school and workshop, we elevate ourselves
Without casting shade on the fair name of this school ;
Our effort is then crowned with success.

5 " Bad company will bring harm no doubt ;
Using snuff and tobacco will make you dull
And unfit you to better your prospects in any walk of life."

The new admission is asked in turn to pay toll with a song. The reason is to break down any strangeness of feeling tending to act as a barrier against his feeling at home. More often than not he responds with a song couched in filthy language, the only soul-degrading verse he has ever picked up from street companions to set his heart in tune.

when the hours lagged for want of occupation. But what a change has come over the sentiments of the school, for a smile of disapproval breaks forth from many a placid countenance, and the master quickly raises his hands in horror, spurting out a request for a change of song.

For a few months the fresher is segregated from the rest of the school, till such time as he gets accustomed to his new surroundings, adapts himself to the discipline of the school, and learns to appreciate the advantages which taken at the flood will lead him on to fortune. His first smile soon shows the change of feelings that is rapidly developing.

When he is permitted to mix freely with the other boys his individualism shows itself in his little world of activity. One type of boy readily takes unto himself a friend and will probably stick to him in after life, especially if he comes from the same town. Sometimes the bond of friendship happens to rest on the slender foundation of having arrived on the same day, and as new arrivals their sympathy goes out to each other. Another boy quickly earns a reputation on the football field, and he draws around him several admirers hanging on to him for his sign of approval.

Then comes the studious boy, who scrupulously attends to the washing of his clothes and to the preparation of his lessons. He is the first to be present at the roll-call, and finds freedom in obedience to rules and discipline and monitorial supervision. He is quick in learning that by such conduct some day the " cap " will fall to his lot.

The fourth type of boy sets himself up in opposition from the start. He seeks for the first opportunity to escape, and always hankers after the forbidden fruit. He really never settles down to work, and is never happy unless he is in hot water.

Lastly comes the born pilferer. Quick at secreting things, he begins by watching his opportunity to either steal vegetable or fruit from the garden, misappropriate a tool or manufactured article, or put his hand into the pocket of a hanging coat. One almost despairs of reclaiming a juvenile of this kind.

With such varied characters it takes time to become

familiar with the individualism of each, while in addition to general treatment, special cases are dealt with by special methods of work.

While castes and classes in the outside world will seldom put aside their differences even in a common cause, it is refreshing to see in the school that representatives from all the various districts of the Presidency mix together fraternally. Great as is the variety of physiognomy and of dialect, it proves no barrier to friendly intercourse. In the hospital you will find a low caste drink from the same bottle of medicine or ounce-glass as the high caste. In the same ward a sweeper boy is attended to with the same scrupulousness as any other, and if anything fatal should happen even to one of the untouchables, the universal feeling of sorrow testifies to the feeling of brotherhood that prevails inside, where every boy is given an equal opportunity to fit himself for the future, and no caste superiority is recognised.

One boy arrives with a suffering, weary look on his face, a few dirty rags cover him, and his hair is matted with filth. Within a month or two the boy is happier for the change of surroundings. He wears a clean suit, begins to smile, and moves about as if the place belonged to him. Another boy arrives covered from head to foot with scabies, nauseous to look at. He is at once segregated, and his skin is mollified and nourished with oil and sulphur, till he puts on a new coat and is fit to mix with his fellows.

Another day, a fine bright-looking boy with lustrous eyes looks one full in the face, taking in everything that is told him with transparent simplicity, and one wonders why on earth he is sent to the school. It soon transpires that some evil-disposed parent, unfit to hold the responsible position of a guardian, was using him as an accomplice, either at helping him to counterfeit coins or assisting him in defrauding the public at fair or festival. Such a lad gets trained to good habits, but he does not leave the school as ingenuous as he came in. He has at least learnt to bless the school, and a grateful regard for the blessings received ought to act as ballast in the shaping of his after-career. A third new-comer has a criminal look and an expressionless face—a narrow forehead, ill-formed ears, heavy jaw, flat feet or broad nose, all marks of his inferiority. He takes in nothing at first, but is gradually made to respond to his surroundings, and is given the chance of reshaping his life along with the others.

The day begins early in the school. At the first streak of dawn, when the gong strikes five, the long drawn-out notes of the bugle sounds the *reveille* in the silence of the morning hour, which is a signal for the boys to jump out of their hammocks and file out to their respective tasks. While one half perform their necessary ablutions, the other half is engaged in the general cleaning up of the grounds before regular task begins. If the Deputy Superintendent desires a "Europe morning" he cannot have it, because he perforce gets up with the bugle call, which is sufficiently loud to disturb his slumbers. The head gardener is the first one to call at his house, waiting for the day's supply of vegetables to be inspected. As for the other supplies, the ration clerk sees them measured out and weighed. Then comes a round of inspection work. The store-keeper places his registers for scrutiny, renders up accounts and submits bills for signature.

The little hospital has always somebody waiting to be attended to—the cause is either a boil on the cheek, a sprain in the ankle, a sore on the foot, a bad eye, a wound from hockey or football, a stomach-ache, a cough or symptoms of fever. These have all to be seen and sent away satisfied, even if it is a dose of a little cold water. After visiting the hospital, the time arrives to make the round of the workshops. The boys stand momentarily to attention as the Head walks round, and the various maistries are given directions about the work of the day and how to set machines right when they go wrong. The carpenter has been allowing some boys to idle or the blacksmith disregards the work that is being done by a young hand, or the weaver neglects to push on the dull ones, while the gardener sleeps over his business, thus tempting the urchins to steal a radish, an onion, a lime or ear of mucca-cholum (Indian corn) which evidently tastes all the sweeter for being stolen. The tailor boy is happy enough plying his needle and cotton with an upward jerk, chatting to his neighbour while he works. These the Superintendent will criticise and supervise, giving advice here, a correction there, seeing generally that everything is kept up to the mark. He next goes to the office to attend to correspondence with judicial and educational officers, initial office copies, answer letters from old boys, look into reports from the sergeant or his assistant, listen patiently to the requests or complaints of boys, and adjudicate on breaches of school discipline or more serious offences after the arguments on both sides are heard.

Now it is feeding-time, and an occasional look at the food and a peep into the kitchen to see that everything is served out and nothing held back by the cooks is very necessary. This done, a passing visit is paid to the schoolroom to see if the boys are properly dressed, and the masters are present in their classrooms in time.

The work in the afternoon is similar in nature to that in the forenoon and carries one on till five. The schoolboys, both senior and junior, are out now in the field playing football or hockey till sunset, the Superintendent seeing them at their games as often as possible, and then the bugle sounds the fall-in. The Muhammadan boys in answer to the long-drawn out chant of the boy "Muezzin" calling them to prayer to the words that "God is great, God is great, I give witness that Mahomed is the Prophet of God, come to prayer, come to prayer, come to goodness, come to goodness," assemble in the school mosque and go through their genuflections. The pious little Hindu boy, and they are only a few, will go to his temple and circumambulate it to gain merit, while the Christian is satisfied with his prayer at his bedside before he lays down to sleep.

The Superintendent is then free to retire to his bungalow, and after dinner silence reigns supreme with the sounding of the last post, except for the occasional cough of a boy, the bark of a dog, the croak of a frog or the chirp of a cricket, for nature is never altogether asleep. But the soundness of one's slumbers may be disturbed at any moment during the night by a call from one of the boys who may happen to be suddenly taken ill.

There is not a sound to disturb the peaceful quietness that reigns at night, except the rush of a passing train, or the distant cry of a jackal, and a stranger entering the premises at that time is unconscious that two hundred little minds, bent on mischief of some kind, are in a state of quiescence.

At 5 a.m. the bugle sounds the *reveille,* the gong strikes the hour, my dog 'Cop' begins to howl—but not in tune with the bugles—and 'Mike,' our mascot donkey, takes up the refrain, the whole producing a conglomeration of notes to awaken the soundest sleeper.

This is the signal for the boys to get off their hammocks, tidy their blankets and clothes; and at the first glimmer of daylight the unlocking takes place and the dormitories disgorge their living. The unlocking and locking up is done quietly, in order, and with the least amount of friction. The boys are marched off to perform their ablutions, twigs of branches, charcoal, and red brick dust serving as tooth brush and powder. A gang of boys is told off to do the sweeping up of the place and the brooms go "swish, swish," the monotony being relieved occasionally by the appealing, yet authoritative, tone of the Duffadar crying out, "Who is there?" to some figure lurking under the shadow of a tree. Then comes the opportunity for a villain to pay off old scores towards another boy or a member of the guarding staff.

After a small repast consisting of a 5-oz. ragi chapatti with 1 oz. of molasses, the boys are marched off at 6 a.m. to their respective industries and continue to work till 9.30. Between 9.30 and 10.30 breakfast is served, each boy getting a 2-lb. ragi pudding (the juniors getting less), with 4 oz. of vegetables and 2 oz. of dal in the shape of a curry. The seniors are at general education work from 10.30 to 12.30, while the juniors are at gardening, after which an hour is devoted to recreation, during which interval a 2-oz. hot rice conjee is distributed to the boys. The senior boys carry on industrial work again from 1-30 to 4-30, the juniors being engaged in general education work.

The half-hour before 5 p.m. is given to drill and gymnastics, and between 5 and 6 the first and second elevens are at their games on the playing-field.

Bathing, and the evening meal, which is similar to the morning one, is finished by 6 o'clock, and at 7 the boys are locked in, but are allowed to talk till the "last post" is sounded at 8 p.m. Night school for the preparation of lessons is held from 7 to 8. For a change, rice is given as a diet twice a week (generally on a Sunday or festival day), mutton twice a week, and fish once a week. The daily routine of duty changes of course on Sunday.

Generally everything goes with a swing on a working day, except for one or two loiterers who, on surveying the arrangements made by those in authority, are always on the lookout for the evasion of rules and bounds if they can possibly do it without detection. Occasionally during the industrial hours a row takes place between two boys and a free fight ensues, the rest of the class plunging joyously into the fray. Work for a few minutes is disorganised, while the Maistry or foreman makes repeated attempts to exercise his feeble authority by a torrent of verbal abuse.

When work is knocked off for the morning meal, the boys occupy the greater part of their leisure hour in washing their dishes and fooling about, for they delight in coming late to meals, either from the excitement derived in doing the irregular or on the chance of picking up the crumbs that may remain. Then they make a bolt for school, for latecomers receive a stroke from the Head Master who waits at the door cane in hand. It is wise to raise the standard of offences deserving punishment, for in punishing the lesser ones the bigger ones take care of themeselves and are put out of action. School work now proceeds with fairly frequent interruptions. A boy holds up a finger to his master, which is a sign that he wishes to leave the room, ostensibly to satisfy a call, but really having something at the back of his head to be carried into execution. Some show signs of slumber over a dull lesson and are put to stand on the bench, but an elevated position proves no bar to their enjoying a quiet nap. The class is generally a mixed lot, composed of all sorts and conditions of temperament, age and scholarship; its management, therefore, taxes the energy of the teacher if he is anxious at all to teach on right lines. A few minutes before break up a buzz is audible, acting as a gentle reminder to the master that it is time for books and slates to be collected, and on the first bugle note a general rush is made for the door, indicative of intense relief.

Walk round the school soon after work ceases and you will find on the parade ground various squads at their drill. In one corner of the quadrangle the weak-chested are going through a course of Swedish drill. In another part of the ground, a section of the school is put through physical exercises with dumb-bells or Indian clubs, for general development. A third squad, weak in limb power, is undergoing native gymnastics, figuring out all sorts of shapes in their contortions on the ground. A voluntary class is at English gymnastics, and the trouble is to tear them away from their exercises at meal or recreation time. They take a pride in their performance and in the increase of their measurements, being only too ready to show off to visitors their feats of exhibition, so that little stimulus is required to maintain a high level of efficiency.

Now come the teasers, who seem incapable of looking after themselves or their property. Their clothes are either stained with objectionable provender secreted in their coat pockets or they come with a complaint that a badge has been stolen or a coat has been lost, and with tears they approach the office for satisfaction; but they receive short shrift when they are asked to stump up the cost of the article lost through carelessness, and they depart crestfallen. The pity of it is that the boy who has a grudge against another thinks he is perfectly justified in paying off old scores in this underhand fashion, by prigging his adversary's coat and throwing it into a well or chucking his tin dish over the rampart. This type of misdemeanour, however, is not a common characteristic, but still it raises unworthy suspicions against many an innocent youth so long as the culprit remains undetected.

Nature has been kind to the school in furnishing a swimming tank alongside, the boys having ample opportunities for learning the art of swimming and diving. After drill is over, a row of boys stands by the side of the diving board and leaping off in quick succession, some head the water in fine style, others make a somersault in the air before touching the surface, while others plunge in awkwardly, creating a great splutter in the water, but *le tout ensemble*, creates a merry quarter of an hour, and amuses the onlooker. Immediately after lock up, silence reigns in the dormitories for a few minutes while each boy's head is lowered in prayer offered up in language of his own, there being no set form. Having spoken with the Angels in enforced silence, they compensate themselves immediately afterwards by letting loose their tongues, and the dormitory breaks up into small groups, but what the nucleus or attractive force of each group centre is, one would fain like to know. It is as good as a play to watch the eager faces as they discuss perhaps the chief events of the day. Plots are hatched, friendships renewed, enmity heightened by little acts of meanness, all enacted in the hour before the sounding of the "Last Post." But with the sounding of the "reveille" in the morning feelings become adjusted to work and the heterogeneous crowd fall into their proper places with little or no ripple on the moral surface, while the school sails calmly on, steadied by work acting as a powerful ballast.

The snuffers and smokers hobnob at odd intervals but their society is a secret one, which is a matter for thankfulness. Fortunately one is not born with eyes behind one's back, for it would create a state of unhappiness of which few could bear the strain; in fact the *Custos morum is* forced to half close his eyes to many shortcomings as long as major offences continue to occupy his time. A voluntary night-school is held, where the schoolmaster's task is a simple one so far as the giving of knowledge is concerned, for in leading his pupils up the slopes of Parnassus he is materially helped by a willing climber. The boy works because he feels he has lost ground in the past, having wasted his early years in roaming about the streets, and when he is brought face to face with learning letters for the first time, he enters with relish upon the task of qualifying for the various standard examinations. The unwilling lad who is forced to attend the voluntary class in order to enable him to keep up with the level of his companions gives no trouble either. He fixes both his eyes upon the page of his book, absorbing nothing and giving out nothing. *Requiescat in pace.*

A calm atmosphere is always sought after at eventide, for it is desirable that no disturbance should take place when the roll call is being taken. Confusion would only lead to an intolerable strain on the staff at a time when perfect order and quiet should reign to ensure careful counting up and marching into barracks. But boys burgeoning into prominence are always ready to defy the law on the least provocation, and it sometimes happens that a crowd gathers round over some little irregularity. In such cases it does no good to shout at the revellers. The safest course is to jot down names quietly and announce to the ringleaders that they would have to appear at the office to-morrow.

It will also be found that a few of the big boys at the last moment rush off to the latrine to have a nervous pull in the dark at a cigarette stump while a file is waiting to be numbered. It is rather a pity that one has to lock up the boys at 7 o'clock in the evening, but it is unsafe to do otherwise, and to minimise the mischief the youngsters are allowed to talk till they climb into their hammocks on the sound of the bugle at 8 o'clock. If a monitor is autocratically inclined, he shouts out for silence every five minutes and takes the law into his own hands on his authority being challenged. In another dormitory everything works smoothly for the prefect collects his house together and interests them by narrating stories. When bedtime comes, every boy is expected to go to his berth whether he feels sleepy or not. As a rule the boys are so fairly dead beat that they soon fall asleep, and sleep so soundly that they scarcely turn in their hammocks—one dreads to think what would happen if any careless attempt at this threw them on to the hard paved floor!

The dormitories are lighted, and any irregularities that take place are soon detected by the peons, who patrol the place at night and are relieved of their watch every three hours. The Deputy Superintendent and the Sergeant make surprise visits, to keep the peons up to the mark. In jails, the tell-tale clock system is used, but as the price of a clock is very high and the instrument is liable to get out of order, it has not found favour in the school, particularly as it is not absolutely necessary. It would be much to be preferred if one of the masters could be told off to sleep with the boys. The experiment was tried and was given up because it was a hardship to non-resident masters to take their bed in school. But the present system of supervision by peons and monitors has worked well, and few irregularities have been reported or are suspected of having taken place.

A holiday is synonymous with a festival day, and on such occasions the boys look forward to a special diet and an oil bath, no food being taken till the bathing is over. Country vegetable soup and gingelli oil are served out in a leaf to each boy, and they help one another in working in the oil into the skin of the body, while the head, the eyes and the ears receive special attention. It is almost painful to watch the operations on the eyes as the lids are turned inside out and rubbed till they become inflamed.

Avani Avittam (or the thread-wearing ceremony) is one of the festivals which only the select few can observe, for it would be an impious and indecent absurdity for any other person of equality to claim the same right. The privileged ones are the Brahmins, the highest caste, and also the Asari caste or the artizan class, thus pointing to the high status enjoyed by the art workmen in ancient times. The thread is supposed to be the sign of the second birth, and is worn on the naked body over the left shoulder. It is of folded cotton yarn and consists of three strands to represent the three gods, Brahma, Vishnu and Siva. During the course of the day the boys undergo the operation of shaving, then of bathing, and the Brahmin priest having performed certain ceremonies repeats a few mantharas or prayers before the thread is put on.

Ayudapuja is the appropriate feast of the workmen, when the artizans worship their tools and the students their books. It is a sublime thought worthy of execution that a workman should so respect the tools and implements by which he earns his daily bread as to gather them together once a year, clean them and worship them.

Somewhat of the same feeling must run through the soldier and the sportsman who takes a pride in his rifle or his horse, or the car-travelling tourist, which impels him to see that his automobile is well looked after and that all the parts are cleaned, oiled and in working order. There is, however, the superstitious feeling that by it they are protected from all injury and accident that would otherwise happen to them in the using of their tools. The whole school, therefore, under the direction of their maistries, enters into the spirit of the ceremony, *con amore*, though they be miniature artizans. From early morning, representatives from each trade rush off in all directions in search of flowers, and a ruthless raid is made upon neighbouring places.

Industries vie with one another in beautifying their respective workshops, and great taste is shown and trouble taken to lay out the tools in the most effective manner after they have been cleaned. An image or picture of Sarasvathi the goddess of learning and the arts, is arranged alongside other pictures, beaten rice, coconut, sugar, fruits and flowers being placed in front. Turmeric and red aniline powder are moistened and besmeared over the several tools to be worshipped as symbols of the deity. The Superintendent is compelled to visit in turn every show under a running fire of smiles and attention from the boys, while he is careful to remember Saint Paul's exhortation against eating things offered to idols. A gong summons a particular trade, and the head boy garlands the Superintendent as he enters, incense and camphor being lighted, and a coconut broken in halves. The lighted camphor is taken round to the boys who hold their hands over the smoke and pass them odorised over their faces. The indispensible sandlewood paste, supposed to possess cooling and digestive properties, is passed round to each one, who help themselves to a little, daubing their hands and face with it. The offerings of cakes and sweets are then distributed among the boys, who eagerly look forward to the good things, the rest of the day being spent in munching the beaten rice and coconut, while a running chaff is carried on to the delight of everyone.

The Commandment "Six days shalt thou labour" is faithfully observed in the school, much more so perhaps than in Christian countries where supposed rights are insisted on, and the working-class demand a half-holiday for the purpose of seeing a football match, or a week of 40 hours. Times have changed since the world-wide war broke out, but in the days previous to it no less than in those succeeding it, one was and is inclined to lay more stress on the first part of the command than on the second, for undue emphasis on workmen's rights is fast becoming an obsession. In the Reformatory due observance is paid to the six working days of eight hours each, and to the Sunday as a *dies non.* On the principle that change of occupation is rest, the routine on the seventh day alters completely. Except for one hour in the morning, when the whole place is tidied up, the boys are given absolute liberty to occupy themselves in any way they like, and they spend it in washing their clothes and ironing them.

The "Dhoby khana" is a square pond in that part of the Chingleput Lake that fringes the ramparts near the school. Flat stones pave the steps that shelve down to the water's edge, and when the clothes are battered on them, a slash-slush sound goes on continuously with columns of water spouting up on all sides. A little fuller's earth or soap is used to take out the dirt, but half the boys rely chiefly on their muscular strength to remove the week's filth that accumulates. To look at, they seem to be trying to split rocks with their coats. For the purpose of ironing their trousers and coat, a blanket is used and the process is a simple and effective one. While the clothes are wet, they are folded lengthwise, and placed between the folds of the blanket spread out on the smooth floor of a verandah. The boy then tramples the blanket with his feet for all he is worth, stamping and treading on the garments to flatten them out: they are then left in the sun on the ground to dry. It is interesting to watch the earnestness with which the operation is performed and the care they take over it, while the time it occupies leaves very few idle moments.

Sunday is a day of both fasting and feasting. The usual diet is ragi, but on this day a special rice diet is given and in the evening mutton is served out. The food is relished, but as rice is light fare, it scarcely seems to satisfy the boys' hunger. Soon after, the Sunday moral lesson, or rather informal talk, follows the morning meal, and with the exception of half a dozen boys who never seem to be able to keep their eyes open, it speaks well for the school that they are interested enough to listen to it with attention. The singing is enjoyed, and everybody feels the better for an hour of quiet talk.

The midday is usefully employed in washing out the various dormitories, and for two hours after that the boys are left to themselves to do what they please. Some have a dip in the lake. Others laze in the open, stretching themselves out on the grassy plots while the rest either play or read. At half-past two the bugler sounds the " fall in " for a general parade, half an hour being allowed for dress and cleaning up of badges. The Officer's call brings out the Superintendent who formally walks out to the parade while the band plays the march, " Hark ! the Bonny Christ Church Bells." After inspecting the line the boys march past in column, in double companies, in double time, and in quarter column, followed by various evolutions done smartly enough to satisfy any school battalion commandant. Physical dumb-bell drill, accompanied by music to teach rhythm of music, is also exercised, and before the final break-up, the order for advance, retire, left wheel, right wheel, double and halt is carried out by bugle sounds which the boys are taught to interpret. When the dismiss sounds, they break off in good spirits for their food. The final tune played by the band never fails to attract the musically inclined boys, who gather round and wonder at the sound produced by their own playmates through what appears to them curious shaped instruments, the big drum, of course, coming in for a greater share of special attraction. Off once again to the feeding ground the meal of rice and mutton is partaken of with great relish.

Once more the "fall in" brings the boys together for a walk out through the town of Chingleput or along one of the great trunk roads. The Indian staff that accompany the boys do not relish this item of the programme, for they cannot appreciate the nerve tonic and the psychological effect of a little fresh air and scenery on a boy cooped in for the greater part of the time. The chances are that only a leisurely stroll is indulged in unless special orders are given as to the spot they should be marched to. As a rule the Superintendent meets the cost of parched peas which is distributed at the place where they fall out, and munching goes on all the way back. Some go to the length of drawing out the pleasure to the following day, when evidence of it is visible in the empty shells left beneath the benches when the classes are dismissed after the first lesson. How a boy loves using his jaws and teeth! Perhaps it is an instinct handed down from primitive days when hard comestibles insured digestion by the free secretion of saliva, as well as cleanliness of teeth by the friction of food. Our ancestors believed in no sloppy mess. Sunday closes with sunset, with no night school for preparation of work— a fitting *finale* to the day of rest.

Mottiyan, a Korava boy aged 13, is responsible for the enactment of an exciting scene in the school five days after admission. He discovers that the last escape was pulled off successfully through the vent holes of the blacksmith shop and so decides to effect his escape in the same way; he succeeds, to the great disgust of the whole school. The big boys at once start off to search for him, some with and a few others without permission, the latter evidently for the purpose of roaming about the town to enjoy a sly smoke. What a rare opportunity for them. Information is soon brought from the railway station that a boy was seen clinging to the chain links behind a railway carriage just as the mail train steamed out, but in the act of entering a compartment a railway policeman apprehends him on suspicion and brings him back to school in the evening.

The boy as usual starts of with the statement that he "had no sense" in running away, and cannot explain himself. In the meantime the other boys have all come back from their fruitless search with the exception of two who had gone out with consent and two others who seem to have taken advantage of the commotion to walk out of the school for the ostensible purpose of bringing back the escaped lad. They travelled far during the night and, 18 miles away, the big city of Conjeeveram is reached, where the police discover four lads with close-cropped heads wandering about the town—the ordinary boy, be it remembered, wears a tuft of long hair tied into a knot behind. They come to the conclusion that these have escaped from the school. In the face of the most serious protest their word is discounted, and a message that they are in custody is received the following day through a policeman, who, on learning the facts of the case, suggests that a telegram be sent to the Sub-Inspector, Conjeeveram, to forthwith release the boys.

It all sounds so funny, as we realise the fact that a monitor with a badge of trust, who is fired with so much resolve and self-sacrifice as to offer his services to find the lost sheep, should find himself picketed with his companions in a common police station for want of knowledge on the part of the Police Inspector as to the trust imposed on our boys.

In due course the truant is handed up for punishment, and when asked how he managed to escape, his reply was most ingenious, for he tried to throw the chief blame on to the railway policeman who, as stated by him, having discovered his presence on the local station platform, took him away in the train to Madras and brought him back so as to enable him to frame a charge of escape. The poor policeman therefore comes in for calumny even from the mouth of youthful offenders. The boy is marched up to the triangle and tied up. For some seconds he contemplates this strange engine of punishment with fear, but he receives the strokes fairly well, and the nasty business is soon over. The boy of course regards his offence more as the result of a pardonable ebullition of feeling for his home and freedom than as a breach of morality, but an example has to be made. It is a healthy sign to find that after the corporal punishment has been administered he comes up and pleads protection from the chastisement of his schoolfellows, who generally resent and claim damages to the last ounce for any behaviour affecting the good name of the school.

CHAPTER VII

MOFFUSIL LIFE IN INDIA

WHERE there were few social amenities, my life in Chingleput was dull. There was no opportunity of spending a rejuvenating week-end in the Presidency town of Madras, although only 38 miles away—for it did no good to be away from the school on a Sunday—and surrounded by high walls one felt wrapped in an asylum atmosphere. Were it not for the stimulating influence of working on behalf of unprotected boys, such an existence would soon become unbearable. Invitations from friends and relatives living away are put aside, and the only compensations are of a local character. A game of tennis, an occasional dinner-party or a tramp in the fields for snipe sum up the amusements of the place. There is a club for Indians, but in the present state of unrest it is not easy to mix freely with the members.

At present the political atmosphere is charged with reform schemes which do not seem to satisfy the aspirations of the extremists, while the less favoured classes are opposed to them. Catch-words and expressions like self-determination, government for the people and by the people, are used on the slightest provocation, and offence is often taken at a harmless joke. The country is in the throes of evolution, and the opposition of castes renders progress slow. Bonds of friendship are broken over differences of opinion, and I remember giving offence by a remark at our prize distribution that in the school non-Brahmins, on account of their sympathy with the depressed classes, made better teachers than Brahmins. I alienated for a time a number of my Brahmin admirers.

If the Superintendent has a hobby, he can usefully employ it in the interest of the school.

On my assuming charge in 1904, the bungalow where I was to spend some 15 years of my life was anything but attractive. There were no punkahs, blinds or mats, no weather boards or sunshades to soften the reflected glare from the water of the lake, often so overpowering as to forbid the enjoyment of any outlook from the verandah. All this was altered, and occupied a great deal of my enforced leisure. Rattan mats now cover the parlour, a bamboo mat was laid in the sleeping room, and the floors of all the other rooms were cemented. The verandah overlooking the lake, on account of its position, convenience and comfort, came to be used as a bed, sitting and dining room, in short as a living room in the hot weather. It was treated to an ornamental floor of "minton" tiles, to be in keeping with its beautiful outlook. Built on an old Hindu temple and surmounted by a broad flight of stairs on either side of a corridor, the upper storey of my house was alone habitable. A neat rail, hedged by plants, now surrounds the garden, and everything has been done to make a successor contented and willing to stay. A few woollen rugs on the floor, with artistically carved furniture made by the boys, brass and other ornaments of beautiful design, combine to make it a veritable home. These artistic surroundings are reflected in the general buildings and dormitories, where neat dados cover the walls with a running floral border. Patches of colour from plants are arranged at vantage points and in keeping with the perspective of the general lines of the place. The playground of the boys is adjusted to form a square by the judicious cutting down of a few trees and the removal of a tennis-court and gymnastic apparatus to a spot further down. The rain trees planted round the square in a short time grew up to shade the ground swept by the fresh cool breeze of the lake. The playground outside the school precincts, which was a wilderness a few years ago, is now a beautiful green lawn, setting off with its verdure the approaches to the school.

The verandah reveals a wide and charming view of the

lake, which compensates one a great deal for the isolated position of the bungalow. At times one gets a glimpse of the affairs of the outside world by sudden and welcome visits. The Government chaplain and his friends, an Inspector of Schools, an Examiner of an Industrial Department, interested visitors, enjoy the hospitality of the Superintendent, and the exhilarating talk on these occasions was of fascinating interest to me. Casual visitors were frequent, and a young couple on their honeymoon must be included in the list. The U. F. C. Scotch Mission has a station here, and I often met a few Scotch ladies and the Missionary in charge at their tennis parties, where we were regaled to scones, muffins, cakes and tea minus jokes. The District Judge or Sub Collector also had a tennis evening. Here the tables are laid under a spreading banyan tree with coffee, tea, iced and other drinks to regale the thirsty ones. It recalls forcibly the hospitality of old times when the house of the Collector was the rendezvous of the few people in a station where the number of Europeans was too small to warrant a club. And so day follows day. But the night does not always bring rest. The toads and rats often keep one alive. When the heat tempts one to walk bare-footed on the cool mat an involuntary shock is the result as the foot strays on to a cold, squashy, squelchy toad that makes one's blood run up the spine. Periodically the rooms have to be cleared of these vermin, but the extirpation of the rats is a more serious problem.

If you are not protected by a mosquito net you are startled from sleep by a rat jumping on to you, and if your head is greased the little creatures nibble at it. Even a couple of rats can keep up an annoyance for days. Beds, pillows and cushions reserved for guests are literally riddled with holes which defy repair, particularly when the rat nibbles a hundred openings in the bedding in its search for stray cotton seeds. Traps are set night after night with dainty baits, but the rat is too cunning to venture inside. Poison readily occurs as a means of destruction. In this plague-stricken land the poison is easily obtained in the shape of Barium carbonate which can be completely camouflaged. One part of the powder mixed with two parts of grain flour and made into small balls is placed in various haunts with effective results. A little pudding mixed with the poison also acts as a successful bait. But the use of poison is at times accompanied with disastrous results. The mention of it recalls the loss of a favourite house-terrier. Well cared for and brought up to good habits, my pet dog "Cop" would never attempt to move anything placed on a table. A poisoned piece of pudding I placed for rats lay once the whole night and early next morning untouched, but an hour later the morsel was gone.

Suspicions were not centred on the dog—a squirrel or crow was thought to have made away with it, and the fact of the dog having swallowed it was found out too late for any remedial measures to save its life. The poison had been in him for six hours, and after suffering a whole day the poor animal sank to rest. He was carried away next morning by two boys on the rug on which he died, and was buried under an orange tree in the garden. The death of the dog was a great loss to me, and many incidents in the routine of the school reminded me of him. It attuned its voice to the note of the bugle whenever the boys were at practice. At home it always lay at my feet, breaking its reverie at intervals by a peep through the loopholes of the verandah wall and looking down on the scene below at the fowls feeding or on some moving object. It was a faithful companion on my walks and rounds, heralding my advent at each place about to be inspected. Its death was viewed with genuine regret by the boys for they are now caught napping and are punished. The dog was a betrayer of all my movements, and its mourners therefore were truly genuine in their sorrow.

To hark back, this orange tree bore no fruit for a long time, but it blossomed shortly after a dead antelope was buried under its shade. The animal was a pet of Miss Pakenham Walsh, the daughter of an Irish Bishop.

My professional life would not be complete without a reference to my butler-cook, who performed the double function of cooking and serving at table. He was a good cook, who knew how to roast a duck or fowl, and was first-rate at making a good Madras Curry. In addition he turned out dainty cakes and sweets, having learnt the art of confectionary in a public restaurant. But he had one failing, and that was his fondness for country beer, a little of which was quite enough to turn his head. To inconvenience me as little as possible, he set to and taught one of the senior boys in the school how to cook, so that he could take his place when he was the worse for liquor. It required the least provocation or excuse to set him going. I remember Lord Carmichael, the then Governor of Madras, who was the Chairman at one of our anniversaries, going round to see the boys at their sports. He came across the butler's son dressed in his best being carried about by a reformatory boy. He came up to the child and shook hands with him. An act of condescension which cost me a dinner, for my boy went drunk on the strength of His Excellency shaking hands with his son. It is said that good cooking and soberness never go together in the East. My experience supports this theory.

Few people in England can realise that we are often obliged to live in localities infested with poisonous reptiles, and that there are very few snakes more deadly than the cobra. Persons bitten by these creatures have only a few minutes to look for antidotes and no time to make their will. Fortunately for the English dweller, these reptiles usually keep away from human habitation, but occasionally are tempted to look for shade and coolness in a European's bungalow. One such incident happened to me.

The old fort is full of cobras, but they are seldom seen, and nobody tries to unearth them for they are viewed as the guardian deities of the place. Shy in the extreme, they venture occasionally from their own dwelling-place in search of food or shelter. I remember getting up one morning feeling pretty seedy from the heat, and in a half sleepy mood walking across to the bathroom. Here I saw, as I thought, my little bul-bul bird in the throes of an entanglement, and trying to get its leg free from some cotton. It was in reality the head of a cobra, jerking out its little tongue at me in the space between the door and its frame, the whole of the body being hid from view. It was evidently trying to effect a passage across the room, and resented my intrusion. My bare feet were planted just two feet from it, and while I was debating in my mind whether I should try to catch the bird-like object, or close the doors first and call for assistance, the snake rushed across the room into the next and hid itself under the bamboo matting on the floor. Still innocent of the narrow escape from danger I sent for the Duffadar or Head Peon and asked him to bring a snake-charmer, who shortly appeared on the scene and carefully lifting up one end of the mat discovered a cobra coiled underneath. He raised an alarm, and with a stick broke its back as it tried to get away. Such luck spells long life to the being snatched from the jaws of death, for are they not those whom the gods had conspired to save. This was the comment of the boys and staff, as they wished me eternal good fortune.

On another occasion while proceeding to the office room in my bungalow, something struck my head as I crossed the threshold, and on looking up I found that a fearful looking serpent was balancing itself overhead after having hit me with its tail. A glance at its body with ventral scales and its tail not markedly compressed, assured me that it belonged to the non-poisonous variety. It was in fact a "whip snake," which lives in trees and is supposed to use its tail as a rod for chastisement. A sudden contact with a snake, however, at times paralyses one for the moment, and in this case I gave vent to an involuntary cry.

Another exciting episode in my life was the shooting of a crocodile in the lake. Some half a mile away there is a blind stream of the river Palar which is infested with crocodiles, and during a heavy monsoon when the neighbouring fields were under water, a stray creature, 'for joy' as an Indian sweeper put it, found its way into the lake. When the boys discovered its presence near their bathing place, a hue and cry was raised, and no one would venture into the water to perform his usual morning ablutions. With a view to get rid of the beast a careful watch was kept to see where it would rise to get its supply of oxygen from the air. One day it was discovered basking in the sun on a bank close by. News was at once brought to me. As luck would have it, the police were firing their musketry course at the time, so I managed to obtain a rifle and a couple of rounds of ball ammunition.

I proceeded cautiously to the spot and looking over the rampart found the animal lying a few yards away down below. Aiming at a vulnerable spot near the shoulder and neck, I fired and the shot told, for the reptile opened its jaws and its gape of enormous width invited me to discharge another round when the beast made a plunge into the water and disappeared below. For a long time we watched the bubbles of air appearing on the surface of the water and were convinced that the animal had been fatally wounded. Next morning it rose to the surface. Decomposition of the flesh had set in, and it was handed over to the sweepers who esteemed the flesh in this "high" condition a great luxury. The skin was sent home to England to be tanned and converted into a brief bag. The work was well executed, and the beautiful bronze green shades of tone on it made it a fitting and suitable gift for a Prince, but much too good for ordinary mortals. Thus it comes about that it lies hidden in my cupboard unused and seldom admired.

Occasionally a stray wild monkey ventures into the school. His presence is soon discovered by the shrieks he utters as he climbs up from branch to branch, and showing his fangs threatens harm to any one daring to approach him. He has come from a neighbouring jungle to keep company with our two little pet monkeys, who seem terrified over the visit of the stranger. His banishment is at once resolved on by the boys, for they are uncertain of his temper and harm may result. His capture is effected by tying one of the pet monkeys inside an empty pigeon cage and placing rice in a tin on the floor. The decoy draws the intruder in and the door is closed. The wild monkey dashes its face against the meshes of the wire cage and jumps from side to side, while the school is as much excited as the monkey itself. To prevent it injuring itself, the hockey goal-post net is fetched and held against the mouth of the door while it is gradually opened. The beast jumps forward and thus gets netted, only to be carried away hammock-wise triumphantly to some distant wood and set free. It is an unpardonable sin to shoot a monkey, for its sufferings when wounded are so human.

Wild pigs also occasionally run into the school, when they are too late to make a bee-line for the jungle. They have strayed from the neighbouring hills on the road side for garbage, and being intent on their feed, are disturbed and their return intercepted by the villagers who set out early for their day's work. The boys, however, are not interested in their quarry for the flesh is an abomination to them, but it is a festival day for the Christian members of the staff who enjoy fresh pork and a home-made sausage. The flesh is disappointing, for a wild pig feeds on roots and never approaches a condition of fatness.

The common Indian water lizard or guana is a reptile that crawls into one's bungalow. One of these which lived in a hole by the side of the garden wall came out at noon for its food, and mounting the steps of the bungalow was poking its nose into the corners of the verandah for insects when it was startled by the front door opening, and rushing inside, was chased by the dog. It rushed in and out of the rooms but was at last brought to bay. The flesh is considered a delicacy and said to resemble hare in soup. The animal was handed over to a member of the staff who quite enjoyed it.

The tree-dog or toddy-cat roams freely at night in every large garden and often disturbs one's sleep by moving about, especially in the roof of thatched houses. We have cause to remember one of these, for it deprived us of a most magnificent pet peacock that was kept for safety in a godown while we were away out in camp. The poor thing hadn't a chance of escape, and it was an afterthought that it would have been safe if left on the trees at night. We mourned over the loss of the bird for many days for it was a great favourite and feasted on the sight of its glory as it preened itself in the sunlight. The wound inflicted on the bird was so small as to be hardly visible but just sufficient for the purpose of sucking the blood of its victim. The name "toddy-cat" is given to it because it is fond of the juice of the coconut or palmyra palm. As its activity in climbing is very great the name tree-dog is also given to it. But both the names are inappropriate for it belongs to neither class. It has a brownish black colour, with a few dingy yellowish stripes on each side and a white spot above and below each eye. The head and body attain a length of about 24 inches. The animal moves about stealthily at night, but when one is discovered it means death, for there is a free fight between it and the dogs belonging to the staff. The monkeys join in the chorus by chattering and shrieking till the animal is laid low.

This mean animal is guilty not only of disturbing one's sleep but also of raising one's anger. A big Kew pineapple that had been marked off for a lady friend was watched day by day, putting forth its change of colour as it neared ripeness till it began to smell. And then when it had been settled upon that it should be cut off the following morning for despatch to the lady who had gone to the hills for a change, a tree-dog with all the seeming venom of an old enemy attacked the fruit that same night and ate half of it, revealing to tearful eyes and angry breast the golden syrupy core within. A thousand deaths to such a mean creature!

The tree-cat more or less resembles the civet cat, which is also found about the precincts of the school. One of these civets was caught and caged by the boys but it was never inclined to make friends. Its odour was so overpowering that one scarcely felt inclined to stand near the cage. The musk or perfume is located in two little pouches or turnings-in of the skin just under the animal's tail. When the animal is irritated it throws out the civet or musk, which is gathered and sold as a perfume.

Chingleput is the home of the snipe in Southern India, and travellers going by the mail train from Madras to Tuticorin and Ceylon will remember the excellent dinner to be had at the railway refreshment room, the two favourite dishes being prawn curry and snipe. The former brought by runners from the sea-coast and the latter shot by local shikaris. When the late King Edward was Prince of Wales and when the late Duke of Clarence visited India, Chingleput was selected to give their Highnesses a day's sport in snipe shooting.

The bird suddenly makes an appearance in South India in September, having travelled from the north-east with the setting in of the monsoon and covering a thousand miles in one night. Among the very few pleasures open to the Superintendent of the reformatory to indulge in is snipe shooting. Shikaris soon find their favourite feeding-grounds, and the habits of the bird are such as to make this possible.

The natives believe that the bird alights in a field and never leaves it, and even if disturbed by a ryot would settle down on the spot again. It is curious to note that the crop of the snipe is never full, even after a whole day's feed, giving rise to the belief that it digests the grub or worm before it eats the next. Indians think that the proper mode of eating a snipe is to chew the head, eat the flesh on the chest, and taste its liver, kidneys and everything inside. The flesh resembles that of the pheasant when cooked. The bird is not easily shot. It zig-zags as soon as it rises off the ground and it takes a pretty quick shot to drop it, but it is fine sport.

I remember taking out a Lancashire youth fresh from home. When he got his first snipe, after wasting about thirty cartridges, he glowed with pleasure. We sat down to lunch with a great thirst, and as the beer was ready at hand in the basket, he exclaimed: "Ah! I would not give up this thirst for a pension."

Life has its compensations, and a bungalow cut away from the town by high walls and removed from ordinary scenes has to be counterbalanced with creature comforts. In addition to this nature contributes towards the attraction of the place. A home with an outlook of little hills beyond, trailing along the distant border of a lake, with a setting of massive foliage all around, makes solitude bearable for many years. Such has been the case with me. The attractive lake scenery has compensated me in my loneliness, and having more than the average love for nature and for art, time has run on without being clogged with a sense of *dolce far niente* or of dulness.

On a morning one never sees the same scene twice as the sun rises over the lake. A sunset is generally spoken of as beautiful, but a sunrise can be just as beautiful when a lake and hills conspire together to break up and diffuse the sun's light and add to it their own reflection.

When the early day dawns, the surface of the water is of a uniform leaden hue, but gradually the horizon is suffused with orange which is reflected in the water with a rosy hue deeper in tone. The reflection of the hill on the other hand is softer than the solid body standing out. Thus the sky and the water interchange, in strength of tones, the light orange and the dark hill balancing the deep rose and the soft reflection of the hill mirrored in the water. Once more the truth that nature does her work well and designs her pictures in perfect balance is illustrated. While one colour deepens in tone in the upper half of Nature's frameless picture, its reflection gets lighter in the lower half, and vice versa. Thus all the time perfect balance is being preserved to teach us one of the fundamental laws of design. As we continue to gaze on the water the rose passes into orange yellow and streaks of light cut into the top of the image thrown by the hill, the orange yellow in turn changing into silver with a faint tinge of rose. Gradually the trees on the further bank unfold themselves, standing out from the mist that lies at the bottom of the hill.

Now on the water faint movements are visible of sporting animalculæ too tiny to break the surface but just enough to scratch the blue reflection of the hill and cause a silver streak, getting burnished by degrees as the sky assumes a paler hue. The reflection of the hill takes on an edge of pink and a quicksilvery tinge above it becomes spotted with dark brown or bronze oases. One change follows another till at length the shadows grow into slate, losing their distinctiveness in a liquid with brush work of dark colour drawn through the water. The quicksilver surface spreads all over, covering the reflected image of the hill as it melts away. With the risen sun there shoots out that broad irradiation of silver gold with which he greets all India, a bar of light strikes on the water, piercing the mirrored surface, and a mottled blue-grey tinge shows up while the haze still hangs round the hill now of a sombre green tinge.

For a month or two after the rains have ceased, it is no uncommon sight to find the mist hang like a shroud over the lake, obliterating all the familiar landscape behind it; with the warmth of the sun the mist gradually melts away and in its withdrawal confusion follows, for hills and clouds are indistinguishable from each other till the sun's rays strike bars of gold across the water, taking their breadth from the jagged outline of the horizon and producing a sheen over the lake which is dulled only at the irregular fringe of the water.

On another morning the dawn breaks with a cold steely look on the surface of the water, or the appearance is like to limpid sapphire which turns into polished silver with diffused light yielding in turn to burnished red. On the horizon the hills are outlined by a narrow opening of bright light throwing into prominence the dark clouds hovering above.

When the North-East Monsoon, on which the prosperity of the Presidency depends, as it is usually a rain-bearing wind, sets in, the clouds bank up in full view and can be seen massing together in ever increasing volume only to break out in a deluge when the proper density is reached. Then the surface of the lake is broken into waves and the driving wind obliterates the distant view, giving it the appearance of an inland sea. In India we are thankful that the rains, when they do not fail, come like clockwork in certain months. One can even foretell the break of the monsoon to a day, the official date being the 15th of October, when the flag-staff in Fort Saint George, Madras, is lowered half-mast to protect it from being splintered by the force of the wind. How different from a place like Manchester where it rains eight days out of ten, where no open-air function can be arranged with the certainty that the clerk of the weather will co-operate to make it a success. Says the prophet of weather predictions: "I can always get the kind of weather all right, but I haven't quite succeeded in hitting the dates exactly." The result is that one has to gamble on the chance of having a fine day. It is not so in the East. There is the hot season, the rainy season and the cool season, but one season does not attempt to poach on the preserves of another. The hot season will not pretend to put on the garb of cold weather even for a few days, nor do the rains ever spoil a show in the cool months. This state of things may make for monotony and indolence, but is highly appreciated by the Britisher, who experiences only samples of weather in his native isles.

CHAPTER VIII

FIRST IMPRESSIONS OF A VISITOR

The first impression of a casual visitor is that the inmates have a happy time and that they are not overworked. As regards their physical condition, they appear small and slim compared with average Hindu boys, and this is true, for it is impossible altogether to rectify the errors of heredity. The pupils are in an emaciated condition when they arrive, and while time removes defects to a large extent, the stamp of inferiority always remains with the majority. The visitors notice that.

The boys are dressed in a white suit of a thick plain cloth with a cap resembling a tea cosy. It is stiffened inside with a piece of rattan, imparting the appearance of smartness to the boys. The cap is pronounced by ladies to be quaint, while some of the officials call it horrid, but for smartness, economy and cleanliness there is nothing to replace it. It was a cap worn by the early recruits of the native army in former times. On closer inspection the cap shows a brass badge which is a mark of the trade a boy follows—the sign of his profession—a weaver wears a shuttle, a carpenter a chisel, a blacksmith an anvil, the mason boys have a trowel, and the gardeners a spade. The tailors' badge is a pair of scissors, while the band and bugle sport the drum-sticks crossed on a patch of red cloth. Some boys have a red border to their caps. These are the assistant monitors, and the head monitors wear a cap of blue edged with red.

The monitors are further distinguished by a brass star, and with their brass good conduct badges their breasts are fairly bejewelled. Each boy has a number stamped on his clothing, by which he is generally known and spoken of, and it is wonderful to find how numbers are remembered easier than names. The visitor finds that the boys are under no seeming supervision or restraint; not that there are no facilities for escape, the fort being full of rat holes by which escape is practicable—but the discipline and order is such that regular habits are soon formed and ensure a minimum of trouble. A few wild spirits to whom the discipline of the school is intolerable make an attempt to escape and generally get away by train, hiding under a seat on the approach of the ticket collector—these are soon caught by the police or by our peons, but only to make another bid for freedom unless carefully looked after till they settle down.

The visitor is inclined to question a boy as to what crime he committed to be sent to the reformatory. Such overtures are usually discouraged, as it is somewhat of an outrage on one's feelings to have the past raked up, but the Superintendent himself points out unobtrusively the juvenile murderer and other bad types of youthful criminals, who have all to undergo the same process of treatment as the petty thief. It must be remarked that our reverence of human life makes one regard murder as the greatest of sins, but murder is not apt to grow into a habit as theft is, and the nature of the crime committed therefore is no index to character.

A short walk brings the visitor to the dormitories substantially built of red brick with hammocks slung in two rows, and a few steps across the pathway is the schoolroom, with its neat dado of chocolate bordered with floral ornament. The walls are covered with charts and pictures, and right above there are inspiriting mottoes picked out in white letters on a red cloth ground and hung up in appropriate places, so that the boys in their progress through the schoolroom are brightened and ennobled by a continual series of beautiful mental impulses and images reflected into the soul from the texts which meet their eyes. The golden rule: "Do unto others as you would that they *should* do to you," is one such motto, but the visitor as he reads it adds, "and do it first!"

FIRST IMPRESSIONS OF A VISITOR

Two elegantly panelled boards with carved headpieces containing the names of combatants and non-combatants who volunteered for the front are hung in a conspicuous position, contributing to the traditions of the place. The Superintendent's enlarged portrait in sepia, framed with oak, attracts attention as the best friend of the school.

No one leaves the premises without having a look at the various workshops where the boys are being educated by the hand and eye method that trains them for a vocation, the most attractive of these being the band and bugle classes. They are housed in a hexagonal building situated away from the workshops in the south-east corner of the fort on the rampart wall with the lake for a frontage. A verandah of 7 feet runs round except on the rear side where a storeroom is provided for the instruments. The walls are built of brick in mortar, plastered inside and pointed outside. The roof of the building is of Mangalore tiles topped with a flagstaff for the fluttering of a Union Jack on gala days. The flooring is of Cuddapah slabs. In the walls four large windows panelled outside and glazed inside are provided, and as the roof of the verandah is lower than that of the hall by 3 feet, six ventilators are provided, one for each wall. The pyramidal shape of the roof with the flagstaff gives the building the appearance of an Indian car. The band is always ready to entertain visitors with a tune, and as they play their big toes mark time, while one eye travels furtively around to see how the show is being appreciated by the visitor.

In the verandah of a dormitory boxes may be seen raised off the ground standing on four stones for fear of attack by white ants. The monitors are the proud possessors of these lockers—receptacles of uncertain temper, for information is sometimes given by a boy who is either a prig or a sneak that if such and such a box were searched quickly, something of interest would be found. The search is made, and sure enough either a piece of tobacco or some bread or other kind of food is found hidden away contrary to rules. The usual orthodox possessions are a comb, a ruler, cloths, books, materials for cleaning up badges, post cards passed by authority, a pencil and an odd assortment of trifles. Contraband of course will always find a place and has to be hunted out periodically. There are not many complaints made by one boy against another. Food is generally at the bottom of all fights, and for the rest such trivialities are brought forward as A abused B and B bit A on the arm, or that A has pilfered a cloth or a badge from B, or B is found fault with for keeping company with C.

The kitchen is the centre of all trouble. Cooks have to be watched and the boys who are in league with the cooks. Certain of them are special favourites who are ever ready to clean up trays and moulds and to fetch water. Entering the kitchen the visitor finds the food moulded into blocks weighing about 21 lbs. each. These are served out with some vegetable curry and dholl. The cooks are not an attractive lot to look at, and to ensure cleanliness a loin cloth is issued to them for wear inside the school. The boys having complained that hair from unkempt locks was often found in the food, close-fitting caps extending right over the ears give the cooks an imprisoned look. A sweetened chapatti of 5 oz. is served out as a first meal, and the work of making 250 of them begins at 2 in the morning. The paste is made into a ball and is flattened out over a heated piece of sheet iron greased with gingelli oil. These chapatties are eaten with great zest and are washed down with water.

It will be seen that their food naturally contains no luxuries, but all the ingredients are thoroughly wholesome, nutritious, and the food is ample and of good quality. The visitor is interested to know that the boys make a few requests touching their home affairs. One boy states that his property is going to rack and ruin after his mother's death and that his uncle is selling his lands for drink. Another boy wishes to go back and help his mother as she is very old and feeble. A third asks permission to see a sick relative or attend a wedding and come back. A fourth wishes to be discharged as all the earning members of the family are dead and he would like to take the place of the breadwinner. All such requests have to be refused, but the boys cannot understand the sphinx-like attitude assumed.

It takes an hour for the visitor to get a passing acquaintance with the place and with the information given on the character of the inmates and the working of school, he leaves it with the thought that the system is good, although perhaps the numbers dealt with are too large to give one the opportunity for personal supervision—and he is right—for the school numbers 250.

Letters received from our visitors, both European and Indian, have always been flattering. One day we received an incidental visit from Canon Goldsmith, the Rev. Langdale Smith and the Rev. E. A. L. Moore of the Church Missionary Society. It was an honour, and reflects the attractiveness of the school when three such busy ornaments of the C.M.S. could spare the time to visit the school. It speaks volumes for its reputation, and we valued it more than a visit from anyone else.

CHAPTER IX

INDIGENOUS INDIAN GAMES

INDIGENOUS games occupy the greater part of the recreation hour, and a brief description of the way the Indian youth plays is not without interest.

Pallanguli and *gudugudu-chaplam* are typical national games played by the boys, the former being a sedentary game, but the latter demanding some physical strength. In *pallanguli*, 14 holes are arranged in two rows of 7 each, and a certain equal number of tamarind or other seed is placed in each hole. The seeds from the first hole are taken and dropped into succeeding holes one by one. The seeds of the hole, next to the one in which the last seed was dropped, are then taken and the same process goes on, till the player chances to drop a last seed just before an empty hole, in which case he takes as his gain the seeds of the succeeding hole and the hole opposite it.

In *gudugudu-chaplam*, sixteen boys take sides and a line of demarcation is drawn across. A boy issues forth from the ranks of one party jumps lightly out into the arena and advances into the field of the other, holding his breath and repeating the word "gudugudu." He is expected to get back into his ground after touching a boy on the opposite side and without being seized himself or taking breath; otherwise he is counted "dead." After a given time the side with the larger number of "living" is declared the winner.

The endeavour of the challenger is to avoid capture while allowing the pursuers to come near enough for him to give them a slap, while the pursuers try to seize, throw, and hold him to the ground till he loses his breath, in which case they are adjudged the winners. Great excitement reigns on both sides, and the throws are often accompanied with great force.

Other popular games are *uppu kodu* or *uppu koondam* and *kilhi-kodu* or *kilhi-koondam*, both allied games with a few points of difference. *Uppu kodu* or *uppu koondam* is akin to "Prisoners' Base" in England.

Upu koondam.—Two perpendicular and parallel lines are drawn about 20 feet apart. Horizontal lines as many as desired are drawn across, equally distanced. The number of horizontal lines fixes the number of players a side, each of whom places himself on the centre of the line. The boys, 1, 2, 3, 4, 5, etc., all face one way. The other side (of the same number of boys) oppose these, standing outside. The leader strikes hands with the boy standing on the first line and immediately a rush is made by all to get past their opponents on the successive lines without being touched, for a boy touched pays the penalty of falling out. Those who succeed in reaching the other side pick up a handful of earth and return the same way, trying to pass their opponents. One successful boy makes his party the winners, but a side loses its chance of attack when every boy falls out on being touched. Their opponents then start the offensive in the same way.

The *kili-kodu* or *kilhi-koondam* is only an advanced form of the simple *uppu koondam*. The aim of the game is the same, but an additional boy on the centre line makes it more difficult. The extra boy on the centre line can move along not only on his own line but on the other lines as well to assist any of his team. In this game the parallel and perpendicular lines are 40 feet apart and the horizontal lines are bisected by a straight line drawn through the middle.

Sirki or *girki*.—This resembles hop-scotch and has either been introduced into India by missionaries or has found its way from India into England.

The reader must imagine himself on a piece of level ground enclosed on two sides by the ramparts of the fort and almost surrounded by the waters of the old moat. The grass on it has an unbroken smooth surface and keeps green all through the year, resembling an English lawn. The grassy ground attracts passers-by by its greenness, which is due to the water that percolates into it from the moat, and on a hot day the appearance of the field is refreshing to the eye. Here games go on till nightfall.

To-day there is an unusual crowd of youngsters from the schools in the town. The flags that mark the side lines and goal posts show that a football match is on with some outside school. The reformatory team come out wearing their school colours of red and blue with an R.S. on each breast, while the captain wears a red shoulder sash with a pocket handkerchief peeping out of his vest to mark him out from the rest.

The school team is composed of boys somewhat smaller in stature than their opponents, with close-cropped heads, while the team they meet are heavier in build with long locks tied up in a knot at the back of the head, and some are even married. An outsider acts as referee, and as soon as the whistle goes both sides muddle about in the field barefooted, trying to kick the ball till a chance shot across puts the field in motion towards the goal. The reformatory captain is about to shoot the ball into the goal when an opponent uses his fist and strikes him to prevent a goal. In an instant the school who are spectators rush down the rampart and in the twinkle of an eye the whole field is in an uproar with the excited boys. There is just time enough to jump into the crowd and with an umbrella to stem back the on-rushing tide of our boys and prevent a free fight. The whole place is now a confused mob, some crying one thing and some another, the masters taking the sides of their respective teams without knowing what is up or which side is to blame. The referee, therefore, wisely decides to call a halt. To help the teams to forget the episode they are not allowed to meet each other for a period of two years.

This incident was a most unusual one. The respective teams generally play fair, and the contest is a source of great interest to the spectators.

The school plays a much better game at hockey, first taught them by the captain of the Madras Doveton College

The Holders of the Silver Cup presented by the Citizens of Chingleput and competed for by the High Schools of the Town

Page 106

hockey team, Cecil Coombes, who brought up a few of his chums to initiate us into the game. Shortly after, this lad of 18 years joined the London Scottish and elected to work in a machine-gun section. He was killed in the engagement at Loos, as he rushed forward just as he was accustomed to do on the playing field. Our hockey team heard of his loss with genuine grief, but his influence remains in the school and will be felt for years to come. Thus do our actions follow us.

Being given a good start, our hockey boys play well, and as few Indian schools have taken to the game, while none in the town are inclined to stand the initial expense, we are compelled to arrange for matches with crack police teams at outside stations, and although always outmatched and defeated we are never disgraced on the field. While the *esprit de corps* of the school is developed, the journey to and fro by train and the hospitality offered us wherever our challenge is accepted, is gratifying and tends to raise the self-respect of our lads.

Football is always encouraged, for it is *par excellence* the game for juveniles. Their superfluous energy, which would otherwise be diverted into wrong channels, is worked off, their tempers are improved, and the game introduces a manly influence into the school. Great enthusiasm is always evinced on match days, and the players never know when to stop. I have always found that a boy given to football rarely thinks of stealing or pilfering, whatever wrong tendencies he may otherwise possess. One watches with amusement the pride a team takes to equip itself for a competition. They possess evidently a feeling for the charms of dress. Banians, purchased out of their own earnings, are worn, and handkerchiefs peep out at the neck. Sashes are arranged round the waist with tassels on the side, and, what is more important, the members of the team, by their combination and skill, are able to more than hold their own against a heavier and older one. They altogether take a pride in their play. Immediately after a match is won, they garland the "head of the family," and carry him upon their shoulders in triumph to his house.

Nothing rejoices the heart of a boy so much as to see the members of the staff meet the school eleven in a game of football. He loves to see them knocked about, and a miss at the goal is wildly cheered, while a false kick causes much merriment. All these exhibitions of feeling are not the result of a want of discipline or a desire for revenge, but proceeds from exuberance of spirits and a sense of humour combined, with an appreciation of the altered situation, when the tables are turned and the boys can boss the show. The disposition of the staff team is always a difficult problem for scarcely can five good runners be got together. The best is made, however, of the material at hand, and the game begins. The goal is taken by the Headmaster, whose one idea of the game is to stand between the posts, firm and immovable, with the off-chance that the ball may hit his anatomy and be deflected from its course. If it chooses to pass him, he puts on a smile to disarm his critics, The extreme left wing is protected by the Head-Clerk, a Brahmin, who on the approach of the ball gathers together with two hands the skirts of his loin—a cloth round his limbs reaching to his ankles—and with a dot one and carry two stride makes a fruitless attempt to get level with the ball. At sight of this screams of laughter choke the members of his own team, to say nothing of the uproar of the onlookers.

One of the lower form masters has a style of his own in running. He hops along and chases the ball all over the field, getting in the way of the few who do play. The Band Master tackles the game more earnestly and puts on a vicious countenance. He means to try his best, and succeeds in deriving satisfaction from a vigorous attempt at kicking the ball, but it is too gentle to be effective. The rest of the team play in all seriousness, but the clever passes of the youngsters, who are able easily to dodge them by wriggling past their shoulders, sends the school into raptures. The result of course is a foregone conclusion, but the defeat only tends to strengthen the *camaraderie* that prevails between the masters and boys. The latter soon go off to their dormitories to discuss the evening episode till they fall asleep, but next morning the out-of-school intimacy is forgotten and the masters are top dogs again until the next match comes off. This doesn't happen till a fairly long interval of time has elapsed, for it would never do to sail too close to the familiarity-breeding-contempt stage of human nature.

CHAPTER X

PRIZE DAY AND ANNUAL SPORTS—COVELONG

PRIZEGIVING Day all the world over is looked forward to with unalloyed pleasure: another red letter day in the school world is the day fixed for the annual sports—when both functions are combined, as in the reformatory, and the various events spread over more than one day; little imagination is required to appreciate the keenness with which the pupils look forward to the *tamasha* involved in these events.

For months before the time they conjecture the nature of the prizes to be awarded for work done during the past year, and practice for sports is steadily carried on. The various trades vie with each other to secure the largest number of prizes, all of which count for championship. The awards are certainly small in value, and it is to their credit that the competitors look upon them from a standpoint other than monetary. The pleasure of being recipients of an honour is enhanced by the presence of a large company of friends and well-wishers, who reside in the neighbourhood. It must be added that the presence of parents, if that were possible to secure, would prove a valuable asset in encouraging the boys to strive for distinction. The ceremony therefore is gone through in the absence of the parents or guardians who live at some distance from the school. But a distinguished chairman, who distributes the prizes, and a large gathering of keenly interested townsfolk who assemble to witness the show, make amends to a large extent for the absence of parents.

The Report is generally read in English, a tongue unknown to the majority of the boys, and on occasions it is just as

The Anniversary Meeting, with Sir John Wallis in the Chair, supported by Sir Henry Stone (page 110)

well it is so, for it cannot be gratifying to hear, amongst other things, about the crimes they had committed before their admission to the school or their escapades while in school. I have always found it helpful and illuminating to tell the boys at the next Sunday lesson the salient points in the Report relating to their progress and the chairman's remarks on the work done. I must confess that the pupils do indeed value their prizes, though there is little real thirst for knowledge. No small part of the success of the prize day is due to the bearing of the juveniles on the occasion. He is proud of his achievements and receives his reward with keen pleasure. He differs, however, from the average Aryan schoolboy in that he scarcely desires to be instructed in booklore, nor does he strain at the leash in his effort to grasp at knowledge. Drill, gymnastics and sports he delights in, and shows his best in everything that tests his capacity as a vigorous animal, but he shuns mental exercises.

It is amusing to find that every boy, whether he works for it or not, looks for a prize on the most slender pretext, and to draw up a list of prize-winners so as to ensure a minimum amount of heart burning takes some pains. The chairman, who is generally a high-placed Government official, is first received with a general salute by the boys drawn up in open order: they then march past and go through their various evolutions with smartness and precision. Their clean white uniforms shimmering in the bright sunlight as it forces it way through the surrounding trees, gently moved with a languid breeze blowing, but not too warm, produces a most picturesque effect, and encomiums of praise flow in on every side. The several items in the sports are next contested by the competitors, and the comic items are as much enjoyed by the boys themselves as by the crowd. Tilting at the bucket, pillow fighting, football in sacks and wrestling pick-a-back are general favourites, while climbing the greasy pole in which the coconut tree climbing boy expertly mounts up like a frog with the use of his feet rather than his hands, keeps the whole company in good humour. Wrestling may be regarded as a national game, and the boys regard it as a fine art and treat it as a natural pastime. The two competitors to engage in a bout stand up stripped, ceremoniously salute the crowd, shake hands, then bend forward—glaring at each other waiting for an opportunity to seize the hand of the opponent and jerk him down or to get hold of a limb and trip him up, or grasp him round the body and knock his legs from under him, the object being to make him lose his balance. Both fall, and then the struggle begins, each one trying to turn his adversary on his back. Then the top dog gets his left leg round the left leg of the other and tries to lift him bodily and turn him over. If successful, both shoulder blades of the lower one must touch the ground, and then the game is up.

At the conclusion of the whole function a day's holiday is usually granted, often at the request of the chairman, followed at times by a treat. Bedtime is unusually silent in the dormitories, for everybody has had a strenuous time, but the following day is spent in thoroughly discussing and enjoying the various incidents. Groups may be seen gathered together to enjoy the reading of their prize books, the victors stretched in languid repose and others in every conceivable posture of ease, content with himself and his little world. With such an experience it is no wonder that a prize day becomes a red letter day in the memory of the boys, is treasured in after years, and becomes one of the pleasant memories which link the ex-pupil with the old school.

We all need sympathy, human kindness, cheer, good fellowship—the thousand little things of human love—as we tramp this dusty road of life, and one of the most difficult problems I had to solve was how best to circulate these little coins of affection among the lives entrusted to my care. It is easier to suppress evil habits than to inculcate positive virtues. The moral sense has become atrophied and some powerful stimulant is required to bring it to life.

A birthday in a Christian home is a time of good fellowship—differences are sunk, injuries healed, kindnesses are remembered, and the day affords an opportunity for the expression of the love and esteem that exist. Thoughtful

The Superintendent garlanded on his Birthday (page 113)

gifts add to the pleasure of the day, and many an old age is brightened by the memory of a jolly birthday. In the homes from which my boys have come the annual observance of a birthday is unknown, and I felt that any event which helped to produce a feeling of esteem for the Head of the institution and one of good-fellowship among the inmates themselves should be fostered, not to speak of the opportunity it affords of giving the boys a treat.

Preparations for the celebration of the "father's" birthday begin about two months before the event, with weekly practices of the special song composed for the occasion in stanzas of Tamil, Telugu, English and Hindustani. The spare time of the boys moreover is fully occupied in the study of their parts for the acting of a drama or the performance of a Kolattam dance. Paper garlands are made in profusion, and an address, which may be described as a personal roll-call of the school, takes some time to receive the autograph of every boy. The proceedings begin at 5 o'clock in the morning. The school band with a stirring march just below the bedroom disturbs my peaceful slumber. It always put me in mind of a merry Christmas greeting, and cheered my heart for the rest of the day. In the meantime batches of boys veer round in front of the verandah and go through various dances in my honour. At 6 o'clock the day starts with nominal work, and as I go on my rounds I am covered with garlands, the various workshops vying with each other to do honour to the chief actor till the scene changes from heroic drama to one of light comedy. At 9 o'clock the plot thickens, and great formality is observed in the reading of an address to me, the garlanding and the acclamations that follow. Then comes the human touch that springs from affection, resulting in a terrible onslaught that almost results in suffocation. Picture to yourself 250 lads, with good feeling and little formality, each with a garland trying to be first in the game of hooking it on to one's neck.

The birthday song, specially composed for the occasion, is sung to the accompaniment of the violin, drum, cymbals and harmonium. Addresses or dialogues in Tamil, Telugu,

Hindustani and English are delivered and a display of acrobatic feats ends the business for the time.

The meeting of the old boys on the birthday of the "Head" is in many respects a welcome feature of the festivities. They enter their old haunts with new feelings as respectable citizens, move freely among the pupils in their best rig, sporting the uniform of a regiment or that of a reserve police bugler. To the admiring gaze of the scholars present they look like those who have passed through a period of transmigration, as evidenced by the altered tone in speech, by the glittering jewel on the ear, or the embroidered cloth around the hip. The past has shrouded them in mystery, and brings with it lessons and hopes for their own future. The old boys' meeting is presided over by one of their own number, and as each one relates his experiences in life he is listened to with greater attention than is ordinarily commanded by a master. An old boy's appeal, through speech, manner and tone, never fails to do good—for is not the hearer hewn from the same rock as the speaker? There is this differenee, however, that there is an outer layer of respectability in the latter which is inspiring, wholesome, and tends to lead the others into rightful thinking. A hockey match between the old boys and the new generally ends in a win for the latter, for, as the old boys say, their limbs are stiff and their breath short for want of practice. When the new beat the old they are delighted at their opponents failing to score even a single goal.

And now for a short description to show how thoroughly the boys enjoy the good things prepared for their picnickety feast. Plantain leaves are arranged in rows in the garden, and rice and dal are ladled out with the various curries, the chicken curry being so thoroughly appreciated that not a single bone is visible in the leavings taken up, the poor stomach being left to tackle a tough job. Ducks' eggs, salt fish, sweet mango curry and fruit served at the end are all, needless to say, luxuriously viewed and sampled to their hearts' content. The delights of the various dishes are crystallised in verse, and previously sung by the boys as part of the programme. The zest with which it is sung makes the blood circulate quicker at the thought of the coming feast, which all too quickly becomes a memory only to be revived as the months roll along. By the aid of verse the epicures and gourmands have at their beck and call a cheap instrument for reduplicating with lessened effect the delights of a previous feast.

The expressive way in which the two following letters convey their congratulations are worth reproducing:—

Letter from Venkataswamy, Muniswamy, Nallayan, and Kanuswamy, ex-pupils Nos. 690, 605, 1003, and 37 respectively, to their father, the Superintendent, Reformatory School:—

WORAIYUR, 4/6/17.

We consider that you are as kind as the eye-lids are to the eyes, as bright as the lotus in a tank, and God Himself to the poor. We worship you with the sweet flowers as rose and jasmine and prostrate. We are doing well and we pray that you are in good health. 6th June is your birthday. Though we do not come there for the occasion, we have here your photo and pay our respects to the same.

(Sd.) VENKATASWAMY and 3 others.

BELLADE, 5/vi/1915.

May that Being that is worshipped as Shiva by the Shivites, as Brahman by the Vedantins, as Buddha by the Buddhas, as Kartha by the Naiyayikas, as Arhat by the Jais, as Karma by the Mimamsikas, as Jehovah by the Jews, as Allah by the Mussalmans, as the Christ by the Christians—May that Father of All shower His Choicest Blessings on you this day and forever.

K. RANGASWAMI.

BIRTHDAY GLEE—SIXTH JUNE

1. Come and play, Come and play,
'Tis the feast of COOMBE's Birthday;
Quit your books, clear your looks,
All be bright and gay.
Analysis and paraphrase,
Arithmetics and Algebras,
Transitives, Intransitives,
Let them sleep to-day.

2. Happy we, Happy we,
Reformatory (chums) in you see
Father dear, Mother dear,
Nowhere known as here.
Fathers, Mothers, come and go,
You are not so, indeed no;
Long live dear, father dear,
Lead us in God's fear.

AN ENGLISH TRANSLATION IN VERSE

6—6—13

KUMMI

1. Six month notices "sixth" by hand,
Early morning cheering up with band,
Garlands lovely comparing favourable,
Shining father Coombes adorable.

2. Morning coffee simply a treasure,
Bread getting in post-haste, no labour;
Ducks' eggs boiled, adding flavour,
To pounce upon fowls curry a pleasure.

Ready for a March

Mudaliar Trustee of Thirukkalikundram Temple (page 140)

3. Notice the varieties of eatables found;
To sing it out is not possible, pray.
Mahabalipuram and Melrosapuram around
Join us to celebrate your birth day.

4. Going out for a walk means by heaven.
Plenty of eatables to be given.
Lovely Father has plenty to give,
For us to be happy and to live.

Christmas Camps.—The District of Chingleput borders on the Bay of Bengal, with scattered seaside resorts which attract many visitors. What more natural result than that we should be led to fix our camps at these places. The "Seven Pagodas" holds foremost rank in historical importance and salubrity of climate, and no less than four camps were held there at different times. The first camp was in 1911.

The Proclamation of the Coronation of His Imperial Majesty at Delhi in person was so unique an event in the history of India that every Province, District, Taluq, Village, and Institution vied with each other, when the intended visit was announced, to celebrate the event in a manner befitting the august occasion. The Reformatory School was no less affected with sentiments of loyalty than the outside world. The problem that the authorities in charge of the school have to face on occasions such as these is how best to mark the festive occasion and yet retain the educative and reformative character of the process daily going on. Opportunity is always taken on Royal birthdays, Empire Day, Gubernatorial visits, and distributions of prizes, to draw out the finer feelings of the pupils and make them feel that they are in future years to take their place as useful citizens of the State.

To a large number of boys a tamasha, or ceremony, involving a little relaxation from the rigour of semi-military discipline on the great occasion would have appealed most, and it was therefore proposed that a week's holiday to the seaside would combine amusement, relaxation from unnecessary control, instruction, and a better field for celebrating the festivities arranged in honour of the event.

It was not without a certain amount of diffidence, therefore, that the project was placed before the authorities. To mark the year of the royal visit to India, it was suggested to Government that the pupils should spend their Christmas holidays in camp at the seaside, and the Seven Pagodas at Mahabalipuram, was selected as a site for the "Margate" camp.

Who has not heard of the city of the great Bali, with its monolithic temples dating from about the sixth century? People from all parts of the world visit them, the rock temples being particularly admired for their beauty and variety. The first represents a cell; the second and fourth are square in plan and are copies of Buddhist Viharas, which served as the prototype of all Dravidian temples in Southern India. The third, with its oblong base, gave rise to the gopuram, or gateway, that has in modern times assumed such enormous proportions as to eclipse the importance of the inner shrine. Surrounded by such antiquities, the camp was bound to be, from many points of view, a success; but the experiment of taking out into camp the reformatory youth, if at all sporting, was a risky one. The experiment, however, was worth trying in order to discover whether a juvenile in this country could be made to feel that there was such a thing as honour and trust, to which he might be called upon to respond. It was felt that reformatory work was bound to fail if it tended to produce negative virtues alone. A boy's active co-operation on the side of honour and right-doing was imperative for success in after-life. It was thought that the youth should be given the air of freedom, and be placed in a position demanding right sentiments on his part, and if he obeyed them he was the better for it. Industrial and truant schools for this very reason have been more successful in their methods. A youth is called upon to put forth certain activities in order to meet certain responsibilities.

The Director of Public Instruction and the Madras Government took a most liberal and sympathetic view of

The Zemindars with the Reformatory and Lighthouse Staff at a Picnic (page 151)

General View of the Camp (page 118)

the application. Permission was not only granted, but a money grant was sanctioned to meet the incidental expenses of the undertaking. Madras has given the rest of India many a lead, and the Chingleput Reformatory was the first in India to attempt to carry out successfully the idea of camping out in order to make the pupils feel that they were not criminals who could not be trusted, and that good behaviour brought with it the freedom it deserved.

Before starting for camp each boy stood up and gave his word of honour that he would conduct himself well and do nothing that would bring disgrace on the school. The idea of leaving well-trodden ground for pastures new was so novel that the school was all excitement two days previous to starting, and when it began to rain their spirits were damped, for it seemed as though the very elements were against them. But the sun broke out cloudless on the morning of December 26, 1911, after a very wet Christmas, and revived drooping hopes. Early at four o'clock on the 27th the carts in solemn procession filed out of the school, carrying kitchen utensils, band instruments, the requirements for a small hospital, tents, and food supplies. It was an exhilarating sight an hour later to see the boys fall in, and when the order was given to roll their blankets up, with their suits of clothes and tin dish within, to note how they carried their kit across their shoulders and marched out in fours, headed by the band and bugles, the Union Jack being hoisted aloft, with the bandmaster in front. The European sergeant took up his position at the end of the column, where the smallest boys were placed, but when he found that the big boys were taking too rapid strides, he turned the column about so that the small ones gave the pace. The long stream of white wending along the road could be seen a mile off, and attracted the attention of the village beauties, old dames, and the hardy agriculturist. The women stood gazing with gaping mouths and chins resting on the palm of their hands long after the little regiment of white marched onwards. Children flocked as they heard the sound of the bugles, and a few who could speak English inquired whither our footsteps were leading.

The first stop was made at the ninth milestone, near Tirukkalikundram—the place with a temple situated on a hill, which is daily visited, it is said, by two sacred kites from Benares in order to be fed, the priests disposing of the remains of the sacred food for gain. The Hindu, of course, treats the kite as a sacred bird. After an hour's rest the jubilant party started again to do the remaining ten miles, which they accomplished in three hours. The Buckingham Canal alone remained to be crossed. Having arrived at the canal, the boys were packed in four boats, the buglers and the drums being placed on the top of the leading boat to herald the advent of the little tramps. Having arrived at the camp, pitched on open ground—the camping-ground of former Governors—the school fell in for dinner at six, and by eight o'clock that evening every soul was soon fast asleep.

The next day was spent in clearing away brushwood and prickly-pear from the immediate surroundings, and making things look shipshape. A cattle pound served as a kitchen, and a mantapam was fitted up as a hospital and segregation shed. On the third day the boys were marched off for a ramble among the ancient world-famed temples. The boys were shown the pastoral group in the Krishna mandapam where the cattle are being tended and milked. The next object of interest was Arjuna's penance, which represents him standing on the great toe of his left foot with his arm and right leg withered and chest and ribs prominent, in order to gain his lost dominions from his cousin Duriyodhana by obtaining an incantation from Siva. Then the shore temple washed by the dashing waves; the spirited representation of Durga, wife of Siva, seated on a lion and conquering Mahishasura, the giant demon; the boar incarnation of Vishnu, and the gigantic figure of the same god reposing on a bed with a huge snake wound about it in many coils by way of a pillow for his head, attracted attention. These records left by the Buddhist faith were objects of great interest and wonder to the pupils.

The sea, unknown to more than half the pupils, was a vast expanse of awe to them. It seemed to make them feel that

1. **Feeding the Sacred Kites from Benares** (page 120)
2. **A School Drama**

there was a mighty power beyond that made them shrink with a feeling of helplessness. It was arranged that there should be a daily sea-bath, and with the Hindu idea that sea water possesses the efficacy of purging sin from the body, the first bath was eagerly looked for. The boys jumped in, and one little fellow was nearly being carried away by the waves of this treacherous coast, when fishermen were sent to his rescue. The plan was then arranged to have a semicircle formed by a rope held by fishermen, and in it the school was turned out, and as each breaker dashed and foamed it sent line after line of little heads bobbing over the surface, grasping at some support or clutching at the water. The breakers would swoop back to gather themselves for a mightier leap, and as the boys felt the great billows rise and sink, the buoyant water furnished them with endless amusement. The waves played havoc with them, and tossed them about in their wild frolic. It was found that the sea-bath had an invigorating and most beneficial effect on everyone.

On the fourth day it was arranged to take the boys by boat to Sadras, an old Dutch colony, seven miles away. Four boats were engaged, and about eighty boys were packed in each boat captained by one of the masters. As the breeze was in our favour, sails were hoisted, and the excitement of passing one another afforded great sport, each successful passing being marked by cheers. On our way back fresh fish was purchased, and the boys had a good square meal of rice and fish. The towing back was done almost as quickly as the sailing, for the boys helped the boatmen.

On New Year's Eve, His Excellency the Governor and Lady Carmichael paid a visit to the camp. His Excellency recorded the following remarks :—" When visiting the Seven Pagodas on December 31, 1911, I had the good fortune to meet the boys of the Chingleput Reformatory, who had come to camp near there. I was very pleased indeed to see them. As a whole, they looked smart and well set up. My ignorance of the vernacular languages prevented me from talking to them as I should have liked to do, but I gathered that they were pleased at coming to camp. I look forward to seeing the Reformatory before long and learning more about it. I thought the band played very well. Mr Coombes' interest in the boys is, I think, clearly great, and I can't help thinking he must be doing good work."

The last day was spent quietly in camp, as the packing had to be done for the homeward return, and although the boys enjoyed themselves they seemed glad to get back to their "home." They did the march splendidly, and arrived looking very fit, as everybody remarked. It was noticed for some days that an alertness was visible in their movements, produced evidently by the fresh air, and that sense of freedom which must have acted like a tonic on the nerves of imprisoned youthful spirits. The citizens of Chingleput were right glad to welcome the boys back, as their absence produced a void felt in the town, for Chingleput is nothing without the Reformatory. As one person pertinently remarked, the place had an air of "chilliness" without the boys. The experiment was pronounced by all to have been a great success, and contrary to the popular idea, the boys behaved splendidly. Realising their own responsibility, they acted up to it. The camping was not done for the sole purpose of ceremonial display to mark a great event, but was equally educational and moral in its purpose. The pupils were able to see and study many various objects of interest. In addition, the trip had a distinctly moral value, and brought out the boys' good qualities, as well as their inner character—a valuable asset in the hands of the reformer.

As an exercise in composition, and as a test of the powers of narration and description, the Mahabalipuram camp was given as a subject. The results may be seen in the following extracts, and is interesting from a psychological view :—

VENKATASWAMI, 4th Class.—On Wednesday, December 27, 1911, I woke up at four in the morning and prayed to God that He may bless our master and his intended trip to Mahabalipuram, so that nothing untoward might happen to mar the proceedings. At 6 a.m. we started, after making necessary ablutions, to the strain of the bugle and arrived at Periakulam. Palmyra roots and the morning meal relieved us a good deal, and after some rest we started again and arrived at the Buckingham canal. We now had a glimpse of the Lighthouse at Mahabalipuram, and as we neared the village our *Dorey* pointed our resting-place, and we enjoyed rest after a long walk. The next morning we got up and paid a visit to the rocks.

KRISHNA, 4th Class.—We had no lock-up in that place. Our *Dorey* said: "In this place there were originally seven pagodas, of which you see only one now existing. The remaining six were all submerged in the ocean." We saw representations of the lion, the elephant, and others showing Arjuna's penance, etc., all made of one single rock. There is an anecdote connected with Vishnu and the hobgoblin. The latter solicited for and obtained the gift of being the most powerful animal in the land; but when Vishnu asked it to name the several animals over whom it wished to exercise its sway, it forgot to mention the name of the pig. Now it happened that the proud hobgoblin went on molesting a number of animals in the land even when no harm was done to it. Vishnu, who saw this, got enraged, and as he had not promised that the pig would not kill it, he took the form of a pig and destroyed the cruel animal. When we were explained what the representations meant we were very glad. In one place we found Arjuna making penance, but the most curious thing was that animals, such as the cat, the sheep, the deer, the monkey, etc., were also engaged in penance with Arjuna. Such pleasing sights we never witnessed in our lives. This pleasant trip will never fade from our memory. During our stay there, we inhaled good and pure air, which conduced to make us healthy and strong, so that we are now able to do our work in the school with strength and activity.

KANDASAWMY, 4th Class.—During our stay in camp we saw the rocks in which there were a number of fine representations of the horse, the lion, and the elephant. We saw the cars and mantapams cut out of one single rock.

Arjuna is engaged in penance, and his example is followed by the cats, rats, monkeys, etc. We went up and saw the Lighthouse. . . . There are so many colleges in India, so many high schools and primary schools. Not one of these was ever destined to enjoy so much pleasure as we enjoyed in our trip. That we were able to derive such a rare blessing was not owing to the luck of our parents at home.

VELU, 4th Class.—The next day after our arrival we went to the sea, and after some time came back to enjoy the gramophone entertainment. In the evening we went to the sea again to have a bath. The bath finished, we returned, and after eating fish and rice to our entire satisfaction, went to sleep. Early the next morning we started to feast our eyes on those splendid sights afforded by the rocks, viz., Arjuna making penance, Kunthi Devi's curd-well and the figures of the monkey examining the head of its friend. We also saw figures representing Maha Vishnu measuring the whole earth with his foot, the five cars of Pancha Pandavas and the miracles of Sri Krishna. There were also figures representing the throne, the lion, the elephant, the cat which stole the butter, the cow-dung cakes that were left over after Bhima's cooking, the wonderful lighthouse, the surviving Pagoda and Ranganatha sleeping in the temple. We enjoyed these pleasant sights and felt exceedingly glad. On January 1 our master enjoyed a dance. The Governor who visited the place saw us all and felt happy. We were also happy to see him. Alavandar gave us plantains and cashew-nuts. One day they gave us a magic-lantern exhibition. Many of us might not have had the opportunity to see the sea or travel by boat, or sleep in a mantapam or pandal. . . .

Never before have we seen or heard of reformatory pupils being taken for a picnic to a distance of eighteen miles. How faithful boys should feel to the father who took so much trouble and responsibilities on their behalf! But *Doreys* may come and *Doreys* may go, has anyone taken us for a picnic like this before?

K. SHASHADRI AIYANGAR, the Gymnastic Instructor,

writes:—The commencement of the New Year was celebrated with great pomp. At 5.30 p.m. a dance was performed and the Deputy Superintendent took an active part in the same. The band played splendidly. The boys were very joyful on the occasion.

Among the teachers, two non-Brahmins had good accommodation for lodging, having made previous arrangement, and had their own preparations for themselves. One is an expert in cooking rice, etc., and the other in making good fowl curry, prawns, fish, etc. In their lifetime they never had such pleasant pleasure.

The two Brahmins (Siva section) have no idea to start to Mahabalipuram. All on a sudden, they started as a Desanthri, *i.e.*, a man who intends to travel the whole world without spending any coin for their meals, etc. If anybody happens to give them meals they will take, or they will starve themselves. In the place there is only one temple for a Vishnuvite section because the God belongs to that section. There is no Siva temple there. In the temple there, daily meals were given for two "Desanthris" for charitable purposes. It is conducted by a Vishnuvite widow. Meals were given to the Aiyar-Brahmins the whole of their stay. According to the caste rules Aiyangar-Brahmins are rather conservative and would not be so free as to take meals, even drinking water from Aiyar-Brahmins, but the Aiyars generally have no objection to take meals, etc., from Aiyangars. On account of to fulfil the stomach at the present, one of the two Aiyars changed his caste mark—that is, bearing a *namam* Vadagalai or otherwise called U mark in his forehead, to show outside appearance for others as a Vishnuvite Brahmin.

In 1913 a second camp was held at the Seven Pagodas. The experience gained two years ago at camping out helped in many ways successfully to organise the present camp. But the problem was always a difficult one for the authorities to face, inasmuch as restriction of movement to ensure safety had to be veiled under the garb of camp life. There are reformatories and reformatories, and when one ordinarily hears of a reformatory going out to camp, it may be taken for granted that it is an institution which is akin in its character and constitution to that of an industrial school; but when a reformatory admits inmates of various types, ranging from the innocent pilferer to the murderer, then the development of the sporting instinct in school life is the only element that can be relied upon, coupled with that trust which the generality of boys appreciate. To youths accustomed to barred doors and walls, half of whom had never seen the sea, the fascination of camp life by the seaside must necessarily appeal more strongly than to an ordinary boy, who is daily brought into contact with the outer world and life. It seems to lift them up to a healthy enthusiasm when they set forth upon the great adventure of a week in camp.

The arrangements for the long march of nineteen miles was the same as on the last occasion. The Union Jack was carried in front, immediately followed by the bugles and drums, to the strains of which the boys marched in fours.

We reached camp by two o'clock, but the long string of carts that followed did not allow of any settling down till 7 p.m., when dinner was served in the open by the aid of two Washington lamps that lit up the entire ground. The camp was pitched on the same camping-ground, and consisted of two long sheds, one for the junior boys and the other for the senior, while Mr Coombes' tent was pitched close by. The Union Jack was hoisted on a temporary flag-staff, and other flags over the sheds helped to brighten up the place. Camp life is a good thing for discipline, but it is a discipline which tones down but does not crush out by its cast-iron rules the individuality and character of the boys; but, such as it is, it has to be obeyed implicitly. The monitor, with the cap and badge of his profession, exercises authority with a big A, and a Chingleput Reformatory lad knows how to do this, both on the march as well as in the carrying out of the routine work allotted to him.

The spirit of adventure seemed to seize the whole school on the first morning, and they set out in various directions to explore the mystery that hung about the whole place, for they were previously told about the struggle between the Pandavas and Kauravas, and in consequence thereof the penance undertaken by Arjuna, the son of Indra, to gain extraordinary psychic powers. They naturally take an interest in these antiquities, for they were executed between A.D. 600 and A.D. 625, under the auspices of the Pallava Kings, who had their capital at Conjeeveram, a place close to the school and known to them. Three mornings were spent in visiting the three groups of antiquities. First, the five so-called Raths, some square and some oblong, the square ones becoming models for the modern Vimanas of South Indian Dravidian architecture, while the oblong were the originals for the Gopuram, or the gateways of temples, which in time formed more important parts of the Dravidian temples than the Vimanas themselves. Next came the cave temples and sculptured work depicting Arjuna's penance, Vishnu supporting the universe, Laksmi rising from the sea of milk. The bull in Krishna's Mantapam, the boar incarnation of Vishnu, and last, but not the least interesting, was the less ancient shore temple dedicated to Siva. What Hindu boy's heart will not be touched by these?

On the evening of Sunday, December 28, Miss Pakenham Walsh gave a magic-lantern exhibition for the benefit of the children of the lighthouse people, to which also the pupils of the school were invited. The school band played for half an hour, and a most enjoyable evening was spent. With the aid of Washington lamps, the band is able to play every evening right up to dinner-time, so that, with the exception of three hours during the hottest part of the day, the whole time was well fitted in. An occasional game at hockey or football completed the round of amusements. As usual, the sea-bath proved a great attraction, and with a dangerous, shelving coast, the boys were protected by a rope forming a semi-circle and held in position by fishermen. The camp, on the whole, was a pleasant and a lively one, and an instructive one to boot. The boys looked upon the outing as a great game. They got back to nature and primitive times, and they returned to school, having, no doubt, learnt many a lesson, and with their health and spirits improved.

In 1914 the seaside hamlet of Covelong was selected as

the site of our third camp, both for its historical and religious associations, the presence of the shrines of three great religions attracting many visitors.

About three centuries ago Covelong was the centre of some activity, the interest in the place being due to warlike expeditions, trade relations between east and west, and religious fervour. In ancient times it was a town of a Kautham —*i.e*, "ten miles area," and Muhammadan accounts state that it was a Shahar or great town, with many suburban adjuncts. The site was selected by the Dutch in the early part of the seventeenth century for the construction of a fort to protect their trade interests in the East, the approach from the south and south-east being dangerous, in consequence of a rocky shoal projecting upwards of a mile into the sea in that direction.

In 1722 the ambition of the Kaiser Charles VI. led to the formation of the Imperial Ostend East India Company, which founded a settlement at Covelong, but this was short-lived, for in 1731, consequent on the treaty with England, the Company was suppressed. The remains of the old Dutch fort seem to have altogether disappeared, and in 1745 Anwaruddin, the first Nawab of Arcot, built another fort, and called the place Saadar Bandar, or auspicious port. This was occupied in 1750 by the French by stratagem. It is recorded that a ship anchored in the roads was observed flying signals of distress, and the Captain reported that his crew was so disabled by scurvy or some yellow sickness, that it was absolutely necessary for their recovery that they should be allowed to land. Thirty Frenchmen landed, and during the night overpowered the garrison, having carried arms concealed under their clothes. In 1752 the fort was taken from the French by Clive with 200 Europeans, 500 newly raised Sepoys, and artillery consisting of four 24-pounders. The French garrison consisted of fifty Europeans, 300 Sepoys, and fifty cannon of large calibre, which had been captured by Labourdannais at Madras. The English force arrived two miles west of the fort, and Lieutenant Cowper was deputed to occupy a garden 600 yards south of the fort, but in the engagement Cowper was shot. Between the garden and fort Clive completed a battery on the fourth day, and was about to open fire when the commander offered to surrender, provided the garrison was allowed to carry away its private property, which consisted chiefly of snuff and turkeys. The fortifications were then blown up.

The Covelong of to-day is animated by religious enthusiasm and local veneration by devotees of the three great religions of the world—Hinduism, Muhammadanism, and Roman Catholicism. The Tamil equivalent of the name "Kovalam" means a headland, but in Sanskrit the place is called Nithya Kalyana Pura, meaning the "daily marriage city"; and the famous Hindu temple about three miles away, known as the temple of Nithya Kalyana Perumal, of hoary age and heightened faith, attracts pilgrims from the surrounding country. It was built in honour of the Vishnu Avatara Perumal, of Supreme Bliss, who is reputed to enjoy felicity every day.

With the Muhammadan the place is of peculiar sanctity on account of the interment of the Saint Thyam-mum-Ansari, of lineal descent from the Arabs, who were living in Medina when Muhammad came from Mecca. Tradition has it that in the year 538 (Hijra) a box floated down the coast of Covelong, and some Hindu fishermen on seeing it approached it with the object of laying hold of it, but to their astonishment the box receded beyond their reach. When they could not get at the coffin-like repository they sought the aid of the Arab fishermen living close by, and on their approach the box remained stationary. When the lid was removed, the well-preserved corpse of a Muhammadan was discovered with a roll in Arabic characters at the head, stating that Thyam-mum-Ansari, during his stay in Arabia and while engaged in trade, was a man of great piety, and that on his death the chief of the place wished to bear the expenses of his funeral, but as the honour of doing so was also disputed by the people, the corpse in consequence remained unburied for several days. Ansari then appeared in a vision to the chief, and communicated his desire that neither party should bear the expense of his funeral, but that his effects were to be sold for the purchase of a box, to be floated on the ocean with his corpse reposing in it. The Arab fishermen on reading the manuscript attempted to lift the box, but being foiled in their endeavours they began to commune with each other, when Ansari again appeared in a dream, and communicated his desire to be buried at the spot where the box had formerly floated. Perplexed in thought, the Arabs could not understand how the box was to be buried under the water, but to their surprise the sea receded a hundred feet, and allowed them to bury the corpse and build a tomb over it. In the days of Nawab Saadat Oollah Khan, a mosque was erected over the tomb, and enclosed by a wall to keep away the gaze of the "unfaithful."

Covelong once more is hallowed by the presence of a Roman Catholic Church, an almshouse, and an orphanage, founded and supported by grants from the De Monte family, formerly rich merchants of Madras. Native tradition states that Mrs John De Monte in a mental aberration wandered about in Covelong. "Our Lady" appeared to Mr De Monte, and promised to heal his wife if he built a church in her honour at Covelong, and accordingly the beautiful little church of "Our Lady of Mount Carmel" was erected. The fact was that De Monte, seeing that the great distance of Covelong from Madras rendered it difficult to comply with the obligation of saying Mass and other precepts of "Our Holy Mother the Church," and wishing to remedy this inconvenience, completed the church originally commenced by Father Carmeleta. He finished the walls and the dome, the work costing 2,000 pagodas. In return, the privilege and right of nominating the chaplain was granted to him, as it was in no way prejudicial to the right of the royal patronage of the Crown of Portugal. An annual Roman Catholic festival is held at Covelong, when great crowds are drawn to it. Till lately a valuable painting of the Madonna by a European artist of some repute hung within the walls of the church, and proved an object of adoration, but to the regret of the faithful visitors the painting was transferred to the Cathedral at Mylapore.

John De Monte was a man remarkable in his time, who

lived in advance of the spirit of his age, and his memory deserves more than a passing notice. He married a Miss Mary Bilderbeck, and his son of promise predeceased him on February 8, 1860, in the twenty-second year of his age, in Germany, while on his way out from Europe to India, and his remains were brought over and laid in the Covelong Chapel. Five years after, John De Monte died in his fifty-sixth year, possessed of an ample fortune, the reward of diligence and integrity in commercial pursuits. He was the joint founder of the late firm of Arbuthnot & Co., the firm being then styled " Arbuthnot, De Monte & Co." His heart and hand were alike open to the cries of genuine distress or the calls of public utility, without respect to differences of religion or nation, as witnessed by his will. His remains were, at his request, interred in the church at Covelong. He left his mansion at Covelong to his wife, and laid it down as a condition that it should not be sold or mortgaged, but, strange to say, the owner of it now is the relict of the Rev. R. B. Feast, a former incumbent of Christ Church, Madras.

De Monte left 5000 star pagodas, two-thirds of the interest being set apart for a requiem to be said on his anniversary day, and that of his wife and his son. One-third of the interest was for the purpose of celebrating weekly Masses at the Church of Saint Thomé and Covelong for his soul and for those of his family and relatives. He also left legacies for Saint Mary's Church, Fort Saint George, Madras, the interest to be distributed annually among the poor and orphans: the Monegar choultry, the Poonamallee church, the church at St Thomas's Mount, the Bible Society, and the different English and Protestant schools then established, and of which he was a subscriber. He also devoted 50,000 pagodas for a hospital and charity house at the Luz, Mylapore, for all nations and of every religion without distinction of caste or quality, and all these acts of charity he did " solely for God's honour and glory, and not from any vanity of this world."

John De Monte is therefore a bright example to the members of a community who are not too well off in this world's goods. Raising himself from small beginnings through commercial activities, he amassed a fortune, and the inscription on his tomb truly describes the man's public life, that "he adorned the prosperity with which Providence blessed him by humility, moderation, and active though unostentatious benevolence."

The site of the Old Dutch Settlement was selected some time previous to the evening call paid by the German cruiser *Emden* at Madras. Imagine therefore the feelings and conjured-up visions of the pupils when they discovered that Covelong was only twenty miles south of Madras, the idea uppermost in their minds being that in her exploits to sweep the Bay of Bengal the little camp might serve as a possible target. But as India had thought it humorous that the *Emden* should have stirred up placid Madras, and as the officers of the vessel had behaved with courtesy in their subsequent acts of warfare, instinctive fear gave place to lively expectations of seeing a real man-of-war, particularly when rumour was afloat that the *Emden* had actually anchored off the little cove and sent a boat to provision herself with fish and goats. History thus repeated herself in the strangest manner, for tradition has it that the first *Emden* expedition was made two hundred years ago, when a German company founded a settlement at Covelong.

Some people, however, viewed the situation differently. The wife of the Superintendent of a sister institution up in the north wrote as follows: "I wonder what you all would do if a German man-of-war took a peep at you! Cut and run!" But fears, expectations, and hopes were all brushed aside when the news arrived that the *Emden* had been sunk, and the boys started from the school in the early hours of December 28, 1914, determined to have a right good time in camp.

The little column, headed by the bugles and drums, wended its way in the dark with the aid of a Kitson lamp till the sun rose.

For miles the hot, dusty road ran, rising and sloping, through green fields and forest land, interspersed with coconut or palmyra, and when Tirupporur, the town famed for its temples, was almost in sight, it seemed hard to believe that sixteen miles had been covered in so short a time, and that the last part of the long day's sweltering and delightful tramp had been reached. This last weary stage was buoyed with the expectancy of a welcome meal, for through the kindly offices of Mr Karimullah, the Tahsildar, arrangements had been made for light refreshments in the shape of cakes and coffee. After resting for an hour, the little troopers started off again to the strains of the bugles and drums, to finish the remaining five miles. When the canal was reached it was a refreshing sight to see the boys wading through the water and crossing over the deepest part in boats. They marched through the little village of Covelong, to find that the camp had been pitched in the compound of the Roman Catholic Mission, who had very kindly placed their grounds at the disposal of the school. The village munsiff was responsible for the arranging of the camp, which was well laid out, some foliage and bunting giving colour to it. After a square meal of rice the boys went to bed, feeling a "sweetness in the langour of aching limbs."

Next morning the bugles sounded the "fall in" for a general parade at 8 a.m., when the whole school was inspected and went through a few evolutions, and was dismissed for the rest of the day to tidy up their temporary dormitories and rest themselves. A long table was placed under the shade of a tree, and on it were arranged a large number of illustrated periodicals, and for the more active, football and cricket proved, as usual, attractive. In the evening the boys were marched to the seashore for a bath, and came back with a ravenous appetite. They thoroughly appreciated the rice and fresh fish prepared for them. After dinner they enjoyed their national games by moonlight, and retired at 8 p.m., when the "Last Post" sounded.

The following day the boys started on a route march of six miles to view the old temple of Nityakalyana Perumal (ever-prosperous Perumal), and in the evening the usual sea-bath brought the second day to a close.

The third day was spent in a boating trip four miles down the canal. Six boats were requisitioned, and captained by various masters, and there was a race going down as well as coming up, and cheer upon cheer arose as one boat outstripped another.

On January 1 a Proclamation parade was held. The school was drawn up in open order and a royal salute was given, followed by a *feu de joie*, the National Anthem being played by the school band. Three cheers were given for the King-Emperor, and the boys then marched past.

In the early hours of the New Year the Duffadar entered the tent of the Superintendent with a garland of flowers and a lime, to pay his respects. The occupant was disturbed from his sleep and garlanded, with the request for a blessing couched in the following words: "God I have not seen, King-Emperor George I have not seen, but I see in you their deputy. Give me your blessing." What an awful responsibility on those, even, who do not live in the fierce light that beats upon a throne!

In the evening a concert and a little dance were arranged, at which the few European inhabitants of the village were present. The following day the boys derived great sport in dragging nets across the old canal near the salt factory, the quantity of fish obtained being sufficient for one meal.

On Sunday the programme was the usual one observed all the year round. In the morning the boys tidied up their dormitories and had a walk to the bar of the sea, passing the old fort Saadat Bandar, built by the Nawab Anwaruddin in 1744-1749, and captured from the Mussalmans by the French by stratagem, and by Clive from the French in 1752. In the day the boys assembled to hear the school's new year motto explained to them, "Play fair in your games." In the evening there was battalion-drill and physical drill set to music, and the day of intercession was observed by Christians, in regard to the War, in Mrs Feast's bungalow.

On the last day Father Marianandham gave the school a treat of cakes, and during the day the boys romped about in the shady grounds of the village munsiff of Covelong, who was "at home" to them. The school is greatly indebted to the Roman Catholic Mission and to Father Marianandham for his extreme kindness in allowing the camp to be pitched on his grounds and for his help in various little ways.

COVELONG

It was to be expected that the dumping down of the school in Covelong would disturb the natural life of somnolency that possessed the village, but the inhabitants must have welcomed the change. They felt a just pride, and realised that they had been raised in dignity in the eyes of their little world. The whole camp was a great success, and the boys thoroughly enjoyed themselves, their behaviour being even better than on the last two occasions. The health of the school, which had run down on account of the presence of malaria during the past year, improved, and the outing raised the resistant power of the boys against any attack of fever that might still be lurking in Chingleput.

Extracts from the composition of two boys follow :—

KARIM, 4th Class.—On our way we found several wonders of Nature. We started direct to Covelong in a boat on the shallow breakwaters adjoining the seashore. After going a mile we met another boat with a widespread sail. Our boat was pulled by two people with a tight rope. The rope gave way in the middle and the two people fell into the water. A young man came swimming to the boat to prevent it from going back. Meanwhile the opposite boat with the sail was moving towards us very fast. We were all terribly afraid that the boat would dash against ours, and we were neither expert sailors nor were in a position to suggest some remedy or other. We were all panic-stricken; but we still prayed to God to preserve our lives, which He did accordingly.

After having gone three miles we got at the shore opposite to Covelong. We were very happy to see Covelong from the shore. How varied are the images arising to our sight! The glorious creation of God—the world with its creations, the deep blue sea with its soft breeze. Much more so is the pleasure of talking to each other about these wonders.

SRIRANGAN, 4th Class.—Health is most essential for man. Every thinking man knows how he can obtain the best health. A good climate, good water, pure air, sweet food, and, lastly, a clear head, are all necessary. This successful function of arranging an excursion for Covelong was chiefly and only due to the initiative of our father.

On December 28, 1914, early morning Monday, we started from our school for Covelong. We halted at Kattukulam. Each of us had two cakes (ragi). After two miles we had a nice drink of coffee, rice-cakes and good plantains from the Tahsildar. Departing from the place, we had again boiled palmyra roots, and after walking five miles we got on boats and reached Covelong.

Next early morning we rose from our beds, cleaned our teeth, and prayed to God. We played a little while. Our father inspected us, and we were one and all supplied with marbles. We played again, and got some peas and food with fish. After three o'clock we bathed in the sea. We had our evening meal, and went to our beds at 7.30 p.m.

On the last day the munsiff of the village gave a feast (rich and sweet) to all of us. The very day the Covelong people brought a big tortoise before our father, and he seated a small boy from our company. The creature still moved with the weight on, and very much excited our laughter and admiration. A photograph of the view of the above (fun), the tortoise and the little boy, was taken. This closed our sweet days. Now let us feel who will be so kind to us to grant us all an immense delight to mind and body. Of course, it is our venerable father. May God preserve him for many a year!

If there is one lesson more than another that an outing of this sort teaches, it is that happiness follows good behaviour. The complete sense of freedom that is realised from the absence of bolts and bars, ramparts and guards, the unalloyed pleasure that is theirs for the keeping, the moral advantage accruing from the effort to keep promises, are imbibed at a most impressionable age. Of course, so long as human nature is frail there will be lapses; but the chance is there for those to seize who may. The whole profit by it in varying degrees. This training is such that time is economised, space utilised, the best quality in each boy developed in proportion to his physical and intellectual abilities, and a boy soon realises that, first, in his little world bad conduct does not pay. He has already learnt that honesty is the best policy, and when he goes out into the world after his term of probation, when his character is beginning to respond to the training, it is with the full knowledge that personal rights must be regarded, and he is provided with the requisite equipment to prevent him from the necessity of preying on others. Though much is done in the school-house, workshops and gardens, it is the supplementary teaching of the playing-field, the privilege allowed to senior boys of going on errands and doing odd jobs outside the school without escort, to infuse self-reliance and a sense of responsibility, together with these pleasure-trips, that bring home to the inmates the sweets of freedom and pleasure that will be theirs for life by upright conduct. Few, probably, at this stage are able to do right for its own sake, but the foundation for the pedestal is being soundly laid for the building up of their characters.

The average Indian boy of the working-class is brought up within the narrow teachings of his particular caste, trade, or calling. Here he learns the first lessons of sympathy, kindness, co-operation, and consideration for others by communal association. Both in work and at play a boy cannot afford to be selfish or stand aloof. His dependence on others and the necessity for helping others is soon learnt. In the workshop, when a chair, for example, has to be made, the turned leg, the curved back, and the planed seat, are the work of several hands; while in organised games the selfish player finds that he deploringly fails at successful attack. The trade competitions in football and hockey create a healthy rivalry, inspire combination, instil ideas of self-control, and create a friendly and sporting spirit.

The school owes much of its success to the far-sighted policy of the late Mr Grigg, of the Indian Civil Service, who was Director of Public Instruction when this institution was started, and to his successors; to the personal interest taken by the Governors of the Presidency and heads of Departments; and to the careful selection of the educational officers entrusted with the duty of training, who really are the main-spring of the institution; and, unlike the work of other school Principals, the burden of the whole school rests upon their shoulders. To these the institution was ever a school, and nothing else, and as each new-comer is brought to the school under escort, and with an anklet on his leg, he is welcomed as a member of a community where only school discipline is enforced. The Superintendent acts as a father to the boys, who, unaccustomed to be loved, respond freely to the sympathy shown them. The general public find it hard to dissociate the idea of crime from penalty. Few can realise that this is a school, and not a gaol.

The moral value of this bold and liberal action has been fully justified by results, and it is to the credit of the present Superintendent and the Deputy-Superintendent of the reformatory that, while this vigorous policy is given full play in the South, similar institutions in the North of India still hesitate to attempt such a step. The fear is, I think, due to the fact that the authorities do not look at the question from the boys' point of view. There is too much restraint put upon the juvenile, and the master poses as a superior person who ought to be respected rather than loved. Immediately a lad is trusted and feels less restraint he shows his better qualities, which draw forth more confidence. This prepares the way for outside freedom, and lessens the difficulties of holding a camp. Once out in camp, the master brings himself down to the level of the boys without assuming any air of superiority. Although he may belong to a higher caste and freely mix in their games, he inspires the boys to respond to what is highest and best, and they, being trusted, prove themselves worthy of trust, and in this way it is possible to raise the tone of the school.

In this connection the remarks of Mr J. G. Covernton, C.I.E., Director of Public Instruction, Burma, are worth quoting. He states: "I visited the institution to obtain information and suggestions for improvements in our reformatory in Burma. I have been much interested in all I have seen. What strikes me most is the freedom allowed to the pupils and the trust placed in them. From this one may infer that the tone of the school is excellent, and that its effects and methods are educational rather than penal. I greatly wish that the same spirit could be introduced into our own Reformatory."

CHAPTER XI

CHRISTMAS CAMP AT SADRAS

THE Christmas camp has become an important event in the life of the school, and the boys now look forward to it and appreciate it. Sadras, the old Dutch trading settlement, was selected as the site of our Fourth Margate Camp in 1912, not because of its historical importance, for there is none beyond the conference held there in 1754 to arrange the basis of a reconciliation between the English and the French, but it was selected for the reason that it was a seaside resort unfamiliar to the boys.

In the early hours of the morning the school marched out in fours, headed by the drums and buglers. Our plush-coated mascot, "Mike," marched in front with his zebra-marked legs, his plume-ending tail, and a countenance betraying a consciousness of doing his bit on the march. A halt was made half-way at Thirukkalikunram for breakfast and for a peep at the famous temple; our grateful thanks are due to Mr Kumaraswami Mudaliar, a trustee of the temple and chairman of the Union, who was most kind in providing a good morning meal for the boys. The little troopers set out again at eleven o'clock and reached camp at 2 p.m., after a steady march of eighteen miles, out and away from the habitable world, with broad green fields on either side and scarcely a village or homestead in sight.

The Dutch Fort was selected as the camping-ground, where a long hut was constructed for the accommodation of the senior boys, while the juniors occupied the godowns built by the Dutch settlers for trade purposes. A tent was pitched between the dormitories for the Superintendent.

After a hearty meal, the boys retired to rest in their comfortable but strange surroundings, and in ten minutes there was dead silence. The fort was soon a little town of slumber until dawn, and at five o'clock, when the clear notes of the buglers sounded the "valley," a horde of little urchins trotted off to perform their morning ablutions. After a brief inspection they started for a two-mile sandy march to "pay their respects" to the Zamindar brothers. Here an impromptu little ceremony was enacted. The landholders were garlanded and eulogised in verse, composed by the head-master and sung by the pupils. Red plantains and sugar were distributed to the boys. On Wednesday evening the brothers were "at home" to the boys and staff, who spent the whole day on their grounds, and heartily enjoyed the sumptuous meals provided for all.

The usual afternoon sea-baths were arranged for, and it was highly amusing to watch the lads being buried in the "surf of delight," and bobbing up to catch their breath, while the mud-larks thoroughly enjoyed themselves to the full in the sands, all raising an appetite which did full justice to the rice and fresh fish, the usual luxurious camp diet of the boys. The competition for the Rogers' Silver Cup in hockey was keenly contested between the various industries and finally won by the Mason boys. A portable horizontal bar was fixed up, and before bed time each day either a camp concert or a circus performance on a small scale, with band accompaniment, was given under a Washington light, to the great delight of the boys.

New Year's Day was marked by the customary ceremonial parade, and in the afternoon with the sports held for the boys. A great crowd of village folk was attracted to these gatherings, the school band which enlivened the camp almost every evening being the special magnet. At night a drama, entitled *Kumuna Chakravarthy*, was enacted by the pupils in aid of the Serbian Relief Fund—the Zamindars being present—which realised a sum of Rs. 20, a handsome contribution from a village. On Sunday the special service of inter-Christian members of the staff was held, and at the Sunday moral lesson for the boys, the new motto for the year—"Time is money"—was given and explained. At the kind invitation of Mr Ramakrishna Mudaliar, the Zamindar of Mahabalipuram, the school visited the Seven Pagodas, doing the journey by boats and returning in full sail, the five boats competing with each other in a prearranged race. The hospitality of the Zamindar, who treated the whole school with a sumptuous meal, was thoroughly appreciated. The Rev. and Mrs Sutherland were the only visitors to the camp, and Mr Sutherland kindly arranged for a lantern exhibition.

Early on Wednesday, the 5th, the boys started to get back to their "Home" in Chingleput, leaving Sadras alone with the north-east wind, the blue sky, and the feeling that the inhabitants of the deserted and sleepy village were enlivened in their dull surroundings with their juvenile activity, though for all too short a time.

The boys, it is true, have many opportunities for healthy recreation, especially after the recent privilege granted them by Government of meeting outside teams on their ground in hockey and football matches, but these frequent camps have created a new method of developing character, by creating a healthy capacity for enjoyment in the constitution of the criminal boy. Brought up in hovels or in the street, and later on, at a most impressionable age, kept within bounds and interned at night, he becomes dull or morbid and loses his sense of pleasure and to some extent the sense of respectability and citizenship. Even the most degraded likes to be trusted—how much more will the growing youth with the bright future before him? Camp life, therefore, is good for him, inasmuch as by restoring to him his sense of freedom it begets the feeling that he is as good as his fellow beings, which always makes for right conduct.

But some one may ask, does it pay to give the juveniles these outings? Has the percentage of relapses been reduced since the bold and new venture was started? It must be granted that there are a certain number who will relapse whatever treatment may be prescribed for their moral delinquency. But in the borderland which separates rectitude from the region of wilful wrongdoers there are souls halting between two opinions, and these are the ones that are certainly caught and reclaimed.

The Boys on a Boating Trip indulging in a Race (page 142)

But the best results are obtained in the class of boys who have ambition and the desire to lead respectable lives. They study hard, take advantage of every facility offered and rejoice in that their efforts are appreciated when they see that every endeavour is being made to help them. They have strength of will and ability to take care of themselves, provided always that the frowns of the world do not handicap them too much in the race of life. Reformatory pupils indulging in the delights of a camp is a specific that not only raises the self-respect of the inmates of the institution, but also tends to raise the respect of the outside pnblic, or rather to create a respect for the feelings of our boys who as human beings expect to be treated as loyal and law-abiding citizens. And it is a fact also worth noting that the inhabitants of the town of Chingleput are the most loyal in the Presidency, leaving perhaps Madras out of consideration, for in this institution they can visibly and tangibly appreciate the ideals of the British Government.

Besides the physical benefits accruing to the boys in camp life, an excellent opportunity is afforded to the masters to learn more about the individual temperament of each boy, mixing as they do on equal terms with them. The discipline of the school is rigid but not severe, tending to weaken a boy's self-control and power to act for himself. In camp life when no restraint is placed upon his movements an appeal is made to a boy to raise himself above his level, and both initiation and self-reliance are developed in him.

Then again, if any good is to be done in the direction of uplifting the character of the boys they must feel that they are trusted and not treated as suspects to be always under surveillance. They come to the school already branded with the stigma of a conviction. They are kept within walls and are locked up at nights. Camp life therefore offers a grand opportunity of putting the boys on trust, and it has been observed that as a result a different atmosphere pervades the whole school, and a marked change in the carriage and behaviour of the boys is noticeable. For the boy now believes that the staff are really interested in his welfare, and beginning to respect his master, he is afraid to earn a bad name.

Sir Harold Stuart and the Honourable Mr Cardew have both expressed the opinion that such outings were beneficial for the boys, and it is gratifying to think that the Reformatories at Delhi and Trivandrum have followed our example. The late camp was a complete success, and the experiment of putting the boys on their honour has been so fully justified that it is now no longer an experiment. The boys behaved splendidly and enjoyed themselves, and returned to the school benefited in every way.

Our camp at Sadras was a success chiefly through the kindness of some of the Zamindars of this district, and their generosity leads one to ask—how came these Zamindars to belong to the Mudaliar caste and what is their history? Tradition states that in the eleventh or twelfth century, a Chola King, Adondai Chakravarthi, whose history is paralleled by that of the Hebrew infant Moses, except as regards the illegitimacy of his birth, introduced from the present Canarese-speaking country the Vehlalas (with the caste title of Mudali) into this district, after having conquered the Kurumbars, the aborigines of the forest, for the purpose of establishing an agricultural colony to till the land as the place was very thinly peopled. Adondai was the illegitimate son of Kulattange Chola, who hid the child away in a golden vessel on the banks of the river Kaveri. Here it was discovered by the Brahmans and head officers of the state, who recommended it to the king for protection as being like him, and they called the child Adondai, from the Adonda flower growing near by. The king gave the child in charge of the queen, who reared it. The child proved to be possessed of heroic qualities, and when he came of age he cast his eyes about and set out to acquire a kingdom between the rivers Kistna and Kaveri, and as he wished to introduce agriculture, he took with him a number of adventurers of the Vehlala caste to whom he gave large tracts of waste land. The emigrants surnamed themselves Dhonda Mandala Vehlala, after the name of the tree Adhonda or Dhonda, but the name became corrupted into Tonda Mandala Vehlala, while the land was known as Tondamandalam.

In those days the Vanniar or Palli people built a fort for

themselves, and under Kandava Rayan began to vex the agriculturists that Adondai Chakravarthi had placed in the land. They sought protection at the hands of Krishna Rayar of the house of Chandragiri, who sent his chief against him, and after repeated failures to capture Kandava, he received the assistance of the Hindu Delilah, by name Kupachi, who after administering poison, cut off the head of her lover and, placing it in a dish, brought it before the chief, who was able then within twenty-six days of fighting to reduce the fort. This event occurred shortly before the foundation of Fort Saint George, and since that time the descendants of these agriculturists are in undisturbed possession of their lands, which they hold as Zamindars under the British Government.

Manu's dictum concerning the right in land is as follows: "Cultivated land is the property of him who cuts away the wood and who first cleared and tilled it." Open spots would naturally be first occupied, and as cultivation spread, extended clearings brought different villages into contact and boundaries were fixed. The first sort of village was the colony or township, the whole property in which was corporate and the concerns of which were managed in common, the payment of the Government dues being in kind, paid by way of land tax and not as rent. Then came the division of each village into so many shares, which again involved an arrangement as to the quantity of grain to be delivered by it to the king. Finally the king granted to it those rights and privileges which were thenceforth to be recognised as belonging to its inhabitants. The proprietors of these shares were known as Mirasidars, and although the law of primogeniture is not recognised by the Hindus, the eldest male member continues as head of the family while the others live quietly in the village and receive their subsistences out of the common family stock.

The etymology of the term Vehlala has been discussed pretty freely. The word is traced to *vellum* water and *anmai* management. Others derive the word from the circumstance that Siva, who was mounted on a white bullock, and Dharmaraja, on a white buffalo, gave these animals to the progenitor of the race to plough the ground with, and hence the name. Others again state that the general term "Vehlirs" means "those famous in free and very liberal gifts and for their very liberal heart" and hence the term "Vehlalars" connoted the people distinguished for their kind disposition and charity.

There are various classes of Vehlalas, which seem to give support to the theory that there were more than one immigration of these people. The landed aristocracy was formed by those who were skilled in agriculture and in keeping accounts. As accountants they were so skilled that, running by the side of the Tahsildar's palanquin, they could write to dictation and even make arithmetical calculations with the greatest accuracy.

Sub-Assistant-Surgeon P. Lakshminaryana Murthi, who joined duty just a fortnight before going into camp, writes as follows:

"It is with the kind permission of the author I venture to express some of my experiences as regards the Christmas camp at Sadras of the Reformatory School for the year 1915. It is my great pleasure and fortune—pleasure, because I was able to witness a lively scenery, and fortune, because I was just in time to avail myself of the opportunity afforded to compare and contrast the life of the young juveniles at school as well as in camp. All the while, my idea of the Reformatory School was, without the least exaggeration, that it was something more or less of a jail for the boys. But I am compelled to change my views as regards the school ever since my recent experiences of the same, and I shall not hesitate to pronounce it to be a school of technics and of physical culture. It is beyond my power, though not out of my field, to depict the mirth and pleasure displayed by the boys during the camp at Sadras.

"Plenty of exercise was obtained both by physical drill and sea-baths, which I think was proportionate to the number of dinners they received at the hands of several philanthropic Zamindars and the humane populace of the village. We had a pleasant boat trip to Mahabalipuram—I may say a boat race, if I am allowed to call it so, from the lively interest taken by the boys in dragging the boat against the wind to overtake each other. The general health and sanitation of the school at camp on the whole was good. The boys looked more cheerful and happy while at camp than at school, and just to satisfy my curiosity I even went to the extent of weighing some of the boys, and I found a good deal of increase in them. I may say the camp was a thorough success, and every credit is undoubtedly due to the Superintendent of the school."

Thirty-three boys had lost weight in December, totalling 96¼ lbs. (loss in weight). On return from camp these boys were weighed again, and five who were found to have gained on their last weight had still 3lbs. to make up between them, but the remaining twenty-eight gained 68¼ lbs, *i.e.*, 2.4 lbs. per head. Of these, four boys actually gained 4 lbs. each. The figures prove how liberty, fresh air, and extra food contribute towards health.

The little village of Sadras, situated thirty-five miles south of Madras and fifteen miles from Covelong, is now a seaside resort, which a jaded official, accompanied perhaps by his wife, resorts to for a breath of fresh air. There is a comfortable travellers' bungalow, and plenty of fresh fish can be obtained to satisfy the most dainty appetite. It was a Dutch trading settlement in the year 1647 and was famous for its fine muslins. The Dutch erected a brick fort, the ruins of which still remain, with a rusty cannon lying undisturbed on the east front. The Dutch settlements of Pulicat (founded in 1609), Sadras and Negapatam were taken in 1781, but were restored to the Dutch in 1818, and were finally made over to the English in exchange for other territory lying mostly in Sumatra. The fort at Sadras was known as Fort Orange, and the colours of Fort Orange were forwarded to the East India Company shortly after the capture of the Dutch Settlement in June 1781. The flag measures three by four yards and hangs now in the hall of the Victoria Memorial at Calcutta. The middle portion is of a light brown colour (perhaps it is a faded orange), fringed on either side with red with a blue colour at the top and attached to white net below. A white net is also attached to the right side of the flag. I had the pleasure of seeing the flag during a visit to Calcutta and found on it the words: "Fort Orange *Isla'h* taken 21st."

The ruins of the Governor's house are still to be seen, and from a study of the ground plan and walls it evidently formed a model for many a bungalow erected in the Presidency. The old Dutch cemetery is within the fort, and the coat of arms on the tombstones indicates that those with high family connections were interred here, and, in the cemetery outside, the graves of the other settlers are enclosed. The date of the oldest tombstone is A.D. 1695.

In the year 1759 the fort seems to have been taken by the French, and a pleasing incident occurred about this time, redounding to the credit of the Madras boatmen. When Lally attacked the fort of Madras on the 2nd January, some of the European ladies who were willing to run the risk got into three Masula boats and were rowed to Sadras, there to remain under Dutch protection till the conclusion of the siege. In the meantime the fort at Sadras had been surprised and taken by the French, who seized the boats and passengers. They sent the boats back to Madras loaded with military stores and gunpowder for Lally, one French soldier being in charge of each boat. When they arrived off Madras, the boatmen arranged to throw water into the pans of the muskets and to bind the soldiers hand and foot while asleep and to deliver them with the cargo to the Governor of Madras. This they succeeded in doing, and for this act they were rewarded.

To this day visitors to the place dig for broken pieces of Dutch pottery, real delf ware, which are to be found buried in heaps outside the fort ramparts. The fort has the reputation of being infested with cobras, and no one approaches the place at dusk. But the bustle of the school camp proved too much for the guardian deities of the place, for they temporarily left their abode for more congenial silence. Shortly after our return from camp the Sub-Inspector of Police reported that two men died of snake bite, a sure sign of the return of these reptiles to their old haunt.

At the invitation of Mr Arunachella Mudaliar, the Zemindar of Chunampet, the Reformatory School had a most enjoyable outing during the Christmas holidays. Previous camps were held at seaside resorts within a day's march from the school, but on this occasion, as the distance to be covered was about 41 miles, the first 23 miles up to Acharapakkam was done by train, four carriages being reserved for the 250 happy lads, who enlivened the journey with their songs and shouting. There is no philosopher subtle enough to be able definitely to analyse the sort of stuff turned out at the Reformatory, and how to deal successfully with ragamuffins is a problem as difficult as any U-boat question, but there can be no doubt that these camps do an immense deal of good in re-shaping these juveniles.

Arrived at Acharapakkam, our kind host arranged for a dinner at our first halting place, where we slept the night. Early next morning the boys started and marched a distance of 15 miles, reaching Chunampet at 11 o'clock, and after a hearty breakfast they arrived at the camp pitched for them under a grove of palms by the side of the backwater that separated it from the sea. Very few outings can be quite so enjoyable as association with schoolboys in camp. The good humour of everybody and the impromptu settlement of difficulties keeps pupils and staff in a state of comradeship, while the mischief-loving boy has his fun in trying to dodge the monitors, who keep a sharp eye on things around. As punishment is for the time being extinct, those in authority have to carry on with moral suasion alone, which goes a long way towards the moral alteration in a boy's make up. He is in school unfathomable, but in camp, where there is no irksome discipline, a key is obtained to the contradictions in his human nature.

It must not be understood, however, that in camp the boys are at a loose end, or get out of hand, as one would expect with suddenly emancipated youths. Inspection of kit and person, short daily drill and cleaning of badges, keep them up to the mark. Occasional sea-baths filled up the evenings, the backwater being crossed by boats. On one day a visit was paid to the old picturesque Muhammadan fort of Allambara, of considerable importance in the 18th century. It forms a quadrilateral about 250 by 200 yards broad, built of brick, the walls being about 7 feet in thickness. In many places they have fallen, owing to the insecure foundation afforded by sand, on which they were built, but in its prime it was a formidable place and commanded the old coast road running from Madras to the South. On the last day of the year the Zemindar, accompanied by the Hon. Dewan Bahadur D. Subbarayalu Reddiar, the President of the District Board of South Arcot, and Mr Seetharama Reddy, joined the camp. An address was read and a song sung in honour of the Zemindar, who, after being garlanded and cheered, sat for a photograph. As soon as it became dusk a drama, *Kumuna Chakravarthy*, was staged, to the great delight of the villagers. Every night a performance was given by the acrobats and gymnasts of the school, under a Washington lamp and to the strains of the school band. New Year's Day was marked in the morning by a parade and in the evening by the usual sports, the most exciting event being the tug-of-war competition between the teams of the various industrial departments.

The whole camp proved an unqualified success from start to finish, thanks to the forethought and generosity of our kind and genial host, Mr Arunachella Moodelliar, the memory of whose hospitality will always be cherished by the boys and staff of the Reformatory.

" The Seven Pagodas " at Mahabalipuram was for the third time the scene of the Christmas camp of the Reformatory School in 1918. Repeated visits tend only to increase the interest " in these ancient temples, once resonant with instrument, song and solemn dance of festive multitudes." To the average Hindu these monolithic remains of beauty and skill of the sixth century are symbolic of a power that " put down the wrong and aye upheld the right, till for ambition the universal monarch fell." The story of the greatness of the great Bali, the famous hero of Hindu romance, is vividly preserved in stone—his fall is no less distinctly pourtrayed. But to the immature mind of children these gigantic temples and figures are sanctified illustrations of their gods and god-

1. Breaking up Camp

2. The Boys at Physical Drill (page 150)

desses. The interest is absorbing. Every figure recalls an exploit treasured by the young and transmitted by tradition from father to son through long ages. No tale of Robin Hood, St George and the Dragon, or King Arthur is half as inspiring to the English boy as these representations of their great heroes are to the Hindu mind, for to the latter it is a part of their religion.

Imagine the zest, then, with which the boys looked forward to their annual holiday. Some of the seniors had been there before, but this did not matter. All were keen, eager, and impatient.

The camp is also noteworthy on account of the interest shown in the boys by the leading Hindu landholders through whose jurisdiction the school passed, and for their many acts of kindness: Mr Kumaraswami Moodelliar at Tirukkalikundram, our host at Mahabalipuram, Mr Ramakrishna Moodelliar, and his brother, the Zemindar of Pazhanur.

It is not generally known that in this great war, when millions have poured in for the relief of the sick and wounded, the pupils of this institution sent their mites to the Red Cross War Fund. The sum that a boy earns totals a few annas during the month, but he gladly contributed of his little. This is an eloquent testimony to the loyalty and affection which the British Raj inspires in the mind and heart of even the lowliest of her subjects.

The school started for camp at 6.30 on the morning of the 27th December, and after an hour's rest, at the half-way Forest Bungalow, the buglers, who enlivened the boys on the march for six hours, heralded the approach of the little army to the villagers of Mahabalipuram, at about 4 o'clock, after the canal had been crossed by boats amidst great cheering and enthusiasm.

On reaching camp, our kind host, Mr Ramakrishna Moodelliar, the Zemindar, had thoughtfully prepared a dinner for the boys and staff, which, needless to say, was greatly appreciated after the long march. The Zemindar was generosity itself. He not only erected the sheds for the boys just behind his bungalow, but actually went to the expense of sinking a well at the site for their special benefit.

His many treats and his attention to the whole needs of the camp will long remain a pleasant memory in the minds of both pupils and teachers. His brother, the Zemindar of Pazhanur, was also most kind in getting us over to his place to spend a day with him.

Domestic routine at Chingleput runs so much on wheels that the boys get accustomed to be handled with the least economy of effort, although it must be confessed the cooks had their work set out for them in serving so many boys with appetites as keen as mustard. The boys, however, have learnt what "pulling together" means, and with the help of the monitors, the worries of camp life were reduced to a minimum. In point of food, they were extremely well looked after and easily got outside a vast quantity of rice and vegetables. The fish diet, as usual, was thoroughly discussed, and Sunlight soap had to be provided for the washing of hands to prevent the camp smacking too much of fishiness.

The Coombes' Football Challenge Shield and the Rogers' Hockey Cup were competed for by the various trades, and occupied the whole of the afternoons, while the mornings were given to sightseeing. Many of the pupils armed themselves with drawing-books and made sketches of the ornamental forms scattered over several temples. On New Year's Day sports were held, and the children of the lighthouse Superintendent and staff were not forgotten. A Christmas tree was arranged for them, the school band, as usual, enlivening every event that took place during the nine days' outing.

The Hon. Mr Bedford and Mrs Bedford saw the boys at drill and were pleased to give them a treat of sweets. The school thoroughly enjoyed the outing, and the news received in camp that a "Kaiser-i-Hind" decoration had been conferred on the Superintendent enhanced the pleasure of the boys.

In 1918 I was the honoured recipient of a decoration from Government. H.E., Lord Pentland, Knight Grand Commander of the Most Eminent Order of the Indian Empire, presented me with the Kaiser-i-Hind medal.

The boys gave vent to their ecstasy in the accompanying address. If the diction provokes a smile, remember that it is not an easy matter to think in one's own language and express the sentiments in a foreign tongue, the idiom of which has not been mastered.

HONOURED FATHER—

With feeling of unmixed joy and pride we pupils of the Reformatory School, Chingleput, beg to approach you on this auspicious occasion of this evening function social gathering as the recipient of the Kaiser-i-Hind decoration, and offer our heartfelt congratulations and felicitations.

It is not our purpose here to bring out prominently your qualities of head and heart, which have won recognition and reflected undying lustre; nor can we gauge the quantitative analysis and qualitative synthesis of the Reformatory question from different angles of view; to find out your merit and apportion it in the right place.

A French saying is to the point, *Ce n'est que le premier pas qui coût.* It is only the first step which is difficult. Where are we to find the first step unless we travel all over the world with the requisites and perquisites?

For all interests and purposes, we know well that you do not care for the decoration as a personal mark, so much as the reflection of honour on this school, *i.e*, the amelioration of this school in the public estimation.

On the other hand, we have to make an open acknowledgment to the effect that as long as we have you with us, we have plain sailing.

Hence we have every reason to wish you long life and prosperity as embodied in the following sonnet and chorus and to reap unbounding and enduring joy and bliss.

"The wish is father to the thought" is fully emphasized in the Third Master's speech at the Evening at Home on the 6th of June. It loses nothing in its quaint Oriental setting, and was received with much cheering.

GENTLEMEN—

Here I rise from this huge crowd, a very strange figure, quite surprising, just like a rat from this mountain. Yet you need not be so surprised to judge from my mere appearance. I am not what I look to be, but I am what I do not look to be. My story is a mystery, full of history, as big as an estuary, specially fitted for the century. You would have known that, I have the haughtiness, rudeness, readiness, boldness, loudness, wickedness, and everyness to proclaim that I am the only interesting comic individual who is empowered with the sole monopoly of trading with the so-called English words. Of course, in the usual course, from every source and with great force, I dare to say, nothing can better rouse my spirit than this sacred occasion, in this location, without provocation. Beyond all that, I dreamt last night, without fright, under the bright full-moonlight, a beautiful sight. The dream of sight gave me a picture, a caricature of many a gesture and lecture. You will agree with me in saying there exists some divinity in a person, who has some ruling powers. Hence I take the men of power and authority to be themselves deities. The lovely dream conjured up a Council comprising four or five such godlike men of higher power and authority, who seemed to have been passing judgments on the conduct of human beings and discussing the elegibility of such persons as desire and strive hard to seek admission into the Council of God. These deities, in my opinion, were seriously engaged in trying the various competitors to single out the fitting person to be one amongst themselves. It is a known fact that ordinary people, like so many of us here, can't aspire for that throne of grace. Only people of unique capacities, talents, fortune and virtues can only hope.

The applicants were nine in number. They were James, Watson, Cameron, Oxford, Oldfield, Manchester, Bachelor, Evans and Sutherland. In short, their names may be denoted by nine letters, each name being represented by its first letter respectively, as J, W, C, O, O, M, B, E, S. Now follows the order of competitors with their respective applications, to seek admission into the god's Council. Now comes the first applicant, Mr James, the journalist, saying :—

"Good morning, Sirs, I am James the journalist and the editor of the *World-wide Magazine*. I have done immense good to the whole world through my journalism, impressing on the people's mind, that war must end sooner than what we expect it to end, and that to our Allies' success. My work has become very popular, so much so, that my journals and magazines sell well, even in places where they can't be read. The number of copies published, if I remember correct, believe me, Sirs, is, I guess, one followed or preceded by endless cyphers. Such is my greatness that tempts me to apply for it."

The Divine Council replied :—"We regret to say anything good, but for your journalism we would not have given you this interview at all. Moreover you don't seem to have any more trumpets. You may kindly recede. Good-bye."

Comes the second applicant, Mr Watson, saying :— "Gentlemen, I am the surgeon, the specialist. I am doing lot of good to the public at large by teaching them ambulance work to fit them for themselves and for field work. Can you consider my case?

Council.—"I am sorry, Watson. You, doctor, are only a factor of a multiple. Kindly try to be more a generalist than a specialist and try to learn many more arts than your present mere medicine and surgery. Good-bye."

Comes the third, Cameron, the camera operator :— "Good morning, Sirs, I am skilled in camera works and an exquisite artist and painter. I can paint well a landscape, a northscape, southscape, and escape. If you like you can try me on the very spot."

Councillors.—"Surely, kindly escape from us and then get a painting representing that action of yours, we will then consider your eligibility."

Comes the fourth, Oxford, the great pedagogue :— "Here, Sirs, I am the most distinguished member connected with the Indian Educational Service. I am an extraordinary professor of philosophy, theosophy, iconography, geography, ethnography, and orthography, besides being well versed in theology, geology, zoology, psychology, physiology, and eulogy."

Councillors.—"You seem to be too great a man, with too much logic and gossips. Our time is much too precious to be talking to you. Kindly, without waste of time, leave us. Good-bye."

Comes the fifth, Oldfield, the judge:—"Dear Sirs, I am the people's arbiter. People very much like me and my judgments for I have always given judgments more real than imaginative. My presence makes people to reveal and betray their weaknesses and vices unasked. To verify it, permit me, Sirs, a few seconds to stare at your faces; your concealed crime will come out."

Council.—"That is too much for an applicant to talk so much. Too much talk will be treated as a great disqualification; beware you!"

Applicant.—"Pardon me, Sirs, if that is too much I will again tell you something too little. Kindly try to bring about a quarrel amongst yourselves and break your heads and brains together in a private place without my knowledge. Then some one or two of you bring the complaint and I will then show you my prejudicative ability and place before you the real culprits."

Council.—"Thanks for your judgments, but your trial costs only our lives. We are already judges ourselves. You seem to have no other qualifications. We wish you good-bye."

The Sixth (here comes Manchester, a distinguished member of the Manchester Society of Technology):—"Sirs, I am an expert in weaving and in kindred industries. I can handicap all others by my numberless handicrafts. Now, Sirs, do I not satisfy you?"

Council.—"Yes, it is all true, but the whole thing comes to prove your ability to make a chest of drawers for a man. Well, at present we require more than your mere handicrafts. Well, good-bye."

Comes the seventh, Bachelor, M.D., D.D., D.Sc. :—"Here I am, Sirs, the Archdeacon of the Church of England, Rev. Bachelor, by name. I devote my life and all my hours of disposal to the good of the rising generation, by preaching to them about God, His mysterious powers and our love and gratitude to Him and all that."

Council.—"True, it is a good work, but in our opinion it is going far ahead and far beyond your own earthly kingdom. Being man, you must not too often trace relationship with God. Sooner you leave us the better. Good-bye."

Eighth Applicant :—"Sirs, I am the great District Officer, Collector, and Magistrate of netherlands. I represent the king in miniature. I collect revenues and do a lot of other things towards the good administration of a district."

Council.—"Very good, of course, but one word to say, being in charge of netherlands, you know neither dry lands nor wet lands, probably you are a collector of no lands. Very strange indeed. Again, you collectors never recollect what you collect. Hence, we neglect you."

Ninth Applicant :—"I am a scientist, come from the southern lands, my name has far reached the northern lands, my moving camp is in the midlands. Again, all the modern inventions and discoveries that have worldwide circulation in this modern warfare are all the outcome of my special scientific research studies. The motor-car, tramcar, side-car, Ford-car, sircar, Peshkar and sow-car, aeroplane, biplane, monoplane, waterplane high-plane, low-plane, explain and complain are all mine."

Council.—"Very well, scientist, we are only very few in number, your cars and planes are too many, too big, and too fast to insure life. We want a new patent, a plane-car, and we think it will take you some time to bring it to publicity. Meanwhile, please take leave from us. Good-bye."

Now the Councillors were very much dissatisfied and disappointed for not having a good applicant who deserved to be with them. They desired all the above qualities combined in one man, and, strange to say, there suddenly rushed a bold gentleman, dressed in neat uniform with a silver decoration connoting his meritorious service. Besides, he looked to me very serene and thoughtful. Under that bright full-moonlight with his rosy cheeks and smiling countenance I found him calmly approaching the deities with a dignified gait and with the testimony of the combined qualifications as aforesaid; I inferred from this he would have reached fifty. While the application was being considered in the Council I recollect now to have seen then the applicant's name being written as J. W. COOMBES. Ah!

Now I see that each letter of his name in order denotes the trade or science he is an expert in. So, I have demonstrated that Mr J. W. Coombes is the master of several arts and trades, has no equal, and he is second to none. I thought as much that he would be selected, and, strange to say, the Council gods, soon as they saw Mr Coombes, stood gazing at him and had, I guess, some kind of thrill passing in their veins. They welcomed him, and exclaimed with one voice, "Mr Coombes, you are the individual we are longing to have in our midst. You have all that we desire of you. You have the decoration in silver in token of your exemplary service; you are sufficiently aged to possess ripe experience in all fields; we believe you will be nearing fifty. Most heartily we request you to join us." That was my last night's dream, and now to recollect what I had seen in my dream last, I am quite surprised to find just the same person here before us all; probably transferred here. I believe my own eyes, this is my father Coombes. He wears the same silver decoration, and to-day is his fiftieth birthday, also to celebrate his golden jubilee, for which we are all now joined. He looks like the very, why very and all that, the very father of mine to-day now before us, who sought to have been in my dream also. It can't but be one and the same thing. There can't be two similar beings. It is quite providential that his greatness has been evinced in my dream last night. I am doubly glad to have seen him in last night's dream and to see him now before us all. His past years have passed happily and peacefully with the finishing touch of the Kaiser-i-Hind decoration and this fiftieth birthday of his golden jubilee. With these few ideas realised from my last night's dream I beg to end my monotony, lastly wishing of course the father of the day many, many happy returns of his birthday and the diamond jubilee with a few lines :—

Jubilee June, joins Josiah,
Warm weather welcomes Waters,
Concealed cuckoo coos Coombes;
The 6th of June is the day of glee,
And it partakes the golden jubilee.

CHAPTER XII

A BOY'S LAST DAY AT SCHOOL

No greater contrast in appearance can be presented than that between a boy on the first day of his admission, and on his last day at school. A trembling creature with down-cast looks, he is brought to the school accompanied by two policemen armed with rifles with fixed bayonets (to prevent his escape, I fancy !), and forms the centre of a group which may be entitled "weakness and strength." The boy is received in jail clothes with an iron anklet round his leg, and a pair of manacles on his hands; these are at once removed. With education, good feeding, physical exercise, and regular habits, he begins to lose the hang-dog look, learns how to smile, and to put on a happy and contented countenance. When the time for his discharge draws near he is allowed six months' growth of hair, and with it is sometimes observed a growth of slackness and indifference to too closely observe the rules of the school. He is more concerned about the totalling up of his earnings, and the getting ready of his "go-away costume," which generally consists of a suit of some fancy check, a cap and a body cloth. With hair well plastered with coconut oil or vaseline he is the hero, for the time being.

He is conscious of his new dignity. On the last Sunday before the close of the moral lesson, the boy steps out to put a garland of flowers on the Superintendent and presents him with a nosegay or a lime. The two masters who help as interpreters of the Sunday lesson in Tamil and Telugu also receive some offering of gratitude, and while this takes place the other boys, with smiles all over clap their hands to emphasise the act. He now takes his stand by the side of the Superintendent, who very briefly reviews the good points in the boy's life in school, dwells gently on his mistakes, and winds up with a few words of advice, hoping that by his future conduct he will bring a good name to the school. All good wishes are expressed by the usual clap of hands, and last of all a farewell song is sung by the boys, praying that he will keep in mind the lessons learnt in Sunday school, and that God will protect him from the influence of evil associates if he works hard and does his duty. In the dormitory at night, vows of lasting friendship are renewed, promises made of regular correspondence being kept up, and cheers are given by his mates for the one launching out into the world.

When a boy, on completion of his term of detention, is taken before the Collector of the district to which he belongs, and is discharged by him, he is handed over to his people. In one instance, a boy was sent straight from the school to be enlisted in a regiment. Such action was doubtless contrary to the rules of the school and the Superintendent pleaded guilty to the charge when his mistake was pointed out, but added that he preferred to be guided by common sense!

The Collector is requested by letter to do what he can to ensure the boy having a fair start in life in the trade learnt at school and to see that efforts be made to keep him in view under all circumstances. He is further requested to pay the boy's earnings in such instalments as he may deem desirable, or, if the boy prefers it, in starting him in business, including, if he sees no reason to the contrary, the purchase of tools. A boy is generally handed over to his relatives, who may be willing to receive him, altered both morally and physically, and, if given a fair start in life, would settle down to honest living, provided that he is occasionally visited during the period of danger which follows his discharge. Hence Collectors are requested to send half-yearly reports, all enquiries regarding the ex-pupil being made through the district civil officials other than the police, and the enquiries are expected to be made as unobtrusively and in a manner as little inquisitorial as possible. The safest plan seems to be to have probation officers for this purpose. In some cases, we do receive complaints from ex-pupils about the treatment they receive at the hands of a police constable who is perhaps inclined to class our ex-pupils as K.D.'s; but representations to the higher authorities have always immediately checked this tendency. But it cannot be said that a boy in every case unflinchingly stands the special dangers to which he is exposed when he finds himself once again in the old unfavourable surroundings. The influence of past discipline and supervision may wear off within a year, and he then finds himself drifting back to his thieving habits, from the absence of proper control. A magistrate, however, is allowed a certain amount of discretion in the case of a youth belonging to the criminal class, for he has power to dispose of him *without* the consent of his relatives in such a manner as to protect him from the influence of criminal associates. Even then it is difficult to keep him away from the gang to which he formerly belonged, and he soon drifts among them and follows them in their wandering depredations, and is lost sight of.

If a comparison be instituted between schools where the training imparted is principally agricultural and those which teach other industries, it will be found that the number who follow the trade taught them is larger in the former class of institutions. For one reason, as agriculture forms the chief industry of the country, it is easier to find work as an agricultural coolie than as a workman in other trades where guilds exist, with all their caste and trade prejudices, with more or less closed doors to outsiders. For this reason, a training in agriculture should form an important part in the scheme of instruction given in the school, more especially in the case of those boys who do not belong to the artizan class. At present, the industries taught in the school are gardening, carpentry, tailoring, blacksmith's work, metal work, weaving and masonry. There is also a band and bugle class. The object of the industrial training is not so much to turn out skilled mechanics, as to train the hand and eye so as to awaken in the pupils an ambition to pursue a lawful calling, and help them to appreciate the value of a practical knowledge of a trade. To such boys, the railway and other worshops are the only places open for employment, and those who are not fortunate enough to enter them try to eke out a livelihood in a precarious manner in their villages. Even in schools where agriculture is taught in addition to other industries, the same results obtain. In Alipore, nineteen boys were found during the year 1906 to be employed in agriculture as against twenty-five who had been taught that industry at school, whereas only thirty-five were employed in trades and handicrafts taught them at the school out of one hundred and thirty-six who had received training in those trades and handicrafts.

In the Burnham Reformatory, New Zealand, it is observed that a large number of past inmates are engaged in the agricultural pursuits in which they received instruction while under control. Of the lads who have been instructed in carpentry, the greater part of them follow up that trade. Of bootmakers, probably 5 per cent. continue in that occution, while tailoring is unpopular, and few of the lads care to go on with it. Our experience is the same.

In the absence of factories, therefore, the percentage of those who follow the trade taught them in the school must necessarily be small, and under the cirucumstances, it is gratifying to be able to record the fact that from 35 to 45 per cent. of the pupils do follow the trade taught them, especially in a country where occupations are so largely hereditary. At the same time, it is only fair to presume that the boys who follow other occupations have benefited by the hand and eye training which they received in the school. To sum up, the chief difficulties found by boys in following the trades they have been taught in the school are, that trade castes are loath to admit outsiders to their trade, that the boys start life with little or no capital, and few, if any friends, and the stain on their character that remains from the fact that they have been in a reformatory school. Magistrates, Collectors of Districts, influential landowners and charitable organisations, however, could do a great deal to find suitable employment for the boys.

CHAPTER XIII

RELIGIOUS TRAINING

REFORMATORY work is considerably handicapped by a boy's undeveloped moral sense. The pupils come to us with little or no religious training. It is true that most of the Muhammadan boys know how to repeat their prayers mechanically, but they are strangers to the spirit of the teaching of the doctrines and tenets of their religion and morality connected with it. A Hindu boy, on the other hand, takes little count of his religion beyond the ceremonial observance of a few festivals. Both these old religions contain the means of awakening conscience, and religious teaching forms the most valuable means of moral training in the school. It is fitting, therefore, that a religious place of worship should be set apart for each creed, believing as we do in religious toleration. Nor do we consider it right to undermine a boy's faith in his religion while a minor, for it is better for him to have some kind of faith than no faith at all. What is more to the point, however, is that it is far better to have teachers around him living the faith that is in them.

To carry out the object in view, the first step taken was towards the latter part of 1915, when a school mosque was built, at the opening service of which the following report was read :—

"My experience for seven years in the Madrasa-i-azam (the old Nawab's school) has taught me to appreciate to some extent the condition, the aims, and the aspirations of the Muhammadan community, and on my transfer to this school it was quite an easy matter to be able to sympathise with the Muhammadan lads of the Reformatory, especially as they were of lowly origin and careless parentage, and to carry out the policy of the Government towards them. Most of the boys come to us without having received any religious teaching, some of them have even had the rite of circumcision neglected and this had to be performed by us. In a school of this kind where especial prominence is given to religious and moral training the first step towards securing this object was to ask Government for the appointment of a Hindustani teacher, who would be held responsible not only for the secular teaching of the boys, but more particularly for their religious training. This was readily sanctioned in the year 1900.

"But to prevent the boys losing the religious instinct of their forefathers and to enable us to have a religious basis upon which to carry out our methods of reform, it was thought necessary that a place should be set apart for the Muhammadans, where they could say their prayers daily. The Government accordingly gave their sanction to the construction of a mosque at a cost of Rs. 1,300, which is the elegant structure you see before you to day and at the opening service of which the Hon. Haji Muhammad Badsha Sahib, late Turkish Consul, has been kind enough to be present. For this act of good will we offer him our sincere thanks.

"It only remains now to give expression to the hope that the sacred edifice opened for use to-day will not only help to keep alive the religious instinct of the Muhammadan youths in this institution, but will also be the means of drawing down Divine power and blessing on the whole work of the school in as much as the boys have been taught the lessons of mutual help and intercession."

The erection of the school mosque was preceded by the setting apart for the worship of the Roman Catholic Christians, an upper room in the "Ther Mahal," an ancient building used for religious purposes by the Indian Prince who built the Fort in the sixteenth century. It was fitting therefore that the little oratory of Saint Aloysius, dedicated in the year 1914 to the patron saint of students, should find a place in a sacred edifice devoted in bygone years to sacrificial and sacred rites. The Catholic priest celebrates Mass here occasionally, and the catechist pays weekly calls to instruct the boys in their faith.

For the Hindu boys there is an ancient fort temple at the entrance to the school, the sacred vessels of which are in the keeping of one of the members of the staff, while the daily oil for the lamp is replenished as a charge against the school. But the public have been allowed from time immemorial to circumambulate it and make their puja, and as we failed to claim a " right of way "—so often secured to the proprietor by shutting up a road one day in the year, not so much to declare it as his only on that day, but to vindicate his right to it on every day—we lost our sole right to claim the temple as part of the fort to which it always belonged. We are consequently shut out from an exclusive use of it. It was therefore decided to have a small shrine within the school near at hand to the boys' dwelling place, so that they might be daily reminded to turn aside for a few moments and concentrate their mind on the symbolic representation of the God of all the earth, whose character was pourtrayed line upon line at the Sunday moral lessons. The conception is certainly inadequate, and an imperfect mental picture is all that can be aimed at, but there is the hope that it may lead to nobler conceptions in the future, when the light which lighteth every man shall enter even into them.

The image installed in the shrine is Ganesha or Ganapathi, the son of Siva, the God and symbol of prosperity, but the strange part in the whole ceremony is the belief and the acting up to that belief that a stolen Ganesha has more efficacy in the granting of prayer than a newly hewn image, notwithstanding its intrinsic artistic merit. Various reasons are assigned for such a belief, but the most probable one seems to be that antiquity is closely allied to veneration in the minds of these simple folk, and an old standing God is more effectual in his workings than a newly fashioned one. The Gods of another's household were often stolen in Old Testament times, and it is done at the present day in India, with a view to carry off all the luck there is in the camp of the enemy. It is strange to relate that the stealing of another's God sometimes forms the cause of a plaint in a Magistrate's Court, and the form of sentence, whether it is to be light or heavy, depends on the special form of the Deity. So far as the attitude of the school authority is concerned, perfect neutrality is maintained. Tradition plays its important part in religious matters, and we neither hold ourselves responsible to prove or disprove any accepted belief. Effort is concentrated rather on making use of everything that appeals to the Indian mind in the direction of cultivating faith in the unseen powers of good, leading it on gradually from elementary truths to higher forms of faith. Superstition must perforce give way as fresh light pours in, but nothing is done to shock the belief of the immature mind or to remove the glamour of old-world stories, or to displace the growth of religious ideas. Ignorance in worship is a good stepping-stone to enlightened faith, provided always that it is accompanied by morality in the concrete.

The daily life of the school supplies many opportunities for training boys in moral habits and feelings and to teach them what to do and how to do it. There are times when the way is not clear. For instance, examination papers are received in long cloth wrappers, and these are eagerly sought after by the boys, who use them as handkerchiefs to be tied over their ears, evidently for the purpose of keeping out the cold. But the problem for solution is how these are to be distributed among four times the number without raising a suspicion of partiality on the part of the giver. The rule of one at a time comes in handy. It is also useful to teach the lads to consider the wants of others in preference to their own. When opposition to yield is exhibited, the result is a deadlock that makes both boys suffer in being turned away, and a valuable moral lesson is thus learned.

In other similar ways, morality is unconsciously learnt in association with fellow companions who sleep, eat, work together, and fight it out on the playground. Great importance is attached to games on the playing field. The beautiful green lawn with the fresh air sweeping down invigorates the jaded body after a day's hard work. The small accidents in the playground are the source of much merriment, while laughter as a tonic on the spirits of the onlookers, whose only trade or recreation in the past has been the excitement or gain derived from preying on the property of others, has a most refining influence. The elements of the chase, the planning out of an attack, the battling with adverse circumstances, the spice of danger, the alertness demanded for success to outdo and circumvent another, are all appeals to human instincts, and require to be encouraged, fostered and directed into proper channels. The criminal boy, if he is not a genius, is in the majority of cases not a fool. There are praiseworthy qualities in him, including the sporting instinct, which have unfortunately run riot, and have only to be kept within the bounds that hold together the social fabric to make him an asset in the economic development of the country.

Playing for one's side gainst an outside team brings out in him the desire for combination, and later on the broader outview of the necessity of co-operation in the everyday business of life. The sinking of private or petty differences for the attainment of a collective benefit, together with a desire to do one's best, are all moral factors, whereas the team matches between the various industrial departments of the school create healthy rivalry and develop the spirit of competition, a necessary element for success in after life. In a school of this kind, where *esprit de corps* exists to a far larger extent than perhaps in ordinary schools, the clannish feeling of collectiveness has to be ignored, if not discouraged. Any act of seeming injustice or ill-treatment soon brings out the herd instinct which combines the school together, and the evil of it is that the sense of right and wrong is not sufficiently developed to enable them to see an act in its true perspective. The moral lessons on a Sunday therefore come in very useful for the purpose of sharpening the moral sense of the better class of boys, and creating a public opinion on the side of right thinking and right action. Mottoes for the new year, picked out in large white cloth letters on a red ground, are hung up in prominent places, so that he who runs may read. Their purpose is to drive them in like pegs into empty, listless minds. Constant trituration, frequent hammering in, and the incessant dripping on the moral surface often result in sparks of conscience to shape a boy's conduct.

With even the broad distinctions between right and wrong, some direct moral instruction is necessary and does do good, but anything abstract or deep is entirely lost on minds almost a blank as regards the exercise of thought. With advancing years the problem becomes still more difficult, when bad companions exercise a potent evil influence.

The creation of a good public opinion among the big boys, always hard to secure in a mixed population, is one great field for operations. By this means the lazy ones among them are compelled to go in for games, while the wasters are isolated and watched and when they trip they are handed over to their fellows for judgment.

The everyday faults of the boys would naturally form pegs on which to hang moral truths, but a boy appreciates an occasional new truth and listens to it the more attentively if dressed up in anecdotal form, and more so if delivered by an outsider. The blackboard, with recapitulation, is not to be neglected, and all the senses are utilised, including the sense of touch, by a judicious use of the rod. Personal and individual talking has a powerful appeal to the hard-hearted, but warnings, threats and overlooking offences do no good.

It must be remembered that the majority of the boys are lacking in self control and in the power to obey, and therefore strong discipline is necessary to produce good habits in the initial stage, and a brotherhood of discipline and control. Standing steady in the ranks and obeying promptly and intelligently the words of command on parade is a case in point of a power that produces habits of smartness, obedience, and of working together, and these are all moral forces. Next in order to good habits comes the gain to be derived from winning the confidence of the boys, always to be obtained, in the first place, by their discovery that one's work is solely in their interest, and that personal pride and sympathy are root motives that animate the daily routine of the School and vitalise the energies that make for progress. But this confidence has a reciprocating factor to be dovetailed in, and that is the placing of the boys on trust and giving them a little responsibility, by creating a sense of freedom which will engender a feeling of self respect. A rigid discipline will produce a mechanical conformity with and adjustment to surrounding conditions, but the individual growth of the boys is at stake and repression will simply cause the thriving instinct to remain dormant for want of free expression. Let a child be allowed to act naturally, so that the tares may show for the purpose of being rooted out. A constant unyielding discipline and too close a watch does, it is true, save an expenditure of trouble, but only at the expense of individual expression and proper formation of character.

The moral use of punishment depends solely on the elimination of the personal element and on the indirect method in which it is administered. To illustrate what is meant:—

There was a quarrel between Govindan, a Hindu, and Karim, a Muhammadan, and while the Headmaster was inquiring into the case and before he came to a decision, Karim, as an assistant monitor, feeling that he was not getting the respect due to his position, threw down his cap on the ground in a fit of temper, an act expressive of strong personal resentment against the method of inquiry pursued by the Headmaster, who, very wisely and with great moral effect, laid the cane on the boy severely. He was told that by his conduct he was showing very little respect for the Superintendent, who gave him the cap, thus interpreting his punishment as a result not of any personal feeling between himself and the boy, but as the natural outcome of his impertinence and want of appreciation of the honourable position conferred on him as monitor. The moral effect on the boy was magical, and he received the punishment with a candid confession of his thoughtlessness.

Songs prove inspirational in directing a boy towards good impulses, even as hymns more than creeds do to fix and uplift the heart *en masse* of any religious body. The street songs previously memorised, with their obscenity, have, however, to be first unlearned, and in their places songs amplifying and explaining moral truths are implanted and imperceptibly imbibed. Minor in key, the music befits the theme, and to a casual visitor the boys appear to sing listlessly, but when there is an infusion of an English air to suit the subject, the crowd take up the chorus lustily and sing it *a la bonne heure*. In fact, they soon learn an English tune and seemingly enjoy it more than their own vernacular airs, judging from the gusto with which they go through it. The effect does not stop there. Often during the course of the morning, snatches of songs are heard, echoes of old ones whistled, giving vent to the joy in place of the moody temperament in the heart of the individual. The poet, moreover, has set his seal on the efficacy of music to charm the savage breast. No school, therefore, should be without its book of songs for use both in school and retention as a souvenir in after life. They sometimes guide one's footsteps straight when they begin to falter. There are few ties to connect a boy with his *alma mater*, and one such valuable link as this should be well rivetted on. But to fulfil this purpose the whole school should take part in the singing and be provided with song books. A few leading voices naturally form the choir, and the drum, with the harmonium and cymbals, supply the orchestra. The language difficulty, moreover, is not insuperable. The dialects of a province are more or less related to each other, and a boy soon gets familiar with the purport of a song, while the music always appeals to him.

In their methods of dealing with juvenile criminals the American believes to some extent in the power of suggestion, not only during the working hours of consciousness but also during the hours of sleep, when the unconscious self is worked upon to produce changes both in conduct and character.

We have heard and some of us have also seen the extraordinary actions performed by persons subjected to hypnotic influences, and interaction between the seen and the unseen as a belief is gaining ground, emphasised as it is by such scientists as Sir Oliver Lodge and Professor Myers.

That suggestion exercises a great influence in moulding the character of children, everyone will admit, and hence stress is laid upon proper physical and moral surroundings for the delinquent youth and upon the personality of the Superintendent and his staff, but when it comes to the sphere of sub-consciousness in a state of sleep, one is inclined to be sceptical from want of sufficient evidence. It is believed by some that a person standing by the bed of a youthful criminal when he is fast asleep, and making use of the power by suggesting good thoughts and desires, has the power to alter an evil course of life. He stands, so to speak, in the attitude of a mesmerist, and by concentration of thought and will power is supposed to be able to make impressions on a lad when he is in a state in which there is a suspension of the voluntary exercise of the powers of mind and body; and when the senses are unaffected by external objects, the unconscious self is played upon by thought waves strong enough to leave impressions to become hereafter a part of one's self. In this way it is believed that the evil thoughts and evil intentions of a boy may be superimposed by higher thoughts, leading him to follow a change of life.

The sphere of consciousness is much wider and larger than we perhaps imagine, and further experiments in this field may reveal methods of work to secure practical results.

In certain disordered nervous conditions, the accentuated suggestion has been known to dissipate disease, but even here the cures are haphazard and scientifically unreliable. A more fruitful field, however, is the study of dreams as a starting point for educational and moral reforms. Dreams reveal buried memories and desires, which go to constitute the sub-conscious mind, the analysis of which will reveal the causes of mental anxiety, fears, depression and morbidness. This ought to prove valuable in the treatment of mentally deficient children as well as of those who are normal, for after all dreams are our real selves.

CHAPTER XIV

GENERAL EDUCATION

The school is roughly divided into two sections, the senior section and the junior section. But some are rather big fellows who, from neglect, attend school to make up for lost ground. The sections work in shifts, and while the seniors are at their industries the juniors are engaged in literary work and vice versa. In five years a boy should be able to proceed from the infant standard to the IVth standard and secure a school leaving certificate. This means that a boy on admission is unable to read or write, but on discharge he has enough literary education to enable him to carry on his business in life. A special class for drawing and the teaching of English provides the brighter lads with an outlet to satisfy their ambition. A little reflection will show what a revolution takes place in a boy's outlook on life, and advocates of compulsory education have certainly valid grounds for pressing their point if they have this change as an ideal.

The fact that muscular movements are constantly being employed in the various stages of industrial work is a great aid to mental development, and much spontaneous manipulation is encouraged to help the feeble minded. The education through the hand is constantly progressing, and the children are thus prepared for any work through the ordinary mental channels.

Reading, recitation, spelling and writing are therefore very fair in the various standards, while story-telling is accompanied with much dramatic form. It is only when one comes to number and space work that one notices a weakness in the processes of reasoning, and in mental work the standard is below the mark. This is perhaps partly due to the limited mental work requiring reasoning or thought, as, for instance, training in the use of fractional tables for solving mental questions in ordinary bazaar transactions.

To sum up, in reading, writing and arithmetic, the boys are above the level of ordinary primary schools, thanks more to regular attendance and good discipline than to keener intellects; but, at the same time, a visitor is struck with the brightness and animation of the boys. They are more interested in their work than one expects to find in a school composed of juvenile criminals. In certain directions, the intelligence of these boys is keen, *e.g.*, in learning gymnastics, intricate movements in drill, drawing and handwriting. The school has a reputation for good handwriting, and an Inspector of Schools, who wished to find out the secret of it, carefully observed the position and slope at which the boys held their pencils. He was surprised to find that, with little stumps between their fingers, they held them at anything but the proper angle. By the way, an Inspector's visit does not create a flutter among the boys. They have vanity enough to try to show themselves at their best.

In regard to memory, it was found that about 30 per cent. of the pupils had bad memories; and in the matter of attention, 36 per cent. were incapable of closely attending to the subject taught. Roughly, about one-third of the pupils are below the average intelligence of the ordinary school, and of these, some may be classed as degenerates.

An excellent library, consisting of vernacular books suited to the various standards, a reading room and museum are attached to the school, and boys have free access to them. Most of the reading is done by the boys during the holidays.

The present elastic curriculum and flexible course of study for primary schools provides for a series of object lessons, for the teaching of which there are great facilities in the school. They are eminently suited for a special institution of this character, where practical work is so much insisted on, and the course of general education can thus be made to aid their practical work, and vice versa.

At Christmas the school enjoys holidays for two weeks and at Easter for five days; the other occasional holidays mark the Hindu and Muhammadan festivals spread over the year, and total 18 days besides Sundays. With the absence of any summer vacation, the boys are busy at work right through the year for 48 hours per week. The masters, of course, suffer, but they are eligible for a month's leave every year, which, it is scarcely necessary to add, can never be claimed.

Much of this will be unintelligible to those acquainted with the work of the ordinary reformatory. What, holidays for criminals! Who evere heard of such a privilege? To the credit of the Madras Government and the then Director of Public Instruction, a distinguished member of the Indian Civil Service, Mr H. S Grigg, it must be stated that in placing the reformatories under the Educational rather than the Judicial Department, it placed the institution in the best atmosphere for success. This school, therefore, enjoys great privileges in the matter of holidays.

The school work is divided into four periods. In the first quarter the boys get ready for their sports to be held on the anniversary day. Their drill, exhibition feats and shows keep them fairly occupied in mind. The next quarter is devoted to preparations for the Superintendent's birthday. One naturally inquires if it takes three months to prepare for a birthday? Well, it does. In the first place, each boy prepares a drawing or a letter to be presented on the occasion. The programme of songs, dances and recitations has to be rehearsed frequently, and a drama occupies all their spare moments. The next period of four months is devoted to special preparatory work for the Government Technical Examinations and for the Inspector's visit to test their literary attainments. The last six weeks of the year is taken up with the forthcoming Christmas camp, to which the boys always look forward, and naturally for some time previous all their talk is about it. These divisions of the year are only artificial, but there is more in the arrangement than appears on the surface.

Boys from neglected homes as a rule must be made to

think. Cut off from home associations and from the outside world, there is nothing to interest them sufficiently to create thought. A breaking up of the year, therefore, into periods with a *point d'appui* for each, is very necessary to throw an additional stimulus into the humdrum work of the boys.

Cottage homes, so successfully carried out in other countries, is impossible in India, but the best substitute for this form of training is to assimilate the school to one large family, with the Superintendent and staff as its parents.

The inmates are encouraged to think of themselves as members of this household, to look up to the Superintendent as their father. This is done, in various ways, to get them to take an interest in the principal events of the life of the Superintendent. The keeping up of his birthday is, for instance, one of these. It is not the outcome of self conceit or self satisfaction, but is for the purpose of supplying healthy outlets for pleasure and happiness in their school lives. Some lofty purpose must be found to interest them out of school hours. Games supply the physical craving for occupation, but the emotional side must be stimulated, and the celebration of a birthday is one way of fulfilling this purpose.

The importance of teaching Indian music in the Reformatory is now fully recognised. If the school is not large enough to justify a music master, it is desirable that the Indian Headmaster or his assistant should be a person thoroughly versed in the Indian Ragas or melody types, by means of which the heart of even the youngest may be reached when moral songs are sung to their accompaniment. The word Rag means "passion," and each rag has a definite melodic scheme, based on no chords as in European music, but on a key-note or central note, and this is combined with other notes in various way, five or six or seven of them in the octave. This endless profusion of cadenzas with which the melodies are adorned makes it impossible to reduce them to notation unless it is confined to the bare outlines of any musical scheme. Indian music has therefore to be taught by ear.

The so-called quarter-tones of the Indian scale are never used in succession, but only to produce a pathetic effect of flattening or the exhilaratory effect of sharpening an interval by a very small amount. The time system also is a bit complicated. Instead of bars divided into common time or $\frac{3}{4}$ times, the drum is used, and one or more beats are made silent; for instance, 1, 2, 3, 4 is rendered 1, 2, 0, 3, as a division of time, and this is filled in with all sorts of groups of rhythmic figures called modes. Not only bars but groups of bars have to be taken as the unit of time, and the number of beats may be 5 or 7 as well as 2, 3, or 4 and their multiples. With much beating of drum and shaking of head, the singer at last arrives at the proper stopping place, which is a particular accented beat thrown in at the beginning.

The Indian boy, whether he has a voice or not, is easily helped by the responsiveness of the instruments. He quickly gets into line with the beating of the drum and the playing of the violin, and readily joins in the vocal music. While the small orchestra plays, the whole school keeps time with a clap of their hands when they feel extra musical. What an antidote is music for sullenness and moroseness! How contagious the spirit of the song and the dance. Music, therefore, should have its proper place in the curriculum of schools intended for juvenile offenders, in fact in all schools. However melancholy or monotonous an Indian air may sound to the European ear, national airs do appeal to the emotions of the Indian lad who is just as much touched by the sense of sound as any English lad is by his school songs or by patriotic airs. If music charms the savage breast and all boys are little savages, how valuable it can be in the hands of a teacher whose work is to heal a diseased youthful mind (by removing to some extent the obstacles in the way of cultivating the emotional side), few will deny. The influence of song, to which like sensitive instruments the boys readily respond, cannot therefore be lightly valued.

In the reformatory school pupils arrive at ages ranging from 8 to 13. They belong to different races, different religions, different castes, and they speak different languages.

The task of teaching them is carried on for most part in the chief vernaculars of the southern districts, Tamil, Telugu (or Hindustani), as the case may be, and a few are also taught to speak and read and write English. Literature proper and all abstract studies must necessarily take a very secondary place in the school curriculum, and it is difficult to determine how to include them without neglecting the practical training which it is absolutely essential these boys should have. They are, however, familiar with the legends of their own country and their national heroes. During the past few years, when their holiday trips led them to the ancient town of Mahabalipuram, they have had an opportunity of seeing the rock-cut temples and carvings in stone illustrating scenes from the lives of people they have known, and it is quite possible that in their case the deficiency in the amount of literature taught is made up to some extent by the occasional dramatization of these legends.

It is only of late years that play-acting has been appreciated as an educational medium. It used to be thought quite sufficient to read Shakespeare in order to comprehend him. Now it is realised that it is not even enough for a child to see his plays acted by some of the best companies. He must act in them himself. He must absorb the character of the man he is impersonating. He learns diction and deportment. He learns the value of sound, and begins to appreciate the beauty of language. In short, he studies the play much more thoroughly than he would if he were only reading from a book.

Nor is it only in literature that acting is helpful. It can be used in the study of history, and some very charming and simple historical plays have been written for use in schools (Harrap's *Historical Readers* come to my mind in this connection). The children have to study the costume of the period, armour, styles of architecture, furniture, and methods of guarding towns. They learn about quaint, old customs and expressions in speech that have long since died out, and it makes the past a real thing to them, teeming with interest.

More lately still, experiments have been made in acting

In the Temple of Thirukkalikundram

The Drama "Rajah Kumana"

Presented by the boys in aid of the Serbian Relief Fund while in camp (page 178)

as a means of learning a foreign language. This statement does not imply that foreign plays have not been acted before in schools, especially our public schools. But the object in having the play at all has changed. It used to be a show piece, to impress relatives and friends; now it is used as a *means* of teaching, of holding the children's interest while a great deal of dreary work is got through.

In the reformatory school the play is used to supply many needs. It is a means of teaching that literature which these boys need so badly. It teaches them history and it instructs them in their own religion, if the play is a religious one. And—a point not to be overlooked—it gives them a great deal of pleasure and is a reward of good conduct.

For weeks beforehand, instead of the usual evening preparation of lessons, the small actors get ready their play. The hard task of memorising words and songs is bravely accomplished. Conjure up the delight boys take in using the brush, scissors and knife and you will realise the keenness with which the screens, drop-scenes and costumes are fashioned by deft fingers accustomed to doing things.

A few visitors are usually invited to see the play, because it pleases the boys to think they are acting before an audience which is not entirely composed of pupils and masters.

Here, however, it is necessary to describe what one of these plays is like. It resembles the old morality play of the 14th century. It usually opens with a prologue, giving a short summary of the plot. The speaker assures the audience that the players will do their utmost to please, and that if their efforts do not meet with success it is to be hoped they will be pardoned. The piece then begins. It is interspersed with songs and snatches of songs and jests which create a great deal of merriment. The school orchestra provides the music, but the fiddles, harmonium, drum and cymbals do not actually accompany the songs but simply repeat the refrain as it is sung, line by line. It often takes the place of speech and does the duty of the old Greek chorus.

One of the favourite stories selected for dramatization,

and one which is popular with all Indians is *Harichandra, or The Lover of Truth.* King Harichandra, on account of his love of truth, becomes a pauper and sells his wife and son as slaves to obtain money to fulfil a promise. Soon after this the son is bitten by a serpent and dies and the wife being charged falsely with murder is condemned to death, her own husband being appointed executioner. He is offered his kingdom and a pardon for his wife if he will but tell a lie, but he chooses to sacrifice her and all his wealth rather than his honour. As he raises the sword to strike her it changes into a wreath of flowers and falls round her neck, and for his adherence to the truth, King Harichandra is praised and rewarded by Saint Visvamitra.

The play is full of daring contrasts. There is a tragic note right through it which is only relieved by the quips and cranks of the jester and by the "Thoti," or sweeper, whose rustic song and mechanical dance delight the boys. There are sudden and frequent changes from the sublime to the ridiculous, from sobering thoughts to outbursts of laughter; but it is this very combination of philosophy and religion and tragedy with the wildest buffoonery that renders the play as enjoyable as it is. The boys have a keen sense of humour. Few things cause so much amusement, and raise such a boisterous storm of laughter and clapping, as seeing their schoolmates transformed into princes and princesses; no one enjoys the local hits better or appreciates the buffoonery of the clown.

There is therefore a good deal of weeping in the play and some moralising, with a savour of religion and philosophy, all of which appeal to the boys. The songs of woe harmonise generally with their feelings, and as the East is noted for its daring contrast, there is much delight over the quips and cranks of the jester, who occupies a more respectable position than he does in the West. He wears a motley garb, and his light jests thrown in on the spur of the moment are greeted with roars of delight.

The boys are carried along impetuously by sudden and frequent changes, from highest lights into the deepest shadows, and from sobering thoughts to outbursts of laughter. No charge of monotony can be levelled against the Indian Drama as staged by the school-going population.

After the jester, the Thoti or sweeper is an indispensable character, and his rustic song and mechanical dance in rhythmical time cause great outbursts of laughter. His wife is also forced on the stage to be caricatured. His treatment of her while in a state of inebriety, and his justification of his wine-bibbing habits—for does not his profession create the thirst?—produce equal merriment. With two such characters the tragedy of the plot is enlivened with lightning-paced changes of comicality. Thus the play progresses, while the thread of the story is only broken to be taken up again.

Its disciplinary value lies in the fact that for four solid hours after nightfall and lock-up time, hundreds of boys assemble in the open, without restraint of any kind, to enjoy a privilege earned by good behaviour. They establish for themselves just claims to respectability and all that it involves—freedom, liberty and equality—and guarantee for themselves future encouragement by further well doing.

CHAPTER XV

THE HEAD OF THE SCHOOL AND SOME STANDARD MASTERS

The most successful teachers in the literary side of the school have been those who were capable of maintaining firm though kindly discipline, and in full sympathy with juvenile modes of thought and ways. The highest caste influenced by its traditions and upbringing seldom drift into the place, and the preference therefore is for those of the lower castes, and perhaps, for choice, Indian Christians. A further disability is that a Brahmin finds it difficult to live out in camp with the boys, and if he is sufficiently unorthodox to do so and resolves to bring himself down to their level, well, he remains no longer a Brahmin.

The great majority of the boys belong to the non-Brahmin caste of Hindus; obviously, therefore, teachers of the same class find it easier to sympathise with the boys they have to deal with, and take more real interest in the attempt to raise the moral tone of pupils of low social standing than would perhaps be possible for teachers of say the Brahmin caste.

The majority of the teachers in the school have always belonged to the "once born" classes. They receive no special training for their work, but their sympathy covers a multitude of sins and shortcomings. The "Head" is perhaps an Indian Christian educated by the Jesuits. He has a smattering of French and Latin, is able, by reason of his poetic vein, to compose quite easily a song at a pinch, set it to music, and deify the Director of Public Instruction on the occasion of a visit. He sails into the school with a smile that disarms all criticism, with a temperament very difficult to ruffle; but woe betide the boy who has made up his mind to try conclusions with his chief by embarking on any irregularity resulting from a swollen head. His dealings with such cases are summary. A scamp in an unguarded moment is perhaps caught with tobacco and birched; he does not appreciate the treatment, so goes about threatening reprisals. The Head comes to hear of it and advises the lad to keep away from bad company, or rather that the so-called bad company should be warned to keep away from him. He takes no notice of the advice, but retorts that he will continue to choose his own friends. The Head goes away, revolving many things in his mind; but he cannot get rid of the thought that the boy was having the whip hand of him. He returns with indignation to admonish the boy, saying: "I asked you to keep away from bad company, but instead of listening to me you have the impertinence to tell me that you will persist in such company." Then, in the Headmaster's own words, he "received good blows from me," which is an expression signifying that he was well caned. The lad was all the better for it.

As the monitors are appointed by the Superintendent, the Headmaster looks upon them as his natural foes. He is constantly at them for bullying the smaller boys, and one lad complained to me that he was habitually nagging them. I found that this only happened when a persistent evil-doer got on his track. He rubs it into them for a lack of a sense of duty and for their readiness to take advantage of their position to hide their misdemeanours. The monitors, on the other hand, take it all in as routine of the day's work, but they have a quiet laugh among themselves at the old man whom they dub with many nicknames. The policy of a great number of them, however, is to run with the hare and hunt with the hounds.

The attitude of the Headmaster towards the staff is one of tolerance. He allows them to do pretty well as they like, and is always ready to sanction their requests for leave. He tries to work as smoothly as possible, even to the extent of glossing over such irregularities as late attendance, lax supervision, and indifferent teaching in order to maintain a calm atmosphere. If the higher powers insist upon him looking into things more closely, he avoids personal contact by reporting the culprits rather than dealing with the matter himself. As there is a Superintendent, nothing serious happens, and if the teachers of the lower classes are conscientious and with some sense of responsibility, he makes an ideal head, for his good nature and smile carry him over many obstacles, and no friction can be possible under such a régime.

His assistant is perhaps a different type of man. He really works in quiet opposition to the Headmaster and assumes a most deferential attitude towards anyone in power. Such a man is crafty, scheming, and with a moral sense ill-developed. He covers himself with a cloak of religious sanctity, but his heart is not in his work. Such a master never gains the respect of the boys, and ought to be put outside the reformatory. His thought of self sometimes leads him to pander to boys' weaknesses in order to get them to do him small favours irregular in the carrying out. But that never worries him. He lays himself open to reprimands, and as a counterblast attempts to ruin the reputation of his colleagues by bringing more serious allegations than the one raised against him.

A lower form master comes to the school with the reputation of being a bright and intelligent teacher and works fairly satisfactory. Fond of sport, he joins the boys in all their games, and his power over them ought to be great; but he overdoes the thing, and in consequence loses a great deal of influence, particularly if he is inclined to neglect the preparation of any teaching notes for his day's work. He is energetic, but not thoughtful enough, and a valuable asset is thus lost to the school. He is the head of the games, but fails to manage the boys, and struggles along as best as he can. The boys are always inclined to treat him on equal terms and the respect due to him as a master is never forthcoming.

I have always found the successful type of master in the non-Brahmin caste Hindu. He is observant and efficient. Mixing freely with the boys, he is able still to command respect, for he appreciates the work of the uniformly good and industrious lad and watches those who only work so long as they are watched. The mischievous lad has no place in his class, as the teacher's efforts in the interests of the boys are too palpable to be lost on even the thoughtless malefactor. With some few, however, his acknowledged sway is largely a matter of knowing to a nicety how far an adventurous spirit could go without being bit. The character of each boy is known to him, for his dealings with them cover various departments. He keeps the good conduct mark register and is the accountant of the School Bank. Every boy's debit and credit accounts are written up once a quarter by him, but there is scarcely any necessity for checking his work, seeing that a boy can detect even to a pie the difference in his account. The task, however, is a troublesome one, for as only the half of a boy's mark money can be spent in the purchase of things there is great squabbling over the refusal of a demand for a cherished article. But he is patient through it all, even to the extent of suffering as a martyr when unreasoning little minds have to be met with cold logic. This results in biting nicknames coined to stir up strife, containing as they do suggestions that the articles purchased for them were overpriced. Nothing is meant by it, as it is only an expression of opposition to a natural foe who at the same time is respected and loved.

Daily queues wait outside the office, each one presenting a chit or note stating in his own handwriting what he wants, and couched in most courteous terms, such as: "My father, will you kindly do me the favour of according your sanction to the purchase of so-and-so." The chit is initialled and passed on to the master, who carefully files them to check the debit account of each lad. Daily contact with the boys, therefore, inspires confidence on the one side and tact on the other. It is an exacting office, but not altogether thankless. An old boy visiting the school never fails to inquire and look up the master who attended to his little wants, and whose retirement from the school would be unthinkable. He has come to be looked upon as a permanent factor, like the little brook which flows on for ever.

The monitor system works excellently, and from results

it seems almost impossible to run a reformatory without monitors, as it puts an end to many abuses which no master can detect. In Sir Harold Stuart's words, "the boys are taught to police themselves."

About 5 per cent. of the best-behaved boys are appointed assistant monitors and 3 per cent. full monitors, the standard of selection being no mean one. The latter are set apart from their fellows by the fact that they wear a blue cap with a red band, and the former a white cap with a red band and, in addition, the star of their office. A monitor can earn twice as much money, and an assistant one and a half times as much as an ordinary boy. There is therefore great competition among the boys for the position, and much heart-burning among those who think they have a slender claim and who fail to obtain it. They court favour, or "catch crows," as the Tamil language expresses it, by presenting small bouquets of flowers collected from their own plots of garden to those in whose gift the honour lies. But on no account should a suspicious or bad character be made a monitor, in the fond hope that the position may help to steady his character, unless he shows anxiety to assume responsibility and not look upon his position as a convenient avenue to hide his own misdemeanour.

The risks are too great. Outwardly, perhaps, for a time there is a change, but his increased powers will sooner or later land him in grief. A monitor holds immense power for good or evil. He helps to maintain the discipline of the school, takes part as a pupil-teacher in the work of the school, acts as a section commander on parade, and is generally responsible for the good behaviour of the boys in school and out of school. In fact the monitors, who should be picked lads, create the public opinion of the school, to which the boys pay strict allegiance.

At times, however, they overstep the limit of authority and take the law into their own hands and punish a boy for an offence. Little harm results from this, but a more serious drawback is that a boy's head is sometimes turned when he becomes a monitor. He assumes a false pride, uses his authority in a wrong direction and gets into trouble.

On the whole, the system works well, and affords an excellent training for boys to get accustomed to responsibility before they obtain their freedom. To ensure success they are mustered frequently and told not to abuse their privileges or shirk their responsibilities.

If a good selection be made of these monitors, the tone of the school is bound to improve and the help given to the authorities is not to be ignored, particularly as the Indian boy, unlike the English lad, has little objection to showing up the faults of his fellows. But this is not encouraged.

The monitorial system, however, is a good asset in reformatory work. It is difficult to probe a boy's individuality when he is associated with large numbers, but when promoted to monitor he is at once removed from his former associates and occupies a more or less isolated position. It now becomes possible to test the refining influence of the school, for he has full scope to show his good or bad qualities. He is in a position to pay off old scores or exercise the virtue of forgiveness. He can rectify faults in the wayward, when before he had to shun those with downward tendencies. His example, for good or bad, is contagious. In short, he stands revealed in his true nature.

If we analyse the characters of these youngsters, always difficult of analysis, we find that there are as many types as the languages spoken. In one type we have the prim, sedate individual, clean in his dress and person, carrying out his duties with terrible efficiency, which does not stop short of running in a boy bigger than himself, although he may lose in popularity over it. At the same time, he sets an example as regards studiousness, correct demeanour and sportsmanship.

Another type is the prig. While in the ranks he has been sat upon several times by his fellows, but he takes it lying down, biding his time. His progress both in school and in the workshop being satisfactory, he naturally expects to receive the distinction of being "capped," but as soon as he enters upon his office he shows himself up by entertaining likes and dislikes. He treats boys differently. He hauls up his former disparagers and runs them in if they be guilty of the smallest irregularity, such as not getting into file, or leaving the workshop before being counted. And the sting is twofold, for the imp gets the better of his elder brother in his attempt to boss him, while he allows his favourites to do pretty well as they like. But these tactics sooner or later land him in difficulties, for a snorter gets hold of his would-be master in a quiet corner and tries to discover the hardness of his skull with a few well placed blows.

The third type of monitor is the rogue. He enters the school branded as a rogue, and leaves it with a seven-fold degree of acquired merit in the art of roguery, undiscovered till he is close on the eve of his departure. He is up to all sorts of evil practices, cunningly veiled by one prominent appealing and redeeming feature in his character. He is careful not to trip openly, and his many good conduct badges are so many proofs, not of his good behaviour, but of his ability to avoid detection. He "earns" a monitor's badge by making himself useful in little ways, and after being capped overcomes all difficulties by his master mind. He keeps every boy well in hand, gets whatever he wants done, hides all faults unless they possess a personal element, and corrupts boys with impunity. One or two are told off to keep his tobacco to relieve him of any anxiety of mind from fear of being found out, and with a good working team to safeguard his other interests he is well off. But he trips just before his discharge from a nonchalance bred of a feeling of my-time-is-up. Such a boy easily becomes a leader if allowed to have his own way, and in after-life is likely always to lead.

Another type yields to public opinion and outside pressure. He minds his own business, indifferent as to how the others get on or misbehave themselves and never lifts a finger to uphold the honour of the school, being satisfied with his own good behaviour. He treats small boys kindly and avoids any sort of friction with the big boys, and when there is a fracas keeps well out of it. Practically he is of little use in the school.

One more type. The boy who cannot hold a position of

responsibility. The lad is clever, but rubs up everybody in the wrong way and makes an enemy of the whole school. As long as he is without a cap he is as good as gold, but immediately he is given privileges he becomes officious, trips up against the smallest opposition, and goes for his opponent. He is ready to take the law into his own hands against an offender and to smite him right and left. He is soon degraded, but his claims come up again, and are considered, till he becomes a byword for instability of character, but only under conditions which are in his favour. If present characteristics are an index of the father of the man, such a lad should turn out a good workman but never a successful foreman.

On the whole, minor authority in the school is greeted much the same as it is in all communities of boyhood, with a half mocking, affectionate tolerance.

In 1915, at Easter, the school for the first time was given six days holiday, and the holding of a summer camp being out of the question, the boys were asked to play at school with a headmaster and assistant masters selected from among themselves. The first question put was: "How long shall we hold school?" and to this the reply came that "it was a matter entirely for themselves to decide." After the first day's experiment, it was discovered that school work was conducted for three hours, with an hour's interval between, that the boys on the whole enjoyed the teaching of their youthful masters, some of whom it may be remarked adopted unconsciously the Montessori System of teaching, and that the "Headmaster" enforced discipline with the aid of a broom—a form of punishment, so I was told, more effective in its operation than caning on the hands. Eager myself for efficeint methods of control, I suggested that in future it would be well for me to adopt this same mode of chastisement, but the remark came promptly and with emphasis, "Oh no." As a superior person, it would not be in the interests of propriety to imitate as to methods a lower order in the conduct of their social affairs.

One very tangible benefit accrued from this "carrying

on" of the boys. It furnished an outlet for self-expression in a field where no harm could result, and where friendly conradeship tended to solve difficulties in a boy's effort for his fellows. As the right stamp of lad was selected for leadership, school work did not degenerate into a farce. The innate love in the young of imitating their elders formed a valuable aid in keeping boys out of mischief. They enjoyed their holiday all the better for a little study, while one felt that character building went on without hindrance. The trouble is that when routine work is stopped temptations lie at every turn to upset even a normal boy's equilibrium. The idea of social service also found an entrance into the heads of these youngsters, who as a rule revel in selfishness, accustomed as they have been from their youth upwards to anti-social tendencies. Every effort therefore in the direction of weaning them from all such undesirable traits of character is to be welcomed, and when the little stage actors in the drama take upon themselves the task of doing something to accomplish the feat, however small the success may appear on the surface, it is to be viewed as the beginning of bigger things. It is a boy's work—a boy's effort for his fellows—and the result is bound to have some value. This experiment showed the boys that they were not mere isolated individuals, but born to help each other. If one went wrong, the others suffered, and the bigger boys discovered the meaning of the word character and its salutary influence on others. The boys cheerfully took their share in the responsibility of supervising the work of the school, in trying to keep their playmates out of mischief, and helping them in their difficulties.

CHAPTER XVI

INDUSTRIAL EDUCATION AND MANUAL TRAINING

THE terms "industrial education" and "manual training" are so loosely employed that I am led to reproduce my views on the introduction of the latter into schools.

To introduce the Swedish system of manual training or Sloyd into any country is to ignore certain elements of character which distinguish one nation from another. Sloyd is good for Sweden, but not good for India, unless it be adapted to Indian needs. The original Swedish models have no meaning whatever for Indian children, and if any teacher is to make a successful use of manual training in his work, he should study the fundamental ideas upon which the system has been based and get hold of the underlying principles. In these circumstances alone can any value be attached to its teaching. The original intention of the founder of Sloyd—if there be one such individual— was not to make a model, or teach an exercise, but to ensure the harmonious development of the child.

He made use of the most direct activities of the pupil, activities which appeal to the pupil directly on their own account. The child imagines that he is doing and not studying. Froebel and Pestalozzi had the same object in view in the introduction of the kindergarten, and in this connection it is important to recognise that kindergarten is a study and not a show. Kindergarten and original research are factors of the same kind, but only placed at the lower and upper ends of education. In every step, therefore, of a course of manual training, the child should feel a positive power. In the spontaneous and free work, interest will be maintained and self-criticism will come in to help to secure perfection of technique. An improved method of working will offer a stimulus, and when a boy finds he is acquiring power to do better, then the interest in the thing is carried over to the interest in the technique.

A finished article makes a stronger appeal to a child than any number of exercises, which to him are meaningless for the present, and the teachers of Sloyd, therefore, imagine that the whole essence of Sloyd consists in turning out the "useful model," and so many models become so many systems of Sloyd. The reason of the first Sloyd model was to set up a standard, and to make work conform to it, so that good results may be produced.

It is a very good thing to hold up a standard to the child, but the internal or mental product is after all the chief thing to be aimed at. On the other hand, Sloyd does not consist in models of abstract joints and exercises carefully graduated with a view to give manipulation of the several tools and the perfect execution of the various principal joints. Manipulation is not construction, and when any method in manual training exaggerates the manipulative tendencies at the expense of the constructive, the work is not "educational." Manipulation means a delicacy and accuracy of skill on the technical side. It is a training of the hand and not a training through the hand. Construction is the putting of parts together to make a whole, and as selection and arrangement are intellectual operations in it, construction involves an intellectual factor. It is only the whole thing which has a meaning intellectually. To confine work to exercises not only fails to supply strong motives, but is intellectually defective. A finished piece of work which the child can use appeals to it, but at the same time it may be wanting in the constructive element. Even the Sloyd models while they were whole things were just one piece, things involving accuracy and finish, without a thought to the adaptation of the parts to a whole.

If manual training is to fulfil its proper function, practical should not be used in its narrow sense in education for the purpose of following a particular trade but in the intellectual and moral habit formed. Sir John Cockburn, in a

Presidential Address this year to members of the National Association of Manual Training Teachers, said that manual work was the best avenue to the brain and that abstract studies could be acquired in a shorter time by means of it than without it. He predicted that very soon there would be nothing but manual trained teachers in all schools. For purposes of general education, this training must justify itself by the intellectual training it gives. Precision and accuracy of observation in doing things, going through similar processes through which primitive life was evolved, and by which it gained its experience in overcoming the difficulties of nature and material, give power of brain and skill of hand. Models should only be an outward sign of the mental training which a pupil has received. Materials and models are selected where results can be easily tested, but in all work there must be genuine construction which involves selection and formation. Not everything that looks constructive is really construction. If a child is told by dictation first to do this or that part of the work, or if the work be too complicated and the problem too difficult, the finished product does not represent the child's own effort and no construction has been done. Manual training must connote intellectual training given through the medium of carefully graded models involving the spontaneous and active effort of the child in its construction.

The course laid out for a school should represent various exercises, which should be so graded that a boy will have no difficulty in forming a mental picture from a working drawing and be able to put proper parts together to get a whole. The models selected should arouse the interest of the boy, and be in keeping with his physical development. Some of the models should involve freehand work, like curves, which cannot be tested, and which brings into play the child's judgment and sense of form. In short, the course should lead the boy to become critical of self, with a growing desire and love for good workmanship. Whittling, or knife work, should never be attempted in any Indian school. It is peculiar to the Swedish boy and comes to him naturally. Its value depends wholly on the way the knife is used, and the Swedish boy alone seems to fall into the proper position and feel of the thing. He uses his knife in a freehand way, and is able to turn out original work with the sense of form cultivated. The Boy Scout makes the nearest approach to handiness in this direction. Being such a simple instrument, the knife is apt to be misused by the Indian boy, and the work will end in notching and cutting of lines and scraping without any useful purpose in the direction of creative form work. The educational results, therefore, from introducing this kind of work into India are almost sure to be very little, if any at all.

A Reformatory school cannot do its work efficiently unless it combines Literary with Industrial Education, and the work in the Industrial department should dovetail with the work done on the Literary side. Five hours of work, for two hundred and forty days for five years, ensures a thorough grounding in a trade. For the first few weeks, work which aims at improving his physique is carried out—drawing water, working the mhote, digging and manipulating the watering channels mainly occupy the time. Each boy then goes through a course of market gardening and learns the simple elements of agriculture, spending three hours a day for a couple of years in studying the secrets of plant life. This open air treatment is specially good for the new boys, who not only learn to handle the spade, the shovel and the pickaxe, but also take a turn at the two and a half inch coconut fibre rope that raises the huge leather bucket with water from a well for irrigation. Muscles are developed, lung capacity increased, and appetites are sharpened by this process, while at the same time useful information is being obtained about the value of manures, the proper time for sowing common vegetables and the raising of crops like rice, ragi and cholum by means of object lesson plots. Some amount of labour is necessary to produce 65 lbs. of vegetables a day, the quantity consumed by the boys.

Sir Frederick Nicholson's idea to use the fort moat for fish is an excellent one. We hope then to start an aquarium for the boys, and after getting all the assistance we can from the experts who will come here about the rearing of specimens, to add fish curing to the training. In time we shall endeavour to do what Japan does. There, a shallow bed, 18 inches deep, is stocked with spawn. When the crop of fish has been finished, a crop of rice follows, and lastly a vegetable crop is raised before the moisture disappears.

There are, to mention some of the plants in the vegetable garden, different varieties of the edible *Hibiscus* (the mallow family), which are pointed out to the boys. The Bendakai or ladies' fingers (*Hibiscus esculentus*) are used in the vegetable curry, while the Roselle (*Hibiscus sabdariffa*) is cultivated chiefly for its leaves, which, on account of their acidity are antiscorbutic, and there is no doubt that as a school we are free from itch or scurvy. It is pretty to see a bed of Roselle when its five sepals ripen to rosy red; when the leaves are picked off and the red stems show, these with the sepals appear one mass of red in the field. They are collected, and make excellent jellies; while fibre is extracted from their stems, as well as from the stems of the wild variety which is also grown.

In the vegetable garden classification to some extent is taught. Very few lads know that the tomato, the potato and the brinjal belong to the same family (the genus *Solanum*) and can be hybridised. Such simple facts are made known to them. The writer some years ago saw an exhibition of Sutton's vegetable products at Taunton, where some beautiful tomatoes (*Solanum lycopersicum*) attracted attention, and it was discovered that they were the result of hybridisation with the potato (*S. tuberosum*). We were informed that further experiments were in operation with the object of producing on the one tree tubers below and tomatoes above. One experiment was tried in our garden plot of getting a hybrid from the brinjal (*S. melongena*) and the tomato, but it was dropped after the first stage, when a bad tomato was the outcome, losing sight of the fact that it was in the third and fourth generation that improvement was to be sought after.

As plantain, both in the green and the ripe state, is largely used as a food by the Indians, twenty-five selected varieties of it are grown, and among them is the squirrel plantain, with leaves marked with white and brown stripes, the fruit being similarly striped. Plants like the pepper vine and coffee, whose habitat is outside the district, are grown as "freaks" to interest the class. The seedless pappaya, possessing digestive properties, the thornless prickly-pear, an excellent cattle fodder in famine time, and the kew pine, large and luscious, are all of interest to the boys.

Each trade, moreover, keeps a flower garden plot, and as annual prizes are offered for the best kept plot, it results in keen competition. On the whole, great taste is shown in arranging the flower bed, though some of them are overdone artificially with white chunam lines and geometric figures. The Superintendent's garden is looked after by a few chosen boys, whose efforts are concentrated on half a dozen species of flowering plants like the canna, the rose, the large yellow chrysanthemum, *Hibiscus* of different varieties, and the begonia, which are grown with great success. Part of the garden is allowed to run wild as nature would choose to garb herself, where the *Plumiera* tree of the dogbane order may be found producing a mass of fragrant white and yellow blossom, and the Oleander (*Nerium odorum*), the sea-nymph flower which flourishes chiefly by the sea-side. The *Vinca rosea* of the periwinkle family, or the dead man's graveyard flower (a name given to it because it was used to wreathe the bodies of dead children), also belongs to the *apocynacdæ* genus, and flourishes fresh and rosy in this unkept portion of the garden, in strong contrast to the artificially laid out plot. Among other things, the boys learn to trim the hedges of the well-known shrub, the Korukkapuli (*Pithecolobium dulce*), and the Casuarina, largely grown for fuel purposes. Creepers are trained to mount the bigger trees, and during the hot months when the flowers bloom, the air becomes laden with the scent of the Rangoon creeper (*Quis quadis Indica*) and the bridal creeper.

The *Thunbergia grandiflora* (an acanthus), the best looking and the best growing creeper of our garden, with its ear-shaped flower of lilac-blue tint, exactly suited to the

His Excellency, Sir Arthur Lawley, Governor of Madras, Planting a Tree in the School (page 107)

green of the leaf; the scarlet *Antigonan*, with a character for persistent gaiety, make screens of the railing round the garden, festooning several trees. The *Bougainvillea* with its thorns catches on to the branches of a tree, using it for a support to show off to advantage its purple flowers, while the white moon flower of spotless beauty and delicate odour and the morning glory of blue cling round the cylindrical stem of some larger plant, pouring out their wealth of leaf and blossom, the one by day and the other by night. The big shade-giving trees in the school are fine specimens of their kind, bearing on the stems the botanical and the common name, lettered in white on black tin plates. Chief among them all is the whispering evergreen Peepul (*Ficus religiosa*), or Bo-tree, over a century in age, dominating space with its long and pointed acuminate leaves, floating with perfect balance in the air, and sensitive to the least suspicion of wind. The other specimens of *Ficus* in the school are the Benjamina, with its glossy, glabrous leaves, the Nitida, a specimen of which was planted by His Excellency, Monsieur Martineau, Governor of the French Settlements; the *Pterocarpus Indicus* and the *Bengalensis* (the banyan) sending down roots from its branches like pillared trunks.

The timber-yielding trees are the *Swietenia mahogan* (the mahogany), planted by His Excellency, Sir Arthur Lawley, a former Governor of Madras, and the *Tectona grandis* (teak-tree), which takes sixty years to develop its proper growth, suitably earning the right of being called the "Monarch of the woods," and which flourishes best in a rainfall of 120 inches. Round the school parade square stand the *Pithecolobium saman*, or rain-tree, that wonderfully sensitive tree whose pinnate leaves are horizontal when the sun's rays beat, thus affording excellent shade for the boys, but whose leaves move downwards and seem to close when the rain falls—hence the name. Lastly, but not least, mention must be made of the Mogadum (*Mimusop elengii*), with its little brown serrated flowers found scattered on the ground every morning and collected for its odour for temple worship. The flowers make neat garlands, and the fruit, of an astringent taste, is eaten for its medicinal properties.

The gorgeous flowering trees in the place are the *Poinciana regia*, the gold mohur or "flame of the forest," bursting out in one mass of red petals, the *Cassia fistula*, or the Indian Laburnum, with its bloom of yellow flowers on a long central axis, hanging down in clusters at the end of branches and overpowering the atmosphere with its scent. The *Erythrina Indica* (the Indian coral tree) holds aloft its bunches of scarlet flowers like torches. The buds are borne on short stalks, one above the other, along an upright axis, and the first to open are the bottom ones—so full of honey are they that the crows attracted by them may be seen bending their necks and pushing their beaks inside to suck the fluid from the nectary. After the flowering is over, the tree becomes denuded of all its leaves and the seed-pods, like drumstick beans, hang on the branches. For this reason it is known to the Indian as the marriage drumstick tree. The *Lagustræmia flos reginæ* has also very pretty flowers—growing in clusters of lilac bloom of various shades; they also produce a splendid effect.

The *Pterospermum lingneanum* is a very ornamental tree with decorative leaves and white flowers throwing out an odour which on too close a visit proves sickly sweet.

The *Peltophorum ferrugineum*, planted by his Excellency, Lord Pentland, another Governor of Madras, on the occasion of a visit to the school, is commonly known as Brazilatto wood, and is a fine avenue tree, with large bunches of spiky yellow flowers.

The palms must not be forgotten to be mentioned. The tall, slender arecanut, giving out a delicate odour; the travellers palm, with its fan-shaped head of leaves, supplying drink to the weary traveller when probed with a spoon-shaped instrument; and the *Oreodoxa regia*, towering above, its ashy grey trunk tapering upwards into green. For 8 or 9 years, the tree stands out in fine proportion, but after the tenth year the base becomes too thick for the height—due, perhaps, to climatic conditions. In its proper habitat it probably maintains its normal proportions. Advantage

The Weaving Shed (page 199)

is always taken of a Governor's presence to solicit His Excellency to plant a tree in commemoration of his visit, and Lord Carmichael, when he was Governor of Fort Saint George, was pleased to pay us a visit and also planted a special variety of the coconut palm. These trees are selected to ornament the school grounds, and are tended with great care by the boys. They are protected by suitable railing, and bear a label marking the date and name of the distinguished visitor.

Of all the industries taught in the school, weaving takes first place, both as regards equipment and outturn of work. A Jacquard loom, dobby looms, a pattern loom, an improved pirn-winding machine, a cop and pirn-winding machine combined, metal healds, brass and rustless reeds and other improvements were introduced by me to make the weaving shed an up-to-date concern.

And it is in keeping with the economic condition of the country that this industry should occupy a position of first importance, for the hand-to-mouth existence of six millions of weavers in India makes the problem a pressing one. Technical and industrial schools are doing something towards helping the handloom industry, and the reformatory school at Chingleput may justly congratulate itself on the well-trained pupils it turns out year after year, several of whom occupy the position of maistries in the weaving schools and handloom factories of the Presidency. Most of the work done in India is plain-weaving, so that the skill of the Indian weaver, beyond a certain amount of dexterity in weaving, is nothing to speak of. Hence the low wages which he can command.

The reformatory school, on the other hand, tries to improve the skill of the boys in weaving, and has for its object the training of boys in the *art* of weaving. The aim is not only to give the pupil a certain amount of dexterity in weaving, but what is far more important, to help him to determine what changes are necessary to produce a certain effect. Take one class of cloth, *viz.*, towelling. A boy is able to produce any design, within certain limits, on the cloth he wishes to weave. He knows what changes are necessary in the tieing and treadling motion to form a diaper pattern or honeycomb weave. He is, moreover, familiar with the defects in cloth manufacture, and is able to remedy them. In short, he has complete control over the loom. Bring him a sample cloth, and he will produce it on the loom. That is the aim, or rather should be the aim, of every school which proposes to train pupils in weaving.

Colour design also receives attention in the weaving of *daris*, or cotton rugs. A flower is given to a boy, who selects coloured yarn to match the colours of the flower, while he is careful to see that the breadth of the various coloured stripes in the *dari* corresponds in proportion to the amount of colour present in the flower. In this way some extraordinary and original designs have been obtained.

Then again, although one cannot get over the fact that a handloom is a handloom, and that there is no middle course between a handloom and a powerloom, still the school believes in an equipment consisting of various forms of looms, not so much for the sake of the slender increase in the out-turn, as for the excellent training it gives in stimulating the boys to think over the mechanism of the loom and the possibility in the direction of progress and improvement. But this fact has to be constantly kept in mind, namely, that the simpler the improvement the greater the chance of its success. No advantage is gained in making an ingenious form of loom which has all the parts of a power loom, minus the motive power. The expense increases without a proportionately corresponding increase in work. A machine, sound from an engineering point of view, designed for rapid and low cost of manufacture, and at the same time possessing spare parts to take the place of broken ones, and which the Indian will take kindly to under conditions prevailing in a warm country, is what is required.

If any money is to be put into a weaving concern, it should be in the direction of improving the preliminary processes, *viz.*, warping and sizing. The native system is far too slow to make a commercial success of any business. There is a wrong idea amongst laymen that the better the sizing the stronger the cloth. The chief object of sizing is to give the yarn sufficient strength to be woven into cloth, and once that object is gained, no further result is looked for. The reformatory can never undertake the manufacture of warps by machinery. That must be left to private agency, which should have for its object the preparation of short warps to meet the needs of handloom weavers.

The execution of private orders entails no little worry. Listen to my lady friend. She ordered a *dari* for a room and gave the wrong measurements, and when confronted with it, she writes:—

"Dear Mr Superintendent—

This is a business letter, and I mean to *go* for the Superintendent of that Reformatory. Here you confront me with a miserable "scrap of paper," which I consider most unfair, to say the least.

It lies between me and thee and that *tertium quid*, the sub-conscious being, though how we are to shift all the blame on that intangible third I don't know.

As a philosopher, then, if not as artistic Superintendent, I put it to you as you read that letter of mine, would not the context have shown what I meant and that someone had merely blundered?

I think I had explained that my room had been newly painted and I wanted a *dari* for the floor to match the colouring of the walls and that a *dari* "3 ft. by 4 ft" would be needed to cover the centre, leaving a margin of polished boarding on all sides.

Now, how *could* a ridiculous dari 3 ft. by 4 ft. be made to do service in that way in a drawing-room?

You must not adhere so stringently to the letter, but follow the line of the spirit, my dear sir! Then you deal a shock to my system by hurling an official document at my devoted head—and now *this!*

Ah! that Dhurrie ought to be a beauty to compensate me for all these knocks at my integrity as a woman of affairs, and my artistic aspirations too.

I meant to have sent this on H.M.S., in which case it would fall into the hands of your clerk—so I forbear.

There is a word from the sacred text which is a beacon in a dark day: "Let your *yieldingness* be known unto all men" . . .

It is wrongfully set down as "moderation"—*yieldingness* is the word. . . . With this pan of coals on your head, I close, and remain, unaltered,

Yours sincerely,"

"That 'scrap,' underlined red, is to be framed and hung up as a warning not to make business affairs over to an irresponsible sub-conscious being!"

It was coolly pointed out to my lady friend that she had no cause for complaint, that in the midst of business one could not afford the time to interpret orders which were carried out to the letter of instructions. Humble confession is in her outpourings.

I was about to call a halt in the proceedings, in other words, to cease from casting fulminating thunderbolts and to ease off the effusion of lady-like epistolary efforts—really I was—because a reaction had set in. Conscience got busy, and a lively imagination, or may be a touch of second-sight, had shown me an overworked "school-master" sweltering at his desk endeavouring to cope with the voluminous correspondence whereby an inconsiderate dweller on the Olympic heights had elected to submerge him, at a time when submersion, if only beneath such flimsies as written sheets, could by no means be tolerated, with the thermometer at what?—say 100° in the shade.

Could you not see that, woman-like, I was merely trying to "save my face," after making an idiotic mistake in a matter of simple measurements?

Why this viewing of life from the wrong end of the telescope? "A schoolmaster after all with a small world and a narrow outlook!" I am so sorry if my ding-donging brought on an attack of world-weariness. If I dared, *I* should turn preacher and teacher, but as it is, all

I can do is to sit up here in such a favourable placing and worry and tease the toilers on the burning plains.

PS.—This is the fly in my ointment. So little can we voice our troubles, and yet there they are.

The *dari* was in due course despatched to her ladyship, and how repentant and appreciative the feminine can be was shown in her reply.

The carpentry department is second to the weaving in outturn of work, and is very popular with the boys. There is no manual instruction syllabus prepared for the guidance of the instructors, but certain broad principles are followed in the work. These instructors are all skilled workmen and could be trusted to do this intelligently. Good supervision and discipline, however, on the part of the instructor forms the main elements of success in a mixed class.

A boy is taught to use the chisel, the plane and the saw, the very best tools being given him. He next learns to sharpen his tools and acquires facility in joinery and cabinet-making. The senior boys are taught drawing to scale and working these out in wood. No set form of exercises is given, but after the principal joints have been mastered, the boy is put to turning out articles for sale, and as an inducement for good work, he receives a quarter of the profit.

The Indian lad has the knack of acquiring, with remarkable rapidity, a certain dexterity in the handling and use of tools. Where he fails is in giving attention to details and in finish. These points are rightly insisted on.

If a lad is given a finnicky little piece of work to do, like a soap-tray or a toy stool, he does not take as much interest as he would in a big job like a school bench or a table. In the first place he has a substantial piece of wood to plane, and it is easier to deal with things in the bulk. He also sees that he is turning out a saleable piece of furniture in everyday use and his interest is quickened. In after-life, these boys are seldom employed in any work involving originality and design. As workmen, their skill alone will command wages, and an industrial school should have for its sole object the manufacture of skilled workmen who would ordinarily be under the control of maistries and foremen.

The piece of woodwork shown in the illustration was executed by the boys, under the supervision of the drawing master and the carpenter maistry, for the Fine Arts Exhibition held annually in Madras, and gained a bronze medal in 1907. It displays the usual features of Dravidian carved work. As a rule, the school goes in for plain, solid work and supplies much of its own needs. In later years the boys won several certificates of merit and other distinctions, while quite a third of those trained were successful in passing the Government Technical Tests.

The object of these classes is to teach the boys the best way of making the ordinary articles required in their villages. As steam is not used in these shops, all the work is turned out by hand, with the aid of simple hand machines, but the blacksmith's shop is up to date with the latest type of forge. Tools superior to those in common use in the bazaar are employed, and the work turned out comprises simple articles, as chains, rivets, bolts, nuts—also screwing and tapping. In addition, common kitchen utensils in use in their villages and simple agricultural implements are made and fetch a ready sale. Last of all, the little blacksmith is taught to forge his own tools, such as a pair of tongs or pincers, chisels and flatteners, for it will be readily admitted that if a lad cannot make his own tools in places where they cannot be bought, he cannot be of much use as a blacksmith. After having gone through a full course of hand work, the pupil is so competent that he finds it easy to find employment in a railway or municipal workshop, though machinery is used. In the one case, hand skill is required and in the other only hand direction.

In the metal workshop there are great possibilities for obtaining skill of hand. Even with no preliminary cardboard work gone through, a soft metal like aluminium lends itself to the manipulation of a beginner, as it is so easy to work the metal. The juniors especially are encouraged

A Carved Rosewood Bookshelf and Medicine Chest combined

Side View of Shelf and Chest (page 204)

when they find that they can turn out usable vessels of simple shape out of a malleable metal, and having once obtained the power to give symmetry to shape, they are prepared to try their hand at the hard metals like copper and brass. What scope and training there is here for the lad who has to make his eye, hand and brain work together to turn out a finished article! With such an education a boy has a groundwork on which he can build anything, and this especially is the case when supplemented with a knowledge of woodwork.

Masonry is a trade which is in great demand throughout India. This is easily understood, for most ryots build their own houses or use very cheap labour. The transition from mud walls to brick is rapidly going on, so that masons easily find work. The system of imparting instruction in the subject is as follows. The boys are not put on petty repairs, but from the very first they are taught what really good brickwork consists in. They learn the various kinds of bonds in brickwork and the correct laying of bricks in position. They are shown the proper mixing of mortar and the building up of brickwork with the correct thickness of mortar and without a wasteful and harmful use, in excessive proportion to the number of bricks. Training is also given in stone and rubble masonry and concrete work, as used in basements and foundations of buildings.

For the purpose of teaching the boys the building of walls, a few thousand first-class bricks are purchased, and mud is used as carefully and economically as mortar would be. These constructed walls and rooms are pulled down and the same bricks are used over and over again, a sisyphean task no doubt. To give the boys actual experience in the process of mixing mortar and of building brickwork in mortar, the seniors help in keeping the buildings of the school in repair and in the construction of new buildings of simple design. The Sub-Divisional Officer of the Public Works Department is in charge of the reformatory buildings, and during his visit he inspects the work of the boys from time to time and gives them advice about various difficulties which crop up. The complete course occupies four years. The infants start building with their wooden bricks an angle wall or cross wall of various thicknesses, and draw the various bonds on the slate; the senior boys finish with plan drawing and a practical knowledge of simple geometry.

The majority of those who enter the class belong to the Odda caste, who by profession are road makers and well diggers. Their training makes them one degree better than the ordinary average workman, and they have no difficulty in securing employment in after life.

One great advantage in having a mason class is that ugly spots in the school premises can be cleaned up and repairs executed at once, free of cost. Boys also respect the work of their own hands. So there are few or no dirty finger marks on the walls.

Tailoring is a class mainly for the halt, the lame and the boy of indifferent health. A few Muhammadans whose parents are in the trade make up the rest, while three or four Brahmin boys of the priestly class, whose caste prohibits them from learning any trade, serve as ornaments. The idea in this particular department is to make a boy an apprentice tailor with a thorough knowledge of the various kinds of stitches, of stoating and rantering, with ability to make button-holes, and with a general knowledge of the different parts of garments. Girls, it will be observed, ply their needles by drawing it sideways; their brothers, on the other hand, jerk it upwards towards the shoulders and head, occasionally rubbing the needle on their hair to facilitate its passage when it gets clogged with perspiration. As the boys' suits have to be made up by the class, they indulge a little in the art of cutting-out, and with a few outside orders for body garments and trousers a more general experience is gained by the seniors. A lady writes thus of their work: "When I ask my servants what they would like for Christmas, the invariable answer I receive is: 'Please, madam, a coat or shirt made by Mr Coombes' boys; they last a long time.'"

But these little knights of the needle are in one respect lucky, for while they do their work they carry on a running conversation, an indulgence associated with all needlework.

At the same time it must be admitted that it is not good for growing boys to be squatted on the floor with legs crossed while engaged in manual work that calls for no muscular exercise. A few boys learn to treadle the sewing machine, but this only involves leg action. Given to sedentary work, the tailor class do not particularly shine in the field of sports. Were it not for the fact that some delicate bodies require light work, and for the temptation to make one's tiny world self contained, tailoring would soon be wiped out as an industry in every self-respecting institution which aims at turning out boys of good physique, energy and fully equipped to earn a living wage on leaving school.

Among the special features of the school, the reformatory brass band may be mentioned. Besides helping in the matter of physical drill and marching, it has a value of its own in cultivating a refined taste among the boys. The boys naturally have a longing for Indian music, and English music has to be specially fostered. They do not appreciate European music until it is explained to them that European music is an elevating art, that each piece of music has a different story to tell, that each is a story in melody, that these stories are either songs of joy or sorrow. It is further explained that music was also associated with prayer and thanksgiving to God, that when the earth is destroyed, all the arts and sciences would be destroyed with it excepting music, which will live in the hereafter. Then it is noticed that the boys (even those of the rough order) glow with enthusiasm and with a desire to do better than they have done, perhaps under the impression that they might stand a better chance in the next world, owing to the fact of being band boys! Explanations of this sort are found necessary to create an interest in their work, and with practice and experience most of the boys soon were able to tell when a wrong note was played or when a mistake was made. Then comes the desire to hear other bands play, which desire, however, cannot very well be gratified, owing to the peculiar character of the school.

It is a difficult matter to teach European music to Indian juveniles. It is well known that caste Hindus, whatever their predilections may be as regards hearing music, do not take part in performances of music. The high-caste Hindu therefore will not join a band, because it is *infra dig.* to his caste. As a result, the band, including the buglers, is composed of low-caste Hindus, or Pariahs, native Christians and Muhammadans. Occasionally a high-caste Hindu will volunteer for the band, and his intelligence helps him to acquire a taste for music. It was noticed that the Muhammadans were musically inclined, although not as intelligent as the Hindus. The Panchamas were slow. The native Christians learn quickly and make first-rate musicians, but they are, as a rule, lazy. In recruiting boys for the band, the method adopted is to get a newly selected boy to sing a Tamil, Telugu or Hindustani song, as the case may be, and if he sang tunefully he was selected. If, however, after being tutored for a month or two he is found to be dull, he is rejected. In course of time the boys become so interested in their performance that they frequently ask to know the meaning of the piece of music they are about to perform. To mention one instance. Before playing a march entitled "Viscount Nelson" (some of the boys could read English), the class wished to know who Viscount Nelson was. They were told briefly the story of this great sailor and his deeds of valour, and how he was shot down on the deck of his ship after a most glorious victory, and how the whole of England mourned over his loss. The boys seemed to be very much affected, and always played the march after that with great spirit, and tried their best to put into it all the expression they possibly could. From this it may be seen how these boys (although criminals) are susceptible of enthusiasm, and how by a little tact their tender or proud feelings can be drawn out, and how easily they are melted or inflamed. That these boys are capable of learning European music with some amount of success can be proved by comparing them with the band boys of the orphan asylums, which are composed entirely of European or Eurasian lads, and the verdict of opinion is in their favour, notwithstanding the fact that native boys always find a difficulty in memorising minor scales, and that they

Seated for a Meal

The Reformatory Band (page 209)

have not the inbred instinct of playing or singing in parts.

The band is divided into four classes—standards C, B, A and the beginner's class. The senior boys are taught to play, from memory, the various scales, and some of these exercises are transposed by the Bandmaster into tuneful music for collective playing. Thus the aim of the class is not to turn out full-fledged musicians, but simply to lay the foundations for future music instruction and practice in any regular band into which a boy may be enlisted.

In a similar school in the north, it is reported that the school band plays at the dinner-parties given by His Excellency the Governor of a Province when he happens to tour about the neighbourhood, but we are not quite so ambitious down in the south, nor would it be advisable to undermine the health of the boys by night work.

As regards the collective playing of the band, little can be expected, because the older and more experienced boys leave the school just when they become of use, consequently throwing the work of *ensemble* playing on less experienced hands, and this naturally disheartens a Bandmaster keen on having a good school band. Short, easy pieces of music arranged for school bands for the *ensemble* playing of the boys are obtained from Boosey & Co., London. Music copying is also taught to the boys, first on ruled slates and then on music paper. A blackboard is used for teaching the rudiments of staff notation and formation of scales. On one side stave lines are ruled and the other side is plain, the board turning on a pivot so that either side could be utilised as required. The plain side is used for writing notes and rests of various shapes in teaching their time values, while the side with painted staves is reserved for teaching notes or spaces and also clef, and later on the scales.

The buglers are also divided into four classes. The senior boys can sound any call, particular attention being paid to tongueing and to the exact value of the notes. While beginners are not strong enough to sound the higher notes of their bugles, it is astonishing to find how soon they develop lung-power along with the hardening of their lips. From the start correct lip formation is insisted on, and quite a small lad can blow his call with ease and without the strain so visible in older persons badly instructed. The buglers are taught to play a few marches collectively, and it helps the school a great deal in marching out to keep proper step when the strains of the bugles, staccatoed by the beats of the big drum, give the time. It will be seen then that the school band is not a luxury, but a necessary help in the work of reformation, while at the same time it proves to be a training ground for boys enlisting in the army, police, salt and jail departments. The public services therefore have their needs partially supplied by this school, and band boys and buglers find no difficulty in enlisting as soon as they get a fair grounding in music. How well the pupils respond to the training is evidenced by the favourable reports received, and it is pleasing to record that one of our band boys actually rose to attain the responsible position of a Drum Major in his regiment. When he visited the school after an absence of eleven years he came in full dress, wearing the red sash worn across his shoulders, dazzling enough to attract the eyes of the boys, and if one could have read their thoughts at the time, inspiration, pride and admiration must have been present at the back of their minds.

With such a sphere of usefulness before it, it was determined that the band should have a practising room worthy of its position in the school, and accordingly a band-room was constructed and formally opened on the 24th April 1915, at which ceremony the following report was read :—

Mrs Bracken, Ladies and Gentlemen.—It gives me great pleasure to welcome you here this evening to witness the ceremony of the opening of our New Band Room, and before that function takes place, it may interest you to hear a short history of our School Band.

The subject of Bands was recently brought very prominently before us by Kipling, who was pained to find that when his car worked her way through four or five miles of men of the New Arn., in training, there was no music—not even drums and fifes to cheer them. It must have been something of the same sentiment that prompted Mr. D. W. G. Cowie, then District Magistrate of Chingleput, to record in 1899 in the Visitors' Book of the School the following remarks which led to the formation of our School Band :—" It is a pity the School has not a small Band of its own, and now that it is becoming quite usual for the boys to enlist in the Native Army, it might be worth while to form a music class and train musicians for the Madras Infantry Regiments." Dr D. Duncan, the then Director of Public Instruction, cordially approved of the idea, and when the Board of Revenue inquired whether arrangements could be made to have a certain number of pupils trained as Buglers for employment in the Salt Department, proposals for the formation of a Band Class were forwarded to Government and sanctioned in 1900, and the class was formed on the 20th January 1901, with 16 pupils under Sergeant J. W. Moore.

In October 1905 the Reformatory was very fortunate in being able to secure the services of so competent an Instructor as Mr S. Taylor, the late Bandmaster-Sergeant of His Excellency the Governor's Band, and under him the Band made substantial progress, and he left his mark in the School by composing for us in stirring strains the Reformatory School March. He was succeeded by our present Instructor, Mr J. C. Cumine, also from His Excellency's Band, whose interest in the Band is unflagging and under whom the work has more than doubled, the pupils having increased from 16 to 42, including 28 buglers and 6 drummers. With regard to the history of discharged pupils, out of 90 Band boys and buglers trained in the School, 72 per cent. are following their profession : 12 enlisted in the Army Bands, 4 joined Volunteer Bands, 41 enlisted in the Police, 10 in the Salt, and 3 in the Jail Department, the institution thus proving itself to be the " Kneller Hall " of Southern India for trained Band boys and buglers for the Indian Army and various Public Departments.

But during all this time the Band was without a habitation, and, however ideal a spot the rain trees have proved for practices during the dry months, in the wet weather a bolt had often to be made for the nearest dormitory when a sudden shower of rain scattered the players. Mr Stone, our present Director, accordingly gave sanction for the construction of a Band Practising Room at an estimated cost of Rs. 3,520, and you see before you to-day this beautiful hexagonal structure occupying a place on the rampart of the fort, on a site commanding the whole view of the lake over whose waters henceforth our music will softly and sweetly travel to charm, I will not say the "savage breast," but the tuneful appreciative hearts of the high officials, the missionaries, the Vakils and the railway folk of the station, and we trust that in the future the Band which has become a feature of the School will continue its successful career and maintain its high degree of proficiency.

A small museum, to amuse and instruct the boys is attached to the school. I say amuse first: with minds so low down in the scale of culture, interest has first to be awakened before any building process can begin. One of the assistant masters undertakes the curatorship of the place. Various kinds of timber, bark and fibre common to the district are exhibited, as also various kinds of paddy. A dozen species of well-known birds and fish—and snipe, so numerous in this district, the jack snipe, the pintail snipe and the King snipe, are all included. Butterflies, snakes, shells and eggs, collected by the boys themselves, are arranged in glass cases. There is also a small collection of newly finished smiths' tools, yarn of various counts, and shades of all colours of dyed yarn, both vegetable and aniline. Although the whole collection may seem small, it is really sufficient for all practical purposes, and the interest it excites among the juveniles is a revelation.

These natural history specimens and specimens of raw and finished material are inaccessible to the majority of the class of the children who come to us, and on a first visit their eagerness for information shows the lines on which a lesson should proceed. The most troublesome boys can be interested in this way. Then again the art of being able to skin an animal and mount it, of modelling a snake or a frog, or of arranging butterflies calls for skill or appreciation of beauty. The keeping of pets is also encouraged, and the practical management of animals, both mammals and birds, is discovered. With a lake close by, an aquarium is on the road to realisation. Nothing teaches close observation and accurate inference better than the care of creatures whose wants have to be interpreted from their behaviour. The privilege of looking after a pet is also an incentive to good conduct, not forgetting the fact that it is unnatural for a school community to be without something for children to love. Among domestic animals the poultry kept by the Superintendent receives plenty of attention. Ducks, geese, turkeys, Orpingtons and Leghorns form a motley group, and it is amusing to see them trot off to the boys' feeding ground at meal time, while the youngsters are only too glad to throw them a morsel to watch their ways and study their movements. Is it not better to educate children first by the realities of nature than by fairy tales or facts from books?

From time to time various pets are introduced into the school. Pigeon carriers, Singapore doves and pea-fowls among birds, and monkeys, white rats, guinea pigs, civet cats and a donkey too among the mammals, form the little zoo. The peacock preening its beautiful feathers in the sunlight, or seated on a piece of old granite carving in a rockery, with all its grace and beauty of form, affords immense delight. The donkey, "Mike," when small, was looked upon as a mascot, but his play, as he grew older, became rude in the extreme. He would rush at boys and knock them down, or go behind a boy and lift his forelegs on to his back, and startle him with a grip—at times he certainly threatened to take a piece off the arm of a boy. But he taught them good habits too. If any slacker left his clothes or books on the floor he was there to chew them. The little ones were in constant dread of him, and were ready at any moment to make a bolt for their lives when he gave chase, for if he chanced to overtake them he immediately proceeded to trample on them. A little cart was made for him, and the tailor boys turned out a nice piece of canvas harness in which he was driven on a Sunday. But the exercise was insufficient to sober him, and ultimately he became so dangerous that he had to be sent away. We were forcéd to part with him with regret, knowing that he would become a dhobi's donkey again. It is not known what the exact psychological effect of his companionship was while with us, but there can be no doubt that on the whole the keeping of pets is one of the ways to help to turn out normal children.

CHAPTER XVII

PHYSICAL DEVELOPMENT OF JUVENILE CRIMINALS

The juveniles of a criminal population, from hereditary and other causes are, as a rule, poorer in physique than those of a normal population. Precarious living, irregular hours of food, unhealthy surroundings, all contribute to lower the tone of health. And yet the casual visitor is struck with the good condition and physique of reformatory boys, who present on the whole a healthy, happy and contented appearance, and show abundant signs of being well looked after (*vide* the remarks of Rev. S. D. Bawden, of the Kavali Erukala industrial settlement):—

> It has been a great pleasure to me to visit for the second time the Chingleput Reformatory School, especially in view of my nine years' experience as Chaplain of a like school, in the State Industrial School in Rochester, New York.
>
> The Superintendent is to be congratulated most emphatically on the fine physical condition of the boys. Their skins are clear and smooth, almost without exception, and, considering the classes from which many of them come, they are very well set up. I should say that physically they would compare very favourably with any corresponding group outside the school.
>
> But an even more important item is their uniform interest in their work. In every shop the boys were hard at work, and the teachers seemed to have good control and to be securing good results in the work.
>
> The whole place is spick and span in its cleanliness and order, and I take pleasure in congratulating Mr Coombes on the very valuable work he is doing.

Regular and wholesome food, regular hours of work and sleep, enforced cleanliness of body, healthy exercise, and sanitary surroundings work a marvellous change. English and indigenous gymnastics, battalion drill, Swedish drill with deep breathing exercises, and physical culture classes have been introduced to suit various constitutions, but the effects of heredity can never be really overcome, or rather altogether eradicated. A recent medical inspection of the school revealed the fact that few boys suffered from defective eyesight, and the percentage was so low, as compared with other schools, that an expert congratulated us on the fine training that must obtain in the school to produce such results, and proposed forwarding the school statistics to a scientific paper in England for publication.

The pupils are weighed once a month, and the average number who lose weight are comparatively few, the condition of these being carefully watched by the Superintendent. The statistics for the last ten years are as follows:—The percentage of pupils who lost weight is 4.4, those who gained weight 85.6 per cent., and those who remained stationary 9.8 per cent. These figures prove that the physical condition of the boys is satisfactory.

The height, chest, upper and fore-arm measurements are taken once a year, and from figures extending over several years the following averages have been worked out:—

Average measurements of boys at different ages.

Age.	Height.	Weight	Chest.	Fore-arm.	Upper-arm.
11	4′	58⅓	25⅓	6¾	7⅓
12	4⅓′	61½	26	7	7½
13	4½′	68½	27	7½	8
14	4¾′	74⅓	27¾	7¾	8¼
15	4′-10½	81	28½	8	8½
16	5′	89	29¾	8½	9
17	5⅓′	94	30⅓	8¾	9½

From these figures it will be observed that juveniles grow in height most rapidly between the ages of 11 and 12, and 16 and 17, but between 15 and 16, while the increase in height is little, the increase in the other dimensions is greater than at any other age.

The increase at the various ages are given below:—

Ages between.	Height.	Weight.	Chest.	Fore-arm.	Upper-arm.
11 and 12	4″	$3\frac{1}{6}$lb.	$\frac{2}{3}$″	$\frac{1}{4}$	$\frac{1}{6}$
12 „ 13	2″	7	1″	$\frac{1}{2}$	$\frac{1}{2}$
13 „ 14	3″	$5\frac{1}{6}$	$\frac{3}{4}$″	$\frac{1}{4}$	$\frac{1}{4}$
14 „ 15	$1\frac{1}{2}$″	$6\frac{2}{3}$	$\frac{3}{4}$″	$\frac{1}{4}$	$\frac{1}{4}$
15 „ 16	$1\frac{1}{2}$″	8	$1\frac{1}{4}$″	$\frac{1}{2}$	$\frac{1}{2}$
16 „ 17	4″	5	$\frac{7}{12}$″	$\frac{1}{4}$	$\frac{1}{2}$

The average gain per pupil in one year is 2—2/3 in. in height, 6 lbs. in weight, 5/6 in. in chest, 6/18 in. in fore-arm, and 7/18 in. in upper-arm.

A rough scale is thus shewn of weight for height, and for age *cum* height, and it will afford a standard by which a juvenile's health and progress may be tested.

In the case of healthy adult Indian prisoners 5 feet represents 100 lbs. and for every additional inch in height 3 lbs. are added to find the corresponding weight.

The following table was taken from Woodman and Tidy, "Forensic Medicine":—

Age.	Weight.	Height.
10	55.6 lbs.	4′—2.4″
11	59.6	4′—4.5″
12	63.13	4′—6.5″
13	72.13	4′—8.4″
14	81.9	4′—10.6″
15	90.9	5′—1″
16	99.13	5′—3″

For Europeans, the following table is given in Lyon's "Medical Jurisprudence for India."

PHYSICAL DEVELOPMENT OF JUVENILE CRIMINALS

Age.	Weight.	Height.
11	72 lbs.	4′—5½″
12	76¾	4′—7″
13	82½	4′—9″
14	92	4′—11¼″
15	106¾	5′—2¼″
16	119	5′—4¼″
17	131	5′—6¼″

In India, there is a great field for research in criminal Anthropology and Anthropometry. The formation of the cranium and the ear are good subjects for study. Pointed heads, flat roofed skulls and receding foreheads are noted abnormalities, and in regard to the ear, which is very sensitive to nervous disturbances, malformations are said to be more common among criminals than the ordinary type of man—in short, criminals are supposed to present features more akin to the savage races, and to possess corresponding traces of character. From an examination of several subjects, important conclusions may be arrived at in a branch of knowledge which receives little attention.

I had a talk with Professor Boas, the American anthropologist, and he affirmed that crime was not hereditary, but that certain pathological conditions of the mind were so, and these may produce a criminal in the absence of self-control.

The institution of reformatory schools being a comparatively new movement in India, no trustworthy figures are available with regard to the abnormalities of juvenile criminals, and a start may be made of taking the cephalic or vital index of each juvenile and generalising from it as far as possible. With the aid of a pair of callipers, which every school should possess, the breadth of the head can be measured, as well as the length. If the breadth be multiplied by 100 and divided by the length, the result is known as the cephalic index, which is the ratio between the maximum length and maximum breadth of the skull. In this way, heads may be divided into 3 classes: when the index is less than 75, the person is said to be longheaded or dolichocephalic; when the index ranges from 75 to 79, the head is medium or mesati-cephalic; and when the index is from 80 to 85 the head is broad or brachycephalic (the Mongolian type). In juveniles, this index will vary from age to age, and from statistics we may perhaps learn between what ages the intelligence of a child varies, and perhaps whether his index is quite up to the average of his caste or class, *e.g.*, among broad-headed boys, aged 15 years, the average index for Tamil boys is 83, for Telugu 83 and for Hindustani 81. Among the medium-headed, the average for the Tamil boy is 77, for the Telugu 76 and for the Hindustani 77. In the long-headed class, the Tamils measure 73, the Telugus 73 and the Hindustanis 72. Thus, the average for each caste or community may be found at the various ages.

From limited statistics taken in the school, it was found that Hindustani boys are inclined to be broad-headed, and that a small majority of the Tamil and Telugu boys are medium-headed, while an almost equal percentage among them were found to be long-headed—of course, it must be admitted that there is a possibility of the boys who are called Tamil boys not being really Tamils. It was also found that the medium-headed boys showed most intelligence, the Telugus leading the way, while the broad and long-headed showed least intelligence. This observation seems to prove that abnormalities in the size of the head among juvenile criminals may not indicate intelligence, although long-headedness may be a favourable sign among normal children.

It has been noted also, from measurements recorded at different periods, that, taking the average of the various classes, the cephalic index was greatest at 14 and 15 years, while it decreased at 16 and 17, reaching its lowest at the age of 17. The conclusions one is inclined to arrive at from measurements and personal knowledge of the boys are, (1) that no intellectual stress should be placed upon boys of the criminal class between the ages of 13 and 14 years; (2) that most boys between the ages of 14 and 15 are brightest; and (3) that towards the period of adolescence, mental stagnation sets in. A plea, therefore, is set up for a greater amount of general education which taxes the mental power, for junior boys, and for a mechanical training for the senior boys between the ages of 16 and 18.

For the past five years, I have been collecting material with regard to the physical characteristics of hand, foot, fingers and toes; height and age of individual; mental characteristics, surface measurements of head, trunk and limbs, principal measurements and indices; cranial capacity and relation of brain to skull. These measurements have all been taken for five successive years for *each* juvenile so as to judge of his growth.

The results have been handed over to Professor Karl Pearson, who has very kindly promised to reduce the data; but as the working out of the statistics will take a year or eighteen months, the publication of the final paper will form a supplement to this book.

The Americans are keen on the subject of anthropometry and hope to establish useful principles for educative work.

If the Superintendent has no medical qualifications, the Medical and Sanitary Officer of the District is held responsible for the general health of the boys. If the work appeals to him he maps out a plan of operation and adds to the zeal of the staff. He studies the statistics of the inmates, examines the new admissions, scrutinises the diet roll, recommends changes, if necessary, and directs his attention to the weaklings, placing them in a convalescent gang.

A physical examination of the boys often reveals the fact that many of them suffer for the sins of their fathers. Orphaned and illegitimate as many of them are, they are still further handicapped. The small stature of the boys, and their slimness will strike a visitor at once, but this does not mean that they are not physically fit. They work hard and they play hard and with regular feeding they improve, but the physical defects which they inherit can never be completely eradicated.

A weekly inspection is held, and all orders regarding the sick are carried out by the Sub Assistant Surgeon, who is the resident subordinate medical officer. Cod liver oil is freely administered, with tonics, and special diet prescribed for those losing weight, but it is sometimes difficult to find out why some of the little ones belonging to the "rat brigade" never fatten. A great deal depends on an efficient Sub Assistant Surgeon. One too old to tackle new work, or an inexperienced hand has always been a failure. The daily routine of the Doctor is to make the rounds of the place, to see that the sanitation is good, and to inspect the Hospital to discover if his therapeutic orders have been carried out. His duties do not admit of his making a personal study of individuals. It is the medical subordinate who can closely supervise the boys who lose weight, to watch them when they eat their food, and take advantage of the numberless opportunities that present themselves at all times to improve their well-being. There can be no provision in this scheme for subnormal children, who require a specialist to look after them, and a psychologist or an expert to examine them.

Smallpox, measles, malaria and occasionally cholera and influenza are the normal ailments. On the outbreak of any infectious disease the patients are at once removed into quarantine, wells are hankinised, the food is protected from flies, drains kept scrupulously clean, fly breeding places destroyed, and the whole school is fumigated. The Deputy Superintendent is responsible for the sanitation of the place, which suffered at one time for lack of proper drainage, but now recently improved with facilities for carrying off the storm water. The waterings of the kitchen are all conveyed into a receptacle buried in the earth and filled with stones decreasing in size layer after layer, the largest stones resting upon the perforated bottom of the vessel. The fouled water passes through into an underground blind drain where it is absorbed by the loose earth. Thus no smell is emitted, no flies are visible, as is the case where organic matter exists. The layers of stone evidently allow of a growth of bacteria which renders foul matter innocuous. This system of drainage is, I believe, adopted round the buildings now being erected in the New Delhi City.

There are periodical outbreaks of malaria which undermine the constitution of the boys. Living within an old fort—surrounded by a moat and a certain amount of decayed vegetation—fighting the mosquito is always a problem. Stagnant water and weeds prove excellent breeding-grounds. The period from the time when the mosquito lays her eggs until her offspring emerges from the water is about 14 days. The length of flight in still air is about half a mile from the water. Nice stagnant air to fly in, after nice stagnant water to breed in, is his ideal and it exists in the fort. To minimise the evil, all scrub and grass are cut down and burnt, small pools at the edge of the water are filled in and all edges are trimmed. Immediately after a shower of rain the cess pools are bailed out and a hunt is made for old tins and broken vessels which offer suitable harbourage for the anopheles. During the rainy season, quinine is administered as a prophylactic to the whole school, and the wry faces exhibited would make the subject of an excellent moving picture. When quinine is regularly administered for some time, a little calomel is added beneficially, thus confirming the efficacy of "Livingstone's Rousers" as they were called, which the famous traveller gave his followers in the shape of pills containing as ingredients both aloes and quinine. Some boys daub their bodies with a mixture of kerosine and coconut oil to keep the mosquito away. With malaria about, the weights of the boys do not show up satisfactorily when the monthly average is taken, the increase being small, and to compare it with that of other schools is not possible for want of an adequate standard of judgment.

According to the latest expert opinion, the weight of a boy should equal his height in inches by chest measurement in inches and divided by 17. But the formula weight thus arrived at is 18 per cent. more than the actual weight, and therefore proves a false standard of comparison for certain types. If the general health of the boys is good, and if the town on the whole is not unhealthy, which is borne out by the fact that there have been only half a dozen deaths in the school since it was founded 32 years ago, there is no cause of alarm about the physical condition of the children. Matters will quickly mend as soon as the moat round the fort is converted into a breeding-ground for fishes by the Piscicultural Department. It would be well, however, if the Magistrates committing pupils to this school were required to fill in a medical form to certify that the boy was physically and mentally fit for an industrial training.

The boys committed to our care do not suffer ordinarily from eye diseases, nor have they to be inspected for bad teeth, for, as a rule, the Indian boy cleans his teeth regularly with a twig of the neem or margossa tree, or if one is not within reach he resorts to ashes or brick dust. He has to be shown, however, that the twig brush must work down the back teeth as well as the front. After every meal also, he is in the habit of rinsing his mouth. There are odd cases of boys suffering from tuberculosis, but these are promptly reported to Government for discharge. On the whole therefore, the medical attention received by the boys is ample. The time has come, however, for other problems to be solved, and students trained in sociological, physiological and medical knowledge can alone throw light on the moral and legal responsibility of the juvenile criminal, on problems relating to education, and also on problems relating to the causes of criminality and to the need of classification on a scientific basis.

It is interesting to watch the distribution of meals to the boys, as they come up serially in Indian file. The peon starts calling out the first number, really the oldest boy, and no record is made of those who answer to the call which is reserved only for the absentees. Occasionally a boy tries to come round a second time when he hears the sharp snap of the peon—"You've had a pudding before." The hungry petitioner withdraws, cheerfully acknowledging defeat in a game of bluff. All the same, it must be admitted that on occasions the peon does trip and not all the protestations on the boy's part would convince him of his fallibility. An appeal is ultimately carried to the Superintendent, who respects the boy's word and orders the issue of a pudding. The whole serving occupies just a little over half an hour.

The boys are given a *ragi* diet with vegetable curry tempered with gingelli oil (*sesamum til*). The curry powder is made up of chillies 50, coriander 25, turmerie $6\frac{1}{4}$, pepper $6\frac{1}{4}$, venthian $4\frac{3}{4}$, mustard $6\frac{1}{4}$, and cummin seed $4\frac{3}{4}$ lbs. The latter four ingredients aid digestion, and give the curry sauce an appetising flavour.

Twice a week they are given mutton and rice, and once a week, fish. Dried fish is preferred because it is difficult to obtain good fresh fish. Moreover, dried fish contains 50 per cent. more albuminoid constituents than fresh fish. Dal (*canjanus indicus*), which contains 22 per cent. of nitrogenous matter, and is rich in sulphur, phosphorus and salts, is given every day.

The dal given is what is known as Bengal grain, and although it is not quite as digestible as the red grain which is used by the better classes, because it is not as "heating," it is richer in composition, as the table below shows, and the boys thrive on it.

	Water.	Proteids.	Oil or Fat.	Carbo-Hydrates.	Crude Fibre.	Ash.
Red grain ...	10.13	17.56	1.34	61.36	5.78	3.78
Bengal grain	9.98	18.14	4.39	57.94	6.40	3.13

Ragi is a grain that resembles the mustard seed. It is ground into flour and is used as a food by the Telugus to a large extent. They make a sour porridge from it, which they drink in the morning, and they eat it also in the shape of cakes. It is rumoured that His Highness the Maharajah of Mysore includes it as an item in his table menu.

It is found that ragi, which is richer in albuminoids and oil than rice, sustains a boy better than rice, and, with few exceptions, they prefer it; and once a lad gets accustomed to it, it takes a very large quantity of rice to satisfy him. I have reason to suspect that a boy who was fond of his stomach actually threw up his appointment as bugler in the Salt Department, because he could not get enough food to satisfy him. He tried the appointment only for a day. Ragi forms an ideal diet, but for one drawback, which perhaps may not really exist. It is a jail diet, and for a re-convicted boy it may not have the same terrors as it would have for one who was unaccustomed to it. A boy on admission does not care for the diet (and there are certain boys who never take to it), but after two months' stay or so he enjoys it, judging by the zest with which he eats it, going the length even of licking his fingers at the finish! An ex-pupil, who had enlisted in the army, informed me that his comrades looked upon him as a jail-bird, notwithstanding his assertions to the contrary that he had come from a school. Their chief argument was that he was fed on ragi pudding in the Reformatory, and therefore it must be a jail. This was indeed the only drawback to the diet. But now that rice is given to prisoners in jail, ragi is no longer under the ban of being classed as a prison diet.

With regard to clothing, the boys are supplied with a working day suit, and a Sunday suit, wearing respectively for six months and a year. The former is made from a coarse plain weave of grey yarn, 10's or 2/20's count, and is washed by themselves, while the latter is of white drill 2/40 by 40, and is laundered by a dhobi occasionally.

From one of the plates it will be seen that the shape of the cap worn by the boys is somewhat quaint and some men even call it horrid; but for smartness, cleanliness and economy nothing better has yet been devised.

The same shape of cap was worn by the early recruits of the native army. Each boy wears on his cap the badge of his trade. The weaver, a shuttle; the carpenter, a chisel; the blacksmith, an anvil; the tailor, a pair of scissors; the band-boy and the bugler, a pair of drum-sticks crossed; and the gardener, a spade.

The pupils are allowed to purchase body cloths, vests and shorts from their own savings and to write to their parents for any extra article of clothing they may need. They are permitted to wear their own cloths except on occasions like dress parade and during the hours of literary work when they assemble in the school room. The wearing of private clothing saves the wear and tear of their uniforms. It is admitted by all that the boys look well in their clean white uniforms.

The boys are not provided with boxes or lockers for their little all, because these would soon become receptacles for rubbish and forbidden articles, and be an endless source of worry and trouble. The result is that, like the Israelites in the wilderness, they carry their "goods and chattels" with them wherever they go. When a boy's cap is accidentally tipped off his head one finds scattered before him broken pieces of pencil, books, pieces of paper, marbles, sweetmeat, badges, etc., etc. On one occasion a piece of tobacco fell out in the presence of the wife of a District Judge, who innocently removed a boy's cap to examine it; through her intercession, however, the boy was forgiven for having been found in possession of tobacco.

Each boy is suppplied with a tin dish costing two annas (twopence) a piece. His number and the date of issue are stamped on the rim. Used with care it lasts a year, and any boy found to wear it out sooner by ill-usage has to pay the cost of a new dish. The vessel answers the purposes of both eating and drinking out of, as a boy never drinks water during a meal, but just before and after.

With regard to the sleeping accommodation of the boys, the cubicle system, where each boy was locked into a separate cubicle, was at first in vogue. But the system gives rise to prurient ideas, and affords facilities for carrying out evil practices, and is degrading in every sense. Cubicles interfere with free circulation of air and the necessary supervision which should at all times be exercised. They moreover harbour vermin. Hence the system has been condemned by the highest authorities on moral and humane grounds. In lieu of it the hammock system has been introduced; but it has this drawback, that it gives a growing lad little room for turning movements, and the big boys complain that their feet are uncomfortably raised. The pial system, therefore, I consider to be the best, the least expensive, and the most comfortable for the Hindu, who is accustomed to this form of bedstead from his youth.

The school hammocks are made from hempen twine knotted together to give a meshed surface of 6 ft. by 2 ft. This is templed by two rods, one at each end, to keep the width, and the ends are suspended from standards fixed in the ground. By this system the bug nuisance is reduced to a minimum, for the standards can be removed and the hammocks thrown out into the sun, or better still, boiled in water, while a little phenyl and coconut oil daubed at the points of swing drives away the pests. A more com-

Dormitory with Double Row of Netted Hammocks (page 226)

fortable form of hammock is made by stretching canvas on to two bamboo rods, stiffened by two teakwood pieces, making an oblong frame 6 ft. by $2\frac{1}{2}$ ft.; but the drawback here is that the bugs enter the joints and hide between the bamboos and the canvas. A further improvement is effected by discarding the canvas for tape or twine which can be interlaced in the frame, this in turn being suspended by a copper wire or iron rod in place of cotton rope.

In Brazil the natives, to avoid serpents, sleep in nets made from the rind of the hammock tree, and which are hung between poles fixed firmly in the ground. In the reformatory there are no serpents crawling about ready to inject the poison from their fangs. A cobra or a Russell's viper with its spectacled skin is occasionally seen, but the noise in the school is sufficient to keep them away. But there are domestic bugs which are capable of causing serious disease like kala azar, and this is the reason for the use of hammocks. The Navy, I believe, still use the hammock system for lads.

When the school was first started it was believed that it could be run as a commercial enterprise and that the excess receipts over the earnings would pay good interest on the sum sunk in buildings. It was thought that in the course of a few years the institution, if efficiently managed, could be maintained without any cost whatever to the State. In the first few years, therefore, the self-supporting character of the institution was kept in view, and the result was an unsatisfactory condition as regards education of an all-round character, due to an underpaid staff, insufficient accommodation and inadequate equipment. If the boys are to be reformed with any degree of success, there should be no embarrassment to work by the lack of funds, required in every direction to make the institution a real home. This has been my policy, and I have had the most generous support from Government.

The receipts of the school are roughtly one-sixth of the expenditure, and the proportion must be considered good when it is borne in mind that a well-paid staff is employed, that most of the boys are youngsters who are perhaps just beginning to learn the use of tools, and that some of the classes, like the band and the masons, are unremunerative. The receipts slightly cover the cost of materials and workshop contingencies, and this is a fair test of the cost of an industrial institution on the right side. On the average, the cost of the industrial training per boy per month is Rs. 6/11/6. The cost of general education works out to Rs. 5/1/0. The cost of dieting a pupil for a month is about Rs. 3/13/9, under ordinary conditions when there is no famine; and the cost of clothing per annum for a boy is Rs. 9, a blanket and two suits of clothing being issued to each pupil.

CHAPTER XVIII

OFFENCES COMMITTED IN THE SCHOOL

The majority of offences committed in the school relate to contraband articles like tobacco and snuff. How these forbidden articles are introduced into the school it is not easy to tell, but that a large portion is brought by the lower class of menials, in exchange for articles bartered by the boys, has been proved more than once. Smuggling tobacco into the school, one of the seven deadly sins, requires considerable ingenuity, owing to the ban laid upon it by the authorities. The tailor boy comes in handy as an outfitter to pander to this *Olympian* whim, and constructs invisible little pockets which the contrabandist counts upon to ensure success; but sometimes the X-ray glance of a monitor detects the bulge, and trouble follows. The boys have also an opportunity of picking up tobacco during their Sunday walk along the public roads, and the lightning-like rapidity with which they (including good-caste boys) pick it up with their toes, excites a certain amount of admiration which is deserving of a better act. The boys, as a class, are very fond of tobacco, and the taste is acquired at a very early age. Even boys who have not acquired the taste outside soon acquire it within the school, perhaps because it is a forbidden article. The possession of tobacco and snuff leads to a great deal of wrangling and tale-bearing among the boys. The best of friendships is based on the existence of this article, and the greatest enmity is caused by a lack of sympathy which prohibits another to share in the participation of its soothing effects.

The habit of using tobacco is such a common one among

the lower classes of Hindus that the offence in the school is inclined to be treated by some as a venial one. But the Reformatory Act, I think, takes a right view of the question when it lays down that the possession of forbidden articles must be properly dealt with, and persons guilty of introducing tobacco into a school are liable to six months' imprisonment. And for good reasons. When a boy dares to go in for a forbidden thing, thus ignoring a standing rule of the school, there is more than one offence committed thereby, and the tendency of the act is to develop in the youth all the characteristics of a thief. There is, first, the bartering of an article, perhaps stolen or surreptitiously obtained, such as a small knife, an aluminium vessel or an article of clothing, for the tobacco.

Secondly, there is deliberate disobedience of a rule frequently reiterated to the boys, the remembrance of which is brought home to them every Sunday in a specially composed song, the worst culprits singing it with the greatest zest. Next comes the secrecy and cunningness involved in the commission of the offence. A boy waits for his opportunity, and when no one is within sight, he slinks into the latrine and with nervous delight soothes his hankering desire for that which is forbidden. A thief exhibits all these characteristics, and unless deception, underhandedness, unhealthy tastes, and disobedience are put down with a firm hand, a boy is bound to show these undesirable traits in other directions when he obtains his freedom. The boys should be taught to practise restraint during their school days. I have always observed that the best boys are free from even the suspicion of using tobacco, and the offence should never be treated as a venial one.

A craving appetite is a fruitful cause of a number of school offences and irregularities. A boy will rob dal or a ragi chappati, he will steal mangoes and other fruit to satisy his appetite. After the morning or evening food is distributed, a little always remains over, and the wrangling to obtain a share of it makes one long for an appetite as keen; and yet the allowance granted them, *viz.*, a 2 lb. 4 oz. pudding, is no stinted fare. The boys volunteer to perform small services in the shape of drawing water and chopping up fire-wood for the cooks, in the hope of being rewarded with a share of what remains of a meal. During an outbreak of cholera the practice of giving boys *extras* was temporarily put a stop to, to prevent overloading of the stomach, and there were great heart-burnings over it. Gluttony, it must be remarked, is no uncommon trait of character, among juvenile criminals.

The minor offences in the school are such as follow:—Fighting with each other, tearing clothes, going into the kitchen, using bad language, bartering food, sleeping on the ground instead of in hammocks, washing clothes without permission, being absent from drill, picking up tobacco stems on the road, losing badges, neglecting to give clothes for repair, telling a lie, altering the length of trousers without permission, spitting on the floor, not wearing badges, not attending gymnastics, being dirty at inspection, loitering about, etc. I was amused at the artifice of a boy who, to avoid detection, stitched a towel to the inner side of his trousers, in order that it might be washed white by the dhobi, a towel being generally washed by the boy himself.

The mark system greatly helps to reduce minor offences. When a boy does not commit himself seriously, he is either given loss of marks or three cuts on the hand; but the punishment is not recorded in his history sheet and therefore does not tell against him in the earning of a good conduct badge.

Many facilities exist for escape, and, if a boy chooses to do so, the obstacles in his way are easily overcome. The escapes generally happen just before lock-up, but in one instance three boys escaped after being locked up, and in the following manner. They unravelled a hammock and made a rope of it, and, having mounted a cubicle, they threw the rope upwards in such a manner as to pass it round the truss of a beam, and by means of it they got out through the sky-light. Once outside the dormitory it was an easy matter to climb over the outer boundary wall and abscond.

The boys are happy under the moral influence, watchful care, the educational and industrial training they receive, and are too well looked after to wish to escape, and this happens only in the case of new-comers, who perhaps fret after their homes. There was a solitary instance of the escape of three big boys who did not care for the discipline introduced. Peons were sent out after them along the chief roads; one of the peons espied the three boys leaving the public road in the early morning and making for a jungle. He followed them up and accosted them, when the three boys stood still as though transfixed to the ground. It was impossible for a single peon to tackle three grown-up youths if they opposed arrest, and it speaks much for the discipline of the school that the voice of the peon was sufficient to control the flight of the boys. The peon was given a reward of Rs. 5 for his smart catch, and he tried to be still smarter in attempting to earn another reward by instigating a boy to escape and bringing him back the following day! There was not evidence enough, however, to bring the charge home to the peon.

The first case of grave misdemeanour that happened in the school was the result of a quarrel between two boys, one of whom was punished. The aggrieved boy, a Muhammadan, then took the law into his own hands and assaulted the other boy. Knowing that he would be severely dealt with, he ran off to the spot where manufactured articles were sold and got hold of two knives, which he brandished before the office, threatening mischief, and the whole school was thrown into disorder. A number of peons armed with lathis brought him to his senses.

The second case was an instance of rioting. Some of the boys got the impression that the Deputy Superintendent was cruelly severe, and they plotted to take action against him when an opportunity occurred, and it happened thus:— A boy was asked to pull the office punkah, which he refused to do, and when he was being punished for the offence, a dozen boys ran off to the District Court, adjoining the school, and disturbed the Judge in the midst of his Sessions work, representing to him that they were being ill-treated. Circumstances lead one to think that there was a master-mind behind this move, and that an outsider or one of the staff set up the boys to commit a breach of discipline. The outcome of the riot was the appointment of a European Sergeant, to prevent a similar occurrence taking place. The evil result of these occasional riots is that they become a part of the tradition of the school.

A third case of grave misdemeanour occurred under the leadership of a boy who refused to take his food at meal time because rice diet was not given in lieu of ragi on a festival day, and he was able to induce the whole school to refuse their food for a time. There was, it is true, a precedent for the change of diet, but I do not believe that the boy felt the loss of a privilege so much as the importance of leadership, which appealed to his vanity. But, in a criminal population, it is easy for a crowd to follow a ringleader on the spur of the moment, in their excitement, and then, afterwards, to dissociate themselves from him. The whole school had very little sympathy for this boy when he was severely punished.

The more serious offences, such as assault with intention to hurt, should not be dealt with after the manner of school discipline, but should be investigated by a Magistrate, for which provision is made in the school rules. If murderous assault or any other serious offence be treated as a school offence, it is bound to have a bad effect on the discipline of the school.

The Indian youth gets addicted to the use of tobacco from quite an early age, and although public opinion in certain provinces is in favour of the legislature taking steps to prevent juvenile smoking, no one has any very clear idea as to how this should be carried out. Some years ago at a meeting of the United Provinces Legislative Council, the motion to introduce Lala Sukhbir Singh's Juvenile Smoking Bill was thrown out by the large majority of 27 votes to 7, one of the opponents of the measure characterising it as grandmotherly legislation—a type of legislation which, by the way, has always appealed to the leaders of the Congress party. The Bill proposed to prevent the sale of cigars and cigarettes to juveniles, and gave powers to the police to seize tobacco found on the persons of juveniles. The idea is no doubt, an amiable one, and legislation on such lines has long existed in most European countries, but in India it would be unworkable, and if put in force would only enlarge the opportunities of the Subordinate Native Police for petty extortion and tyranny. Then, too, in some parts of India, notably Burma, and parts of the Telugu districts in this province, everyone—man, woman or child—smokes, and these people would regard police interference with this time-honoured custom as an unwarranted interference with the liberty of the individual. The only course feasible at present is to educate the school-going population.

About five-sixths of the pupils admitted to our school have known the taste of tobacco and about one-sixth have smoked the opium preparation called Ganja. It becomes a difficult task, therefore, to drive tobacco out of the school while so many subterfuges are practised to obtain it. A boy will give away his food to a sweeper who promises to fetch him snuff. Another will surreptitiously remove a tool from the workshop and hand it over to a peon dishonest enough to oblige him with tobacco. Ex-pupils who visit the school are cajoled into handing over either money or tobacco to the boys addicted to the habit. Sometimes an incorrigible youngster has the daring to exchange his school cap for a turban or head dress and camouflage himself in such a way as to escape the detection of the peons. He goes across to the compound of the adjoining Magistrate's court, purchases a packet of cigarettes from one of the vendors who are there to meet the convenience of clients, and slips back again, looking as innocent as possible. It is is quite easy, therefore, for a contraband article to be introduced within the walls of the school.

Occasionally we receive an addicted opium eater. Once a "street Arab" who lived by pilfering was sent to us convicted of the theft of a brass pot and some fowls. His age was 14 and his occupation was that of driving a jutka, that fearsome two-wheeled pony carriage which is to be found nowhere except in this province. They are drawn by sick and sorry animals, and the driver, who is filthy and often addicted to intemperate habits, usually increases his fare by accommodating a fifth person on his seat, the pony being an unconsidered partner in the arrangement. Imbued with such previous associations the school proved an uncomfortable training-ground for the juvenile jutka wallah, and he quickly earned the sobriquet of the "good medicine" boy, because he consumed large quantities of quinine as a soothing substitute for opium. He came to us in indifferent health, but within a year he was able to overcome his hankering after opium and even quinine. He began to fill out, put on a cheerful countenance, and took part in the games of the school. He enlisted from the school in the Queen's Own Sappers and Miners at Bangalore, where during his recruit course he fell and broke his arm while negotiating a hurdle. He was in hospital for some time, but alas, on coming out he relapsed into his old habit, which led him to desert his regiment several times. He was court martialled and imprisoned, but was subsequently sent to Mesopotamia after enlisting in the jail corps. His confession as an oium eater is given in his own words below, and describes how he fell a victim to the drug:—

> When I was ten years old one day I was playing in the streets. Then I received a severe wound in my skull. I was bed-ridden for about a month. During this period, to enable me not to feel the pain, my mother used to give me one sixty-fourth tola of opium. Being a boy, I did not know the evil effects of this dreadful intoxicant. The relief and pleasure which it gave me, even when taking a very small quantity, was so great that I began to have a real liking for it. My mother gave it to me as a medicine for about three months. After that I did not like the idea of giving it up. Further, I was often uneasy on the days I was not able to taste a bit of it. I began, therefore, to get somehow or other at least a quarter anna worth of opium a day. This small quantity was taken for a few months. Then it was raised to double that, *i.e.*, half anna worth a day. Then at the age of twelve I began to drive a jutka for hire and I had the opportunity of earning at least 4 annas a day. As

my daily earnings rose, the quantity of opium I consumed daily increased until at last it came to 4 annas' worth a day.

Further, as the daily quantity increased, its companion, Ganja, was gradually increased. Finally, when I was brought to the school, I managed to bring with me one rupee worth of opium, and this lasted for a few days only. Then on the first day when I had to remain without it I began to experience the difficulties that arise, namely, pain through my body at the joints, excessive thirst and uneasiness. For about a fortnight I suffered very much and I had no sleep whatever. Then some of the boys advised me to drink quinine when I was feeling unwell. I followed their advice, and to my excessive joy I felt the pleasures I had while in the habit of taking opium. I began, therefore, to take four ounces of quinine twice a day. The relief it gave me was so great that I never failed to be without it even for a day. It was consumed for about eight months. Now, for the last fortnight, I am without taking even quinine and I don't feel any sort of uneasiness. I am all right now and stronger than I was ever before, and I could easily digest the diet of three boys if I am favoured with the same.

I have already referred to the Deputy Superintendent as the head of the family, but his duties are very varied, and although he does not go through a course of legal training, he is called upon to exercise judicial functions and to inquire into every offence of an anti-social character. Witnesses are heard on both sides and a decision arrived at—based, let us hope, on common sense. He is helped, however, to a great extent in unravelling the threads of a case by the boys themselves; for a boy is a boy after all, and one or two searching questions put to him is sufficient to bring out the truth. The investigation of the cases, however, takes up time, and in addition, every little complaint has to be heard and settled. The facts of the case are then put before the Superintendent, who performs the function of a higher court, in some instances, and passes orders as to the punishment to be meted out.

I knew of one Superintendent who purposely played football with the boys in order that they might know him in a capacity different from that of a disciplinarian and realise that when they were punished there was no personal element in it. The Deputy Superintendent acts also as treasurer of the boys' savings. The whole of the pupils' money is banked in the Postal Savings Bank in his name, and he sanctions all expenditure. "Chits" or notes are presented for signature for the purchase of sweetmeats, fruit, cakes and small articles of dress, such as banians, out of a boy's own earnings. They are then taken to a master who is detailed for this particular work, and he debits the amount to the pupil, and balances his account once a quarter. A running account is thus maintained for each pupil, and a statement showing the balances is posted up periodically outside the office for the information of all boys. The pupil himself knows pretty well how his cash transactions stand, and he soon detects even the smallest error in his account.

On a Saturday afternoon it is amusing to watch a row of from twenty to thirty boys standing at the office with chits in their hands for signature. They have come for permission to take a purgative on Sunday. A Hindu boy seems to relish taking castor oil and asks for it, perhaps because he feels all the better for taking the medicine. How different from an English lad, who dreads medicine, even when mixed with the nicest of syrups!

Much is said of the American "up-to-date" methods in the treatment of juvenile criminals. It is said that they are characterised by deep humanity and optimism. Punishment is not resorted to until advice, exhortation, rebuke, threat and surveillance have all been exhaustively tried. In some institutions self-government is followed, a boy who misbehaves himself being tried before his comrades, to awaken in him the sense of moral shame as well as self respect. This system may work very well in European and Christian countries, where a boy's moral sense and self respect can be appealed to; but in India, where one is handicapped by the almost total absence of religious motives and moral sense as a basis to work upon, it will be found that corporal punishment must play a certain part in the treatment of the juvenile criminal, whether it be flogging on the buttocks or caning on the hands. To the latter form of punishment, little if any exception can be taken; the objection comes in when flogging or birching is resorted to, and the objection is perhaps more or less of a sentimental nature.

A corporal correction league exists in Liverpool, the members of which promise to make known as well as practise a return to the old-fashioned form of corporal punishment. "The only sure way," says the tract of the league, "to make your children have respect and obedience is to whip them if naughty. It is most important to begin when children are quite young, for then they do not fully understand kind words."

The free instructions given are:—"Stop in the middle of the chastisement to tell the child again, having told it beforehand, why it is being punished; give, say, in force, according to the child's age, ten slaps to begin with, then a second talking-to, with the child still over your knee, then, say, six more slaps."

The headmaster of an English public school remembers to have flogged a whole bench of bishops. Surely, then, this form of punishment cannot be objected to; nay, rather it is suitable for juveniles steeped in superstition and ignorance, and with an inherited obtuseness of moral sentiment. I am, therefore, an advocate for the retention of flogging to meet those cases where no other form of punishment will bring a juvenile offender to his senses; but it must be used judiciously. The person also who sanctions the punishment must be known to possess the qualities of kindness and sympathy, if it is to serve the ends which the punishment has in view. The punishment is dreaded, and for this reason it is necessary to retain it as a last resort when other forms of punishment prove ineffective. It is degrading to a sensitive mind, but for incorrigibles it acts as a charm. There are cases in the school where birching has made a boy a new boy and done him all the good imaginable. Once in the history of the school the system of birching was done away with, and the result was that the number of offences increased under all heads, especially under insubordination and impertinence. Caning on the hand was found as a punishment to be practically a farce to a set of horny-handed young scamps who spend half the time in gardening, carpentry or the blacksmith's shop, and who before coming to the school were inured to hardships, fisticuffs and kicks. Such boys take fifteen cuts on the hand without wincing, and can only be governed by fear of flogging until subdued and brought to their senses. The system, therefore, was reintroduced, more particularly as it was found from experience that the certainty of flogging tended to do away with the necessity for it.

CHAPTER XIX

THE STORY OF A PUPIL

KRISHNAN was born in a village in the Telugu country, which covers the middle and north-east part of South India. His father was a small farmer, not over scrupulous as to the way in which he could supplement his slender earnings. He sometimes resorted to dacoity, made a raid upon passing travellers, or carried on depredations on dark nights among the rich Hindus, thus terrorising the surrounding villages. These lawless methods could not long continue in British territory, and both he and his brother were caught at last and awarded long terms of imprisonment. The boy, left with no other protector than his mother, who shortly afterwards had to face the neglect and contumely apportioned to widows in India, soon fell into bad company and started his downward career, consorting with the worst characters of the place. In due course he considered theft an act more or less praiseworthy, according to the skill or daring shown in its execution, and to the success in the subsequent evasion of capture by the police. What more natural course than that the son should begin to follow in his father's footsteps? His first attempt, however, overstepped the mark, and he was apprehended with three others on a charge of house-breaking by night and theft in a building. The case was tried by the Sessions Judge at Vizagapatam, but the jury acquitted the four accused. The Indian Code of Procedure gives the presiding judge the power of referring the case for the orders of the High Court, in cases where he differs from the finding of the jury. Availing himself of this wise provision of law to prevent a miscarriage of justice, a reference was made to the High Court of Judicature, and the Judges passed the following judgment: "While we are disposed to agree with the Sessions Judge that the jury might well have convicted the three accused adults on the evidence, we do not think we ought to interfere with the verdict. The view of the evidence the jury seem to have taken cannot be said to be perverse.

"The accused therefore are acquitted. But as regards the second accused (the youth Krishnadu), there can be no doubt that he is guilty, and we cannot accept the verdict of the jury in his case. We therefore sentence him to be simply imprisoned for three months, but, being of opinion that he is a fit subject for treatment in a reformatory school, we direct that in lieu of undergoing that sentence, he be detained in a reformatory school for three years."

This, briefly, was the history of Krishnan's admission to the school. With this indifferent record he was further hampered with ill health. His physical condition was put down as "bad" in his history sheet, but with regular habits, good food and absence of care, he rapidly gained in weight and grew to be a big-boned boy. He was, on admission, a quiet, retiring lad, who kept pretty much to himself, thus attract
retiring lad, who kept pretty much to himself, thus attract-
selected to be hospital orderly to the Sub-Assistant Surgeon, whom he was required to help in dressing cases and in preparing medicines for the boys in hospital. There were, however, temptations attached to his special job, which he seemingly, at first, was able to resist. Afterwards, an inordinate idea of his position and his own importance grew upon him, and he fell a victim to the admiration of the circle of friends that gathered round him.

Krishnan's inclinations were towards study, and he showed a great love for reading. He might be seen poring over an English book by lamplight or reading aloud to himself jerkily in the foreign tones of a language so different to the soft cadence of his own. He proved an apt pupil, and applied himself with assiduity to the study of English and drawing, at the same time practising carpentry as a form of manual instruction in which he excelled. He also attended to his physical development by exercising himself in drill, gymnastics and games, and he soon became the best athlete of the school. He rose rapidly into favour, attained the position first of assistant monitor, then a monitor, and finally secured the good-conduct medal on the votes of the boys. No wonder, therefore, that he was looked upon as a hero by the boys, especially those of an adventurous spirit who followed him and hung upon his smiles. Promotion came without stability of character, and he was soon called upon to face a very severe test. Either through the evil influence of one of his associates, or at the suggestion of a member of the lower staff, he stole two packets of sterilised cotton from the hospital, which he secreted in the carpenter's workshop. The theft was detected; he was brought to book, examined by the Headmaster and found guilty. With a great deal of effrontery he blurted out that he purposely took the cotton, because he did not want to keep his cap any longer, that is, he did not wish to retain the responsible position of monitor, of which the distinctive cap was the symbol. He was deservedly thrashed for his barefaced lie. I decided, for several reasons, to keep out of the inquiry. If I had anything to do in the matter, I should have taken away his cap, and that would have ruined his future. I wished to save the boy, for to me he seemed so much fine material that could be moulded into proper form for the good of the school and for his own benefit. The staff on several occasions endeavoured to prejudice me against him, but I set myself the task of winning the boy. I allowed him to retain his position as monitor, and as the thrashing did him good he was given a chance to rehabilitate himself. He was further safeguarded by the supervision of the ration clerk, who was warned to look out for any signs of trouble and to advise the boy to keep clear of the assistant sergeant, who seemed to resent the boy's independent way of behaving; it was all I could do to try and keep them apart. Was all this trouble over one boy worth the candle? Well, instinct and intuition told me what was at the back of his mind, and I plumbed into the very depths of his being only to discover that he had all the elements of a born leader, minus the lack of moral balance,

The Chingleput Fort (page 35)

to make him a great power for good. I knew that if ever I thrashed him he would not only have gone to the bad, but would have corrupted others with his evil influence. My anxiety to understand his secret trouble met with no response, for he was both shy and reserved; in fact, he avoided me as one from whom it would be wise to remain at a safe distance.

One more trouble loomed over the part that Krishnan took in a *contretemps* on the football field, when his conduct came up unofficially for consideration, but I was still convinced that there was a great deal of good in him, that through one or two associates he was put forward to take a prominent part in the affair, and that, by studied attention, his want of balance would be gradually restored. I continued my interest in the lad, and as a mark of my favour took him in hand to be coached by me in English, while every encouragement was given to him to make a special study of drawing. He was my companion in an occasional walk out, and a friendly chat soon won the confidence of the boy. I noticed that his influence for evil was thrown into the opposite scale, while the visible progress made in his studies opened his eyes to his shortcomings, humanised him, and captured him for right conduct. He gained so great a proficiency in cabinet-making, drawing and gymnastics as to justify an extension of his course for two years in manual training in the Teacher's College, Saidapet, with the view of adopting it as his future profession in life. The youth subsequently became a joint drawing master and gymnastic instructor, and, as he could now afford it, married and settled down to the life of a worthy citizen. Later, he attained the position of Workshop Instructor and Instrument Repairer in the School of Engineering, Vizagapatam.

It is a typical instance of how a little patience, a little sympathy, a little forbearance, a little interest and a little individual attention influence a boy for good when all else fails! Some boys respond to an ethical stimulus; some react on disciplinary pressure; some are moved by kindness alone—the difficulty lies in knowing what to employ and when to employ it.

Narayanaswami is a big-boned lad who chucks his chest when he walks, and yet carries a girl's heart. Not blessed with much intelligence he worries himself over little insults and suffers severely from depression if not backed up by authority. He is a police constable's son, and was sent here for stealing rice from a bag in a bandy. Soon after his admission into the school he got hold of the third master's tiffin carrier and helped himself to some cooked potatoes. As the master was a Brahmin, the food became polluted by the boy's touch and was thrown away. The master, however, reconciled himself to the enforced abstinence on the ground that his father had often objected to his craving for potatoes, for which his soul had frequently lusted, and that on this particular day he was able to induce his mother and sister to surreptitiously prepare some for him, with the result that he was punished in a natural, and, as Herbert Spencer would remark, most effective manner, for having acted *mala fide* towards his parent. The objection of the orthodox Brahmin to the use of potatoes is a sentimental one, and lies in the resemblance of the farinaceous article to an animal product, the egg of a fowl. They object also to certain kinds of gourds, the seeds of which resemble the teeth of a cow.

This boy and another were subsequently enrolled as recruits in the 2nd Queen Victoria's Own Sappers and Miners, a regiment which proves to be an ideal opening for our boys because it teaches trades, and provides facilities for practising them. The lads were trained here as smiths, and their Commanding Officer in a report stated that they were likely to make good soldiers and that their behaviour had been exemplary. He added further: "They are of good physique and should make good sappers. I shall be glad to take more boys of the same stamp." The boy often writes, and he never fails to state that he prays God to keep us ever in sound health.

Abbu.—One is inclined to smile when one sees an ex-pupil escort a new admission to the school. Some of our boys enlist in the Police Department, and when an opportunity occurs of paying a pilgrimage to the school they do it inexpensively by inducing their superior officers to allow them to escort a convicted juvenile waiting for admission to the school. And it is good for them both, for one can imagine the kind of conversation that would take place between the old and the new. The views of the latter are sure to be given in glowing colours, describing the present state of the place with all its advantages, which were perhaps never realised in the case of the ex-school boy and about which he never concerned himself. With the voice of a brother, he details the regulations of the school and warns him against breaking any of them with impunity. He chaperones the boy till he ushers him into the presence of the Superintendent, and with never a quiver on his lip or a ripple on his face, the old boy comes smartly to the salute. He is, however, impatient to cast off the correct attitude of the Police Constable standing to attention, and longs to speak to his master in the endearing manner of by-gone days, but he dare not for a while. A correct demeanour is necessary to bring him repute, and a sense of pride imposes on him the obligation to stand steady, but it is only for a few minutes.

He means to spend the day in the school and he soon throws off his uniform to get into loose, comfortable Swadeshi garments and with easy familiarity and evident pleasure mixes with the crowd that soon gathers around him. Abu, for that is his name, the scamp of former days, Abu the smoker, Abu the mimic who made his fellows laugh, Abu who was always ready with a rambling legend to explain away his shortcomings, begins to narrate his adventures in the centre of a grinning group, and the nippers after a while begin to chaff him as the small policeman in big boots. He goes for them; they make a bolt outside the fence, and turning round at a safe distance they challenge him with repeated threats to kick him if he came near. He takes it all in good part and with inward mirth, but pretending to stand upon his dignity he threatens reprisals for this insult of theirs if they ever run up against him in the outer world. The time now comes for him to take leave of the school; this he does in high spirits, marching off to headquarters.

But alas! the report received about him shortly afterwards is not very promising, for he is, sad to say, suspected of intemperance, and in the words of his chief: "His conduct is only fairly satisfactory. He is inclined to be impertinent, and thinks it brave to consort with the older men in the toddy shops, but of late he has not given any trouble in that way." The explanation of his behaviour lies in a nutshell. With none of his relatives to guide him, and in the absence of an elder brother to take a friendly interest in him, he succumbs to the seductive influence of his elder companions, but it was his early training which kept him from altogether becoming a failure. Such is the history of some of our lads who enter the public services.

Gomathy.—A boy respectful and reserved, but short-tempered, once fell out with his friend, Padalingam, a henchman of Muthian, an agricultural lad of attractive qualities, with whom Gomathy lost caste because of his association with boys of doubtful character. The whole school was afraid of Muthian, for he made short shrift of any boy guilty of any escapade that did damage to the fair name of the school. If a big boy was suspected of crooked conduct and did not own up to it, he used the common-sense argument of muscular force, but with no undue severity, to extract a confession.

With such a youth, Gomathy had no affinity, and soon after his discharge Gomathy, from a fancied grievance, spread the rumour that he belonged to a criminal class, meaning to imply thereby that he was not within the charmed circle of those who could handle a water-mug, or, in other words, issue water to caste boys. Imagine the uneasy feelings of the school when they discovered that they had been taking water from an untouchable; their faces fell, for hadn't they been taught in their youth that in the matter of eating and drinking pollution was possible, that cleanliness was gauged by the scrupulosity with which pots and pans were cleaned, that while eating with unwashed hands was a mere offence, to take water from a lower caste was much more than an offence—it was unpardonable; it meant excommunication from caste, founded as it was on an ethical basis and sub-dividing with rolling time into ever narrowing circles. Caste to them was the very breath of their nostrils; the atmosphere in which they lived and moved and had their being; the heritage of generations, hedged about by rites and ceremonies, and a re-entrance to which could only be accomplished by a special ceremony needing money. How appalling to little minds to contemplate such a disaster! Naturally they were very exercised in mind, and when the matter began to get serious and an inquiry was set on foot, Gomathy, who perceived that his adventurous spirit had proceeded too far, pooh-poohed the whole affair, while he simplified his argument against any evil design on his part by asserting the fact with weird self-satisfaction that he himself had received water at the hands of the boy. Wasn't it therefore to his interest to conceal the matter if there was truth it it? And he laughed a hearty laugh.

This same youth, Gomathy, on another occasion strolled out of bounds with a companion and was encountered on the way by the Gymnastic Instructor, who brought the matter to notice. The lad first tried to browbeat the master, failing which he argued out the point with the Duffadar to the effect that a person caught in the act of committing a crime was an offender, but one who escaped detection could not be classed under the same category, hence his anger against the Instructor for letting on. With our boys, when they first come, crime consists in being found out. Their moral conception of right and wrong is so weak as not to stand in the way of their committing any offence that can be done without fear of detection.

The youth, however, left the school with different ideas. He joined the police force as a constable, where he received a good-conduct prize during his period of training as a recruit, and his subsequent character, from reports received about him, was uniformly good.

Raman.—This boy started badly, and in a short time made history for himself before the good influences of the school could work round him. He escaped from the institution eleven days after admission, and a year after that he was punished for stealing two limes from the garden; three months subsequently he was guilty of forging in a post card received from his parents, a sentence purporting to give their consent to his transfer from a trade he disliked to another more to his taste. His most serious offence happened when he took it into his head to enter my house one evening while I was away at tennis, and going straight for the bedroom he put his hand into the pocket of my own office coat hanging on a peg and took the whole bunch of coins found in the purse. The boy was so unimaginative as not to peroeive that had he removed only one or two rupees—and it was enough for his purpose, for a pice worth of tobacco or snuff would keep him in clover for some time—it was possible that the loss would not have been detected, but blessed with only youthful intelligence he grabbed the whole of the contents of the purse and made away with it.

A clue to the theft was obtained when some one "let on" that he saw a friend of his knocking about the precincts of the house on the evening in question. That same night the blanket trick was tried upon him and his friend with good results, for the stolen money was brought out from its hiding place in a ledge of the roof. The blanket trick, to explain, is a mild form of lynching practised in the dormitory at night for the purpose of extracting truth. The suspected boy is covered with a blanket and the others go at him with their fists like hammer and tongs till he cries for mercy and acknowledges his offence by handing over what he has purloined.

The last ebullition of moral evil happened after two years' satisfactory behaviour—so satisfactory that it entitled him to enter the ranks of the monitors. Such responsibility, however, seems to have been too great a temptation for him, for it led him to bring about the escape of a boy, unintentional though it was, when ten of them were in quarantine for chicken-pox.

On the day previous to the escape a woman of a criminal tribe and mother to one of the quarantined boys came to see her son and was permitted as a favour to speak to him, but only at a distance as a precautionary measure to prevent the spread of infection. But this act of kindness—

hardly appreciated—brought disaster, for it tempted her to carry on an illicit conversation, and while the man on duty was otherwise engaged, she got round to the back of the place, and having made overtures to her gentle offspring managed to throw him a few coppers. This was, of course, taken charge of by the monitor, who, as a grown-up lad, naturally wanted to put it to the best possible use by the purchase of meats not intended for babes. As evening was coming on he handed over the money to a stripling in whom he somewhat confided and instigated him to remain unseen in the background till "all correct" was given. At dusk he was to clear away to the bazaar to purchase a few packets of snuff, with instructions to turn up before daylight in time for roll-call.

Having bluffed the peon on duty that all was correct when the time for internment came round he retired peacefully to rest, conscious of having done a good stroke of business. The peon, of course, finding it convenient to pass on responsibility, never for one moment doubted the honour of the boy, and the door was shut. But golden opportunities for escape do not always present themselves thus handy, and in addition the romance of an adventure appealed so strongly to the boy when he found himself at liberty that he took his journey (without a ticket) by the first train going into Madras, widening still further the gap made in his feeble moral sense by "bagging" a new suit of silk pyjamas of a recently married Muhammadan travelling in the same compartment. Arriving at Madras he was detected travelling without a ticket, and after a little interrogation he found himself escorted back to Chingleput, but the police instead of handing him over to the school authorities, brought a charge against him of having stolen a silk pair of trousers and lodged a complaint before a Magistrate who very sensibly dismissed the case on the plea that the owner of the lost article was not present, but probably because it was not worth while to proceed with the case which, if proved, could only have one result, viz., the return of the boy to the school.

Raman lost his cap over this breach of trust in allowing

a boy to go out of bounds and thus opening his eyes to a short cut to liberty, but it is pleasing to note that the healthy traditions of the school were not lost on him altogether, for towards the end of his stay he seems to have pulled himself together and gave promise of confining his energy within the limits of study and work. On leaving the school he was employed as a mason under the Chairman of a Municipal City Council, whose opinion of him was that the lad invariably impressed him as a young man quite willing to work and earn an honest livelihood, while his supervisor added that he has been behaving all along satisfactorily and that there was every hope of his improving himself professionally in company with first-class workmen. The last recorded report is: "The young man is working satisfactorily. He has improved in his professional work as a bricklayer and has earned an increase in his wages." This youth has at last made the discovery that it pays one to do honest work. *Quantum mutatus ab illo.*

MUNUSWAMI was a type of boy full of humour who always made his fellows laugh, and sometimes carried things too far in his exuberant remarks about other people. He reached his zenith shortly after he left school, when he was sent as a bugler to the Coimbatore jail. Such a boy is quick to size up character, and he soon discovered that the head warder was addicted to drink. It happened one night that this son of Bacchus was on guard duty, and when bugler Munuswami, who came in late, had to pass him he was called upon to advance and give the countersign.

Failing for the moment to remember the password he coined one of his own and used what he thought to be a very appropriate *pis aller,* and shouted out in Tamil "one bottle." It was an expression that cut to the quick, a bitter gibe as the warder interpreted it, a taunt at his weakness, and resenting it he flared up, demanding once again stentoriously the password. The spirit of tormenting his enraged chief having seized the youthful bugler, he called out this time in his own vernacular "two bottles," which proved to be the limit of endurance. Next morning he was hauled up before the Colonel and reported for insubordination. The old Colonel at once took in the situation, and making an effort to suppress a rising smile, he addressed in solemn language the prisoner at the bar and warned him that he would be dealt with severely if he were guilty of such conduct again. The boy, reduced to his own society, must have learnt meditatively the lesson that humour does not always pay.

One or two incidents will suffice to demonstrate the hold that tobacco has over the boys. When the shades of evening are falling two lads, according to custom, are told off for the special purpose of putting on the lights in the dormitories. The Sergeant prior to marching in the boys stands at the entrance and calls out to make sure if anybody is inside the dormitory, to enable him to check the remaining number.

The youthful cunningness of one of the lamp-boys bent on a night ramble suggested itself that as he was on the outside of the verandah he had simply to stand close to the bars of the windows and in a clever manner project his voice inside to lend support to his answer that he was in. He did so, and the tones of his voice, deflected from the opposite wall, floated towards the Sergeant, who never for a moment doubting that his ears could deceive him numbered the boys and bolted the door. Shortly afterwards one of the peons, whose intelligence was below the average and could not be relied upon, reported to me that he thought he saw a boy rushing across the yard and disappear in the shadow beyond. To make sure, the Sergeant was at once sent for, and he rather resented the question put to him if all was correct. But on asking him to re-number the boys it was found that one was short, and then the coterie of friends of the missing youth made believe that they were trying to fathom the mystery, and after pretending to hold a conclave they began to assure the Sergeant that he would turn up all right in the course of the night, the one idea that obsessed him being not to escape but that of getting some tobacco from a bazaar in the town, either by payment or by fraud—it mattered not. A sharp look-out in the early morning discovers our innocent culprit standing close to the wall of the carpenter's shop ready to mingle with the crowd as the boys filed out, and on being cornered he confessed to his having been unable to resist the attraction of spending a night outside with the certain prospect of procuring tobacco. One was hardly inclined to punish him, particularly as he was sporting enough to return, but the Sergeant looked at it from a different angle of vision, inasmuch as he was fooled in presence of the pupils, and considered that the miscreant ought to be severely punished. He was chosen to administer the strokes, and he did it with all the pomp and circumstance of an official execution. He laid the strokes on well and truly—that much the victim himself admitted by his short, sharp ejaculations.

After his discharge the boy wrote to say that he regretted having given so much trouble in the school, and he prayed that the pupils of the reformatory would behave as members of one family. On inquiry later on from the Magistrate as to his mode of occupation and conduct, the reply came that he was studying the Koran with the object of becoming a priest to his castemen (the Lubbai), to earn his livelihood thereby, and that he had given up the idea of enlisting in the Army. The youth subsequently turned up at the school for a note of recommendation for a tailor's job in the Army Clothing Department to enable him to follow his trade. On this the father, with paternal anxiety, sent us a letter to the effect that his son was anxious to enter Government service, and asking us as a *pis aller* to provide him with some appointment in his native town. He did not expect any material help from his son. All he wanted was that his boy should lead an honest life; and to save his bacon he added that he is one who will have his own way, and as he has resolved to leave home and take service elsewhere, he prayed that we would advise him and send him back to him to help him in his work as a butcher.

The boy, finally, did have his own way, but finding that he could not settle down in India, he emigrated to Singapore, sending us a letter beginning with the words, "With profound reverence and feelings of filial love and gratitude." It was accompanied by a small parcel of silk kerchiefs.

Later on he wrote to say that his marriage had been celebrated, the ceremony lasting for three days and ending in a procession, and that he was awaiting my blessings. He subsequently came back to his native place, starting work as a timber merchant, but as he could not stick to it, he resolved to cross the seas once more and try his fortune again at Singapore. The last report about him was that he was doing well.

Pupil RAMASWAMI was once hauled up to the office on a charge of picking up tobacco on the road during the Sunday evening walk-out. Pupil Pothu Raju, who detected the act, was the informant, and being a lad with some sense of responsibility he waxed warm over the offence, committed, as he said, in spite of repeated advice in Sunday school on the evils of smoking and snuffing. But it was very funny to hear how Ramaswami turned the tables on him by naïvely affirming, with all seriousness that the guilt was on the other boy, for he had instigated him to commit the act.

To the question: "Why, then, does he report you and why did you listen to him," the answer was promptly forthcoming. The two were bad friends, and if he received the caning which the other deserved then there would be no more enmity between them and the traitor-friend would then be satisfied, which was tantamount to saying that if one wished to make up with a friend turned enemy, the strategy was to procure him a thrashing in order to tap the juvenile's heart to set flowing again the milk of friendship and good feeling—a philosophy which is either too advanced or too ancient for our present-day civilisation. But the incident is worthy of note to show how a little eastern lad can go to work to evolve original and fantastic ways of protecting himself when he knows that the odds are against him for breaking a law of the school.

A much-coveted position is that of the Superintendent's Orderly. Select a monitor for the job and he holds office with all the tenacity and authority of a paid member of the staff. It is stated that the peon of a District Official is more powerful than his master in the eyes of favour-hunting subordinates, who believe that the belted knight possesses such an accurate gauge of his master as to be able to divine when the *buddha Sahib* is in a favourable mood—a mood coinciding probably with the period following a good dinner. When no tip is forthcoming, he knows how to throw difficulties in the way of interviewers waiting for their cards to be taken up. Naturally, therefore, the Superintendent's orderly is inclined to make the whole school believe that he possesses no little influence with his master, that he knows all his feelings, the secret springs of his actions, the opinion he holds of each one in the school, and how that opinion can be modified. As a result, everybody tries to keep good with him. He is credited with being able to obtain a more liberal allowance of chapatties (flat cakes) from the cook, has been known to try to blackmail some of the school staff, and behaves as if he were a cut above the other boys. These possible delinquencies necessitate from time to time a reminder that his privileged position carries with it great responsibility, and demanding amongst other things that he should not mix himself up with school politics or take sides in any controversy, that he must bear in mind the respect due to authority, and that he must show himself a pattern for others to follow. Monitors trip at times, but steady themselves again, and on the whole shape well in an atmosphere of liberty and trust. These boys in their after career lead respectable lives, and evidence the effects of stimulating surroundings. They correspond frequently with me, and strange as it may read, they show their respect and affection for their "father" by garlanding and "worshipping" his photo, purchased perhaps out of their little savings and hung up in a private room. One boy who enlisted in the Army made me the heir to all his little possessions, in spite of explanations by the Adjutant that he was expected to make his will out in favour of his own relatives. He was determined to know only one "father," and that a white man.

CHAPTER XX

THE LICENSING SYSTEM

ALL countries recognise the good which results from this system. It places a boy, a year or two before he leaves a reformatory, in a social environment which he will experience when he is finally discharged, and he is for this reason better prepared to withstand the temptations of life. It would be well if every boy could be put out under licence for at least six months before discharge. But the weak point about it is that employers of labour do not, in the first place, possess the facilities for the exercise of the closest scrutiny over a boy's conduct during his off time, nor do they take the same interest which the school authorities evince in supervising him during recreation hours. Frequent reports have been received of boys who have been put out on licence lapsing into crime, and unless an employer of labour is prepared to look after his apprentices during the non-working hours, or some scheme is devised to place such under control during their period of apprenticeship, the licensing system defeats the object it has in view. What is wanted is a philanthropic body which will interest itself in looking after the morals, not only of our licensed pupils, but also of ex-pupils, till such time as they are able to control themselves.

A boy out on license has the widest possible liberty, and his opportunities of mixing with the world are many. He therefore needs to be watched. I remember a lad who came up before the Committee of Visitors, requesting them to put him out on license to a tailor firm, on the ground that he had learnt all that was to be learnt in the school, and he wished to learn the higher grades of work, for which there was no scope in the school. He also represented that he had a little less than a year for his discharge, and as he had no parents living, he would continue to stay on with the firm. The boy spoke with plenty of common sense and his reasons were sound. He was sent out at his request, but within twenty days he was sent back to the school as a failure, having picked the pocket of the proprietor and eased him of a ten rupee note. There was temptation placed before the boy, and being weak willed, he yielded to it. The licensing system therefore proves a success or failure according to the supervision or want of supervision that exists in places of business. In the Burham Reformatory of New Zealand, the licensing system works very well. A large number of lads become useful citizens through the training they receive while out at service under license, and the control of the reformatory. The earnings of the boys are put into the State Savings Bank and are paid over to such of them who, in after years, can produce evidence to the satisfaction of the Minister of Education that the money will be well invested in sound business pursuits.

In the Insein School, Burma, boys have been licensed out only as domestic servants, and have invariably given their employers satisfaction.

The statistics of the Alipore Reformatory School, Calcutta, for five years before its transfer to Hazaribagh, will show that there were two methods of license at that school—(1) *Under ordinary conditions of license* the boys lodged at the place of employment and were under the employers' supervision, resulting in a large number of failures; (2) *Under special conditions sanctioned by the Government of Bengal* boys were housed and fed at the school, and sent to work daily in charge of an officer of the school, resulting in few failures. The latter system of licensing had the following advantages :—

(*a*) The boys did not lose the benefit of general instruction and discipline; (*b*) they were under the direct supervision of the school staff, and did not run the same risk of temptation as boys under the other system; and (*c*) their wages were deposited in the Post Office Savings Bank till their discharge. Under the former condition their earnings had to be spent on their food and clothing. License *under ordinary conditions* was therefore discontinued, but *under special conditions* encouraged. On the transfer of the school from Alipore the boys on license, *under the special condition*, had to be withdrawn; and for want of suitable employers license under this condition is not possible at Hazaribagh. For this reason it was suggested that a depôt, or hostel, for such boys should be established at Calcutta, to admit of their employment on license under supervision in workshops and mills of that city. The Director of Public Instruction, Bengal, stated that while Government fully recognised the importance of the licensing system for training reformatory boys and securing their employment, yet it was feared that the opening of a hostel at Calcutta, unless conducted on proper lines, might be productive of more harm than good, and he asked for the submission of a self-contained scheme. The late Board of Management of this school, resolved in the year 1909, that in view of the temporary nature of the location of the school the consideration of the subject should be postponed, as the school might yet be removed to Calcutta, in which case it would not be necessary to open a hostel there. Since then the Board of Management has been abolished. In 1911 the school was threatened with overcrowding. The proposal was again renewed, but orders were received to defer raising the question of the revival of the license system at Hazaribagh, till such time as the scheme for a hostel in Calcutta had been matured.

In view of the above facts, licensing on an extensive scale was abandoned. Under the ordinary license system one boy was licensed in 1911 to the Pioneer Lock Works at Aligarh. In 1912 two boys were licensed, one to His Highness the Nawab's band at Murshidabad and the other to 63rd P.L.I. The latter boy was subsequently apprenticed for enlistment. In 1913 four boys were licensed: three to 63rd P.L.I. as bandsmen and one to the Bengal Police as bugler. In 1914 no boy was licensed. In 1915 three boys were licensed to the Basumati Press at Calcutta. Out of ten boys licensed since 1911, only one, from the 63rd P.L.I., was re-convicted, while one from Basumati Press was returned to the school on account of suspicious conduct.

With regard to apprenticeship in India, it must be observed that the peculiar conditions of the country do not necessitate any great demand for apprentices. In India, labour is cheap and easily procurable and the necessity for apprentices cannot exist largely.

If a lad is to be apprenticed at all to an individual, he should be of the same caste as the boy and he should undertake to keep him as a boarder and exercise a general supervision over the boy's general conduct outside the factory. There are several public-spirited men who would be glad to take a boy from the reformatory and help the school with their co-operation. A covering letter to them with a printed enclosure giving the general outlines of the scheme, what the State is aiming at, and what help can be given to carry on the work of reformation, would secure much of the object in view. The Collectors in the various districts may be addressed to give the names of those men who would be willing to look after a lad or two. Of course, such men have to be found.

MUSTHAN was a first offender, a Muhammadan, tall for his age, but with a childish expression and way of thinking. After a stay of 2½ years in the school he was sent out on licence to an Inspector of Salt, Abkari and Customs as a bugler on Rs. 8½ per mensem, and out of this he was compelled to deposit Rs. 2 in the Post Office Savings Bank, but two months after joining he wrote to say that as he had no clothes to wear he did not want any deduction made from his pay. The truth of the matter was that he had taken to gambling (perhaps a previous pastime of his), and when spoken to and given beat duty to keep him busy he refused to do it and said that he was sent to do duty as bugler, and that unless the school wrote to say that he was to do extra duty, he declined to do it.

In the meantime, the boy wrote to us to excuse him if he had acted wrongly and wished to be taken back to the reformatory. The Inspector of the Salt Circle asked us not to take any notice of the petition addressed to us direct by the bugler who had been licensed to him, remarking that he had refused to do the duty he was deputed to do and was constantly absent from the lines, gambling in the village. He added: " As the boy has been placed under my charge and as I am responsible for him, all orders issued by me are for his good, and it is impossible for me to maintain discipline if he feels he can offend against any order given by me "—adding that at present there was an inquiry as to the loss of one set of uniform by him, which, it is understood, was pawned in order to pay his gambling debts. After this, the boy seemed to have pulled himself together for six months, when he wrote again that he had no money for clothes and requested that only one rupee be deducted from his pay. His request was recommended, but the reply received from the Assistant Commissioner was to the effect that Sheik Musthan was a most undesirable character and that when the Inspector rightly insists on discipline and departmental rules being carried out, he writes and complains. He asked, therefore, that the boy may be removed at once from the Circle.

Five months after this, the boy was sent out on the licensing system to the Superintendent of Police, Ganjam, as a bugler; but even there he misbehaved himself, joining another boy bugler from the reformatory in assaulting a baker boy and stealing a pound of biscuits valued at one rupee. They both deserved dismissal, but as the Reserve Police would have been without an efficient bugler, and as the Superintendent of Police was anxious to prevent the two lads relapsing into crime, he got the District Magistrate to give them twelve stripes, and retained them in the service.

A month after this he foolishly took part in a strike engineered by eighteen others, to defy authority, and he was suspended and dismissed from the service. He then went to his native place and became a bandy driver, and shortly after fell sick and was for three months an in-patient in hospital, and then came the sad but not surprising news that he was sentenced to six months' rigorous imprisonment for theft. Thus ended a promising life, which, from the want of a little friendly supervision, went astray. Discipline, it is true, has to be maintained, but there ought to be some discriminating difference of treatment in the case of a lad unaccustomed to the world's ways and about to make a start in life.

CHINNAYYA, another failure under the licensing system, was a boy of the weaver caste, sent here for seven years. As in the instance of many another boy, his age was not correctly estimated, which is the difficulty with all Hindu boys, who seldom have records of their birthdays, and consequently his period of detention was longer than it should have been. After a five years' stay with us, he grew to be a big lad, and in growing never lost his smile, while the rhythm in his body displayed itself in a most fascinating way in the Kolattum—an Indian maypole dance. He was just the lad to inspire confidence in his superiors, being obedient and hard working. He preserved a neat figure and was good in gymnastics, which gave him a following and made many a boy hang upon his lightest word. But there was a fly in the ointment—it was his vanity which ultimately landed him in trouble, as soon as he stood on his own feet with a little responsibility thrown in. His vanity found expression in his fondness for dress when, after a good record in school, he was sent out on licence to the Superintendent, Peripatetic Weaving Party No. 2., working at Ellore, on 1st March 1915, where he conducted himself at first satisfactorily. But after a year, just a few weeks before Christmas, the Superintendent seems to have left the boy behind and proceeded to Madras to get ready a weaving exhibit at the Exhibition Camp held in connection with a Park Fair.

During his absence, a veritable sun-shining period for him, the boy "made hay" by receiving advances, which he pocketed, from weavers for looms to be supplied, and joined his master at Madras in the early part of December. He took with him a trunk, suit of clothes, two cloths, English shoes, mirror, socks, necktie, belt, banian safety-pin and comb, all new. On investigation, the Superintendent discovered that he had more money than he could account for, and telegraphed to me to take him back at once as he suspected that the boy intended to escape. He was received into the school on the 10th December and was given fifteen cuts on the posteriors for misbehaviour while under licence. Rs. 13 that he had misappropriated were sent to the Superintendent, Peripatetic Weaving Party, out of his earnings, and the lad had still Rs. 15 to his credit. Three months after this he was able to get away from the school. Tasting the sweets of liberty for about a year, he found the discipline on his return to be irksome, and as he had still one year and three months before him, he sought freedom by escaping from the school. He was rather a big boy, and it was the intention of the authorities to bring him up before the visiting Committee for discharge as soon as he had shown signs of turning over a new leaf, but he forestalled them by taking the matter into his own hands. He seems, also, to have been able to induce another boy to accompany him. There is no reason why this second boy should have escaped, as he had only four months and twenty-three days for his discharge from the school, and he had earnings, too, which he would forfeit.

Alluring promises were evidently held out to him which made him throw in his lot with the other. The lad Chinnayya never came to any good afterwards. He was fond of gay companions and led a fast life, and although he escaped re-conviction, he cannot be pronounced a success.

CHAPTER XXI

THE ARMY AS A PROFESSION

WITH the almost total disbandment of the old Madras Army, it is difficult to obtain enlistment for our ex-pupils, who make excellent material for the Native Army. They are accustomed to discipline, they have a fair knowledge of company and battalion drill, and they are skilled in a trade.

With the outbreak of the great War on 4th August 1914 the Madras Army once more came back to life. Composed in the early days of British rule in India of a few hundred peons employed as factory hands, armed with matchlocks, pikes and other primitive weapons, the old coast army, composed mainly of Muhammadans, evolved into what was known as the Madras Army, which served with Clive in Bengal and took part in the battle of Plassey.

It was only in 1758 that Madras Sepoys were formed into regular companies and muskets had been issued in place of matchlocks. Six battalions were formed in 1759, and in 1767 the establishment was fixed at sixteen battalions, each consisting of ten companies, of which two were grenadiers, and recruiting took place from various classes of Muhammadans and Hindus, including Rajputs. In 1770, the Madras Army was formed into three brigades of six battalions each, and ten years later the famous corps of Sappers and Miners was formed, into which most of our boys now enlist, as they are able to follow their trade in the regiment. It is interesting to recall that in 1800 a Cadet Company for Europeans was stationed at Chingleput, and elaborate orders as to their dress and discipline were issued. The

Boys at the Front (page 262)

The Greasy Pole (page 111)

orders for discipline were practically the same as those which obtain at the cadet college established in 1917 at Wellington in the Nilgiris.

Since the advent of the War with the Central Powers recruiting has gone on apace in the Madras Presidency, and quite 10 per cent of our boys enlisted every year in the various regiments, besides those who joined the military, Labour Corps and the Porters Corps. There is a growing demand from the Native Infantry bands for our band boys and buglers, who are quite ready to enlist. A great deal has been done in fostering the idea among lads by recounting the valiant deeds of Indian V.C.'s ever since the coveted distinction was thrown open to the Indian Army, the two first being Daudabad Khan and Naick Darwan Singh, the former for holding on to a machine-gun and putting it out of action before he retired, being the sole survivor, and the latter for leading his company into the German trenches with bayonet in hand, and although twice wounded, he dashed along, mounting "traverses" where there was no trench, regardless of life.

Our boys are proud to do service to the State in return for what it has done for them. The uniform, it must be admitted, is also an attraction. I know of one instance where a boy who was trained by a first-class firm to be a chauffeur had his future decided for him by a looking-glass. He happened to don a military pugaree when he stood before a glass hanging in my house, and like Narcissus, he became enamoured of his own looks and straightway went and joined the Army. Most lads join the Sappers and Miners for choice, for they are encouraged to seize every opportunity of improving themselves in the trade taught them and of keeping their hand in.

The records of the lads who have joined the colours show that they like the life. A few, in former days, saw service in South Africa, in the N.-W. Frontier, Tirah Expedition, and in China, and recently not a few volunteered for Mesopotamia. Some have earned clasps and medals for services on the frontier. The following is the translation of a letter received from three lads who served in the China

Expeditionary Force:—"They state that they belong to the China Field Force, and that Government had for five to six years educated them, trained them to industries, fed and clothed them and gave them good advice, and made them men. They hope to fight bravely in this war and bring credit to the Reformatory School, even at the risk of their lives; when they remember the benefit Government has conferred on them, they feel strong in their spirit to fight for Government. They hope at any cost to vanquish the enemies of Empress Victoria and then to return to India."

The boys who are trained as musicians in the school enter the Army bands and continue to follow their profession, while a similar benefit is enjoyed by the carpenters, blacksmiths, masons and tailors in the Sappers and Miners. The return visit paid to the school by the boys from the front is always appreciated, and the hero in khaki uniform is honoured as a demi-god walking among the children of men, while the troubles he gave as a law-breaker are all forgotten. The masters congratulate him and the boys admire him, magnificent from top to bottom. He is asked to say a few words in school about his experiences, but his shyness will allow him to bring out only a few sentences stating nothing in particular, except to advise the boys to be true to their *alma mater* when they leave the school and to learn to obey while they are in school—sensible and well-needed advice. When the time comes for leave-taking, he does so in a halo of hero-worship.

Some of the lads corresponded regularly from the front, and evidently had pleasant memories to recall on my birthday. One lad writes: "It is nearly 2½ years since I joined the Army. When I only think of your birthday, but not hear anything about it, I am very much moved. How happy I would feel to hear about your birthday from this long distance." Another writes rather affectionately, with the help of somebody: "Dearest Dad,—I am quite well, by the grace of God Almighty, and trust you will be the same. I received your kind letter safely to my hand, and I understand all the contents therein."

Roll of Service (page 262)

Hindu Temple for the Boys (page 166)

The School Mosque (page 164)

THE ARMY AS A PROFESSION

St Thomas Mount,
25/9/1917.

Most respected and kind Sir,—

I am one of your student, Nathaniel, writing your honour my simple letter. Our Regiment, 85th Carnatic Infantry, again arrived at St Thomas' Mount on July 1916. Lately it was at Cananore, Secunderabad, and at Poona. When it was at Secunderabad I was sent on Field Service, overseas in a hospital ship. In that ship I went to England, Southampton, France, and other new places. After one year service I was relieved by another man from that ship. Now I am at Saint Thomas' Mount with the Regiment. I am very anxious to see you all. I will take leave here and come over there to see you all. I close this letter with best wishes.

Your faithful servant,

Nathaniel,
85th Carnatic Infantry.

The boy Nathaniel deserves more than a passing notice. Being by birth a Telugu, he had all the grit and bone of his caste, who reside in the northern districts of the Presidency. He won a silver badge in the school for proficiency in music, joined a regimental band before the War broke out, and automatically became a Roman Catholic Christian, for all bandsmen in the native regiments are Christians, and a caste boy can never mingle with them without being "converted."

Soon after leaving school, his regiment was transferred to Fort William, Calcutta, when he had the pleasure of blowing the Royal Salute when King George V. came out to India to proclaim his Coronation. He, with another, stood at the entrance to the fort, and on sounding the Royal Salute, the King stood to attention and returned the Salute. Such honour falls to few reformatory lads. The way this boy narrated the incident to me revealed the intense pleasure and pride he felt in recalling the glorious moment of his life. His letter gives details of his trip to England and France, and on his return to India he attained the rank of Drum Major in the 88th Carnatic Infantry and visited the school wearing the officers' red sash across his shoulder. The boys felt proud of him. His quiet chats with a few of the seniors must have raised their respect for the ideals of the school. His presence certainly proved that if a General's baton does not await them, an officer's sash at least lies hid in the knapsack of every recruit from the school.

Some good would be done if we were allowed the liberty of teaching, with their consent, those boys who elect for a regimental band the elementary doctrines of Christianity, that they may be better fitted to take their place in a band. But the orders of Government prohibit any active part in missionary work, directly or indirectly, and a schoolmaster in charge of Hindu boys has to be strictly neutral. In one instance when a band boy, after his discharge wished to embrace Christianity, and arrangements had been made to baptize him in the schoolroom by a Government chaplain, a missionary addressed me in the following terms:—

"I presume you will be arranging to baptize the boy who has decided to become a Christian. As no reference has been made in the matter to this mission or church, I presume you are not aware of the laws of comity recognised among most missionary societies.

"As there are several extenuating circumstances in this case, I do not wish to lodge a formal protest, but as there is a question of principle involved, I could not let the matter pass without bringing it to your notice."

A boy, therefore, is allowed to decide such matters after joining a regiment, and when he is his own master. The danger of his becoming only a nominal Christian for the social advantages enjoyed in a regimental band, wholly composed of Christians, is also avoided.

To sum up matters and put them on a definite basis, a general order may well be issued by the military authorities that a recruiting officer should periodically visit the school for the enlistment of suitable youths, and that allowances be made in the case of those boys who do not quite come up in measurement to the standard requirements, for the reason that they are growing lads and that they would soon reach the required measurements. The school also should be made a recruiting ground for Regimental Bands,—a Kneller Hall for the needs of South India. It is true a few of our boys do enter regimental bands, but one would like to see a larger number in them. In England from 600 to 700 Reformatory pupils on the average enlist in the army every year, of whom 250 join the band.

During the South African War many of them gave their lives for their country, and Lord French was not ashamed to say,—pointing to the list of names of old boys who had fallen in the war, when he was unveiling a memorial tablet, "They were your comrades, they were my comrades." Out in India, a great deal more might be done to encourage the enlistment of our boys in the army in the piping times of peace, especially in those Regiments where skill in some trade is necessary. As reformed juveniles, they possess qualities which enhance their value to the army. If enlistment is encouraged, it becomes an easy matter to foster in the school the idea of service to the State.

The world-wide war with its storm centre in Flanders has sent its wave force along the surface to reach, though in ripples, even this distant small corner of the Indian Empire. The war-fever seized our boys from the start and the bigger ones were glad to enlist. Their patriotism caught on and the occasional Sunday talks on the War helped the school to take an intelligent interest in the events of the great struggle. They have practically shown their loyalty and sympathy by subscribing out of their own earnings, which is little enough, a pice a month or 3 annas a year towards the War Funds and the Hospital Ship "Madras." When there was a rush at the start they willingly did extra work in cutting out pyjamas and weaving operation towels. On 'Our Day' they went round with boxes and quite easily collected a hundred rupees from the citizens of Chingleput. At their yearly Christmas camp they staged dramas in aid of Red Cross work and to their great delight on one occasion the "Illustrated Times of India" published a photograph of the actors which finds a place on the walls of the Library—framed and hung.

In their private prayers, they have remembered the sick

and wounded, and the success of the British Arms was a subject of continued supplication.

The visits of their old chums in uniform gave the needed stimulus to a desire for efficiency in drill and in physical exercise with a view to attaining the standard measurements for the Army. They were careful to discipline their bodies and offered to do gratuitous work such as working the water-pump for the purpose of developing their chests and biceps.

They learnt also to economise in their work and to do without little fancy articles. The scarcity of yarn and metals and the non-importation of certain metal sheets taught them how scraps may be utilized in work, thus doing away with extravagant methods in all the workshops. The purchasing of coloured paper for making kites and garlands, little tin boxes, vests, English sweets and biscuits was given up willingly. Some of their money was invested in the 5 year Post Office Certificates, while the boys at the front sent remittances to their parents or to us to be banked in their names. But not among the least of the many lessons learned was the admiration of brave deeds done particularly by the first Expeditionary Indian Force that left for France after the declaration of War. The wily Gurkha scout, the brave Sikh, the daring Rajput, and the loyal Punjabi who fought side by side with British troops and won glory on the field appealed immensely to a class of boys whose vision is devoid of social imagination. For them, the common grave where India's heroes sleep with England's sons is a sanctified spot though far away under another sky.

CHAPTER XXII

PARENTS—LETTERS—CASTE

PARENTS are allowed to see their boys on any day, and correspond with them as often as they like. Of this privilege chiefly those living close to the school avail themselves, but instances have been known where a mother has come from a town some 250 miles away to see her son. Once a woman walked the whole way by stages and when asked why she put herself to such hardships, her maternal instinct came out with the reply that her *Athma* or soul called her to the school. Her son, however, was most unworthy of such solicitude as he scarcely took advantage of the many opportunities for self-improvement. When his mother asked him why he was so backward in his lessons, he told her that his "tongue would not twist properly." He was once brought up before the office for an offence, and on that occasion the Duffadar neatly summed up the boy's character by saying that if you treat him kindly he will bite, if you treat him harshly he will bite—in short, that he was a pig. When the lad was about to leave, the mother made a special request that "her son should be employed by the Government somewhere," which goes to prove that even in the lowest social stratum there is much confidence in the benign character and fair dealing of the Sircar, although some people would have us believe that there are villagers who are still ignorant of the existence of the British Raj. The boy, however, was not allowed to enter Government service to perpetuate the folly of his more educated folk, and consequently took to agricultural work, but only for a time, for later on he emigrated to Penang like so many of his compatriots who wish to better their prospects. There they are able to look after themselves and hold their own. Poor indentured cooly—what tons of literature have been written for political and other reasons to raise his status in the eyes of the world?

Another mother belonging to the Dhobi or washerman class—travelled all the way from the Nilgiris by train, over a distance of 325 miles, in order to see her son. The journey cost her Rs. 12, equal to a month's earnings, to be made good by instalments to a kind mistress who advanced her the money. The woman approached me with vivacity exhibiting in her hand the post cards written to her by her son as proof that she was bona-fide the mother and no false knocker for admission into the place. She turned also with pride and pleasure towards her son to show him that she had indeed received all his cards. What evidently pleased her was to know that her boy, who was not able to read or write when he left home, could now write and tell her all about himself.

Then there is the parent of the criminal tribe boy, who periodically pays a visit to keep in touch with her son, lest his filial feelings may get estranged, and his modes of thought altered at seeing things from an angle of vision in the school different to that from which he has seen things in his own home. The brazen faced creature is all affection for her offspring and in strange jargon communicates to him the domestic events that have taken place since he left home. She is careful to enquire when he will be discharged and never fails to turn up at the proper time to accompany her son in the same train, keeping at some distance for fear of the peon on escort duty, her intention being to snatch away the lad all too soon after he has secured a decent post and stealthily convey him to his former haunts to be sworn in among his brothers. "If you want a wife you must join us" prevails in the end and good intentions are cast aside as easily as a cobra sheds its skin.

There is the parent who desires that his son shall profit by the training and earn a living afterwards and he suggests reading, writing and an acquaintance with the English tongue to enable him to get on in life. No mention is made of teaching him a trade for he wishes his boy to fill the post of a petty village officer and the industrial equipment of the country does not trouble him. Reply post cards are periodically received from him to ascertain the progress made by his offspring. Luckily this school is saved from the interfering parent or the parent who objects to his son receiving corporal punishment and rushes into print as is sometimes the case in ordinary schools, especially if a Christian missionary happens to be the offender.

It must not be assumed that every lad is favoured with a parental visit, for five-sixths of the school never receive more than an occasional post card from home, and thus it comes about that when a parent does enter the school, a crowd of urchins look on while the interview between parent and son takes place. They are curious to hear the advice that will be given and bits of family news to be recounted while eyeing the cakes, sweets and articles of extra clothing like vests that are handed over to the favoured one.

Advantage is taken of parents' visits to inform them of their son's conduct. If a boy's record is not a good one, the parents' counsel to the following tune follows :—

"What, my son! is this why I brought you forth into the world? Have you not learnt sense yet? If you behave properly and learn a trade, you are not going to benefit us, but yourself. If you keep good, I shall come and see you again, and when you come out I shall get you married"—and so on.

Sometimes the scene of the meeting of parent and child is a heartrending one, and the interview ends with a promise from the son to behave better in future. Such visits help to keep alive a tender spark in the heart of the boy, and, for a similar reason, free correspondence under supervision is allowed by letter between parent and boy, however bad the boy may be. He is punished in various ways for his offences, but his correspondence is never stopped. Some officers hold a different view, and refuse all interviews for the first six months after admission; perhaps, because it is believed that a lad's mind becomes unsettled, and he gets home-sick, and attempts to abscond to his parents. There may be a little truth in this, but the compensation is too trifling to be considered, and, with proper guarding, escapes can be prevented.

The old boys are distributed all over the Presidency so that it makes it impossible for one to expect every old boy to revisit the school, scattered as they are over such a wide area. It is generally the Madras-boy or the boys living in districts close to the school who are able to run in for the day to see their *alma mater.* If the parent has means, a boy even travels a long distance to recall old memories, but at the outside we never see more than 10 per cent. of the old pupils who have passed through the school. Every boy who joins the Army unfailingly pays a visit, because for one thing he is proud of his uniform, and he likes to strut in it before his old masters. Then their military discipline engrains into them a spirit of loyalty and of *esprit de corps* and they find satisfaction in revisiting the old haunts.

One is often tempted therefore to set apart a room for them and fit it up with a few odds and ends, but the great hold that tobacco has on our class of miscreants makes one hesitate to provide a common room for social purposes lest it should encourage old boys to pass tobacco to the little teasers who now fill their places in the various class forms. Even money is sometimes handed over to them. To these they unbend freely, dallying even a cigarette before them on the sly. To minimise these irregularities the Superintendent sets apart a spare room downstairs in his own quarters —which gives him ample opportunities of listening to adventures and recalling old days. At the same time absolute freedom is given to them to visit the old workshops, to mix with the boys in their class rooms or on the field and to be present at the Sunday moral lesson when they are asked to say a few words. Their remarks always contain sound words of advice, though few, for the old boy has mixed with strangers and the experience gained has brought home to him in striking contrast the fostering care of the school and the cold shoulder to be expected in the outside world. Of this, he warns his hearers.

So it speaks well for the work that is done in a Reformatory school when the old boys thus take an interest in it, and keep up their connection with the old school. In an ordinary school, one always thinks well of a boy who looks back with affection to his old school days of pleasant memories and does not forget his *alma mater*. That a reformatory boy should do the same, and evince even the smallest interest in his old school must be regarded as a favourable sign of good work being done in the institution, where, perhaps, the memories are not of the pleasantest nature. The case of their admission into the school, the special punishments that are ready at hand to meet offences, the curtailment of liberty, the discipline, all militate against the drawing out of a boy's affection for the school. It is therefore a very pleasant surprise to find that many an ex-pupil revisits the scenes of his school days, showing that he is not ashamed of his connection with the school. There are various motives which prompt a lad to do this: one boy perhaps cannot find work to do and he travels miles to seek the protection of the school. Another comes to renew old friendships and old scenes; a third, to pay respect to his masters, which is usually shewn in the form of garlands and the accustomed lime. These visits, needless to say, are always encouraged, especially from well-behaved boys who thereby exert a powerful influence on the inmates of the school. When the latter see their former companions respectable and doing well, either as sepoys, constables, or as artizans they are most favourably impressed. An ex-pupil in uniform is always a centre of attraction. Opportunity is not lost on these occasions to make them contribute towards the athletic fund of the school, which they gladly do: opportunity is also taken to get them to counsel the boys in the school on the way they should meet the temptations to which they would be exposed on their discharge—temptations which they themselves have experienced.

A few Madras boys have been known to visit the school immediately after a theft in the town. They evidently break their journey here to have a look at the school, dressed in all their fineries, which have been purchased from the hard earnings of somebody else, thus converting ill-gotten money into clothes of respectability and show. Thus much for the seamy side of visits from 'old boys.'

Some of the pupils correspond with the members of the staff, and I give below the translation of a letter written in Telugu by an ex-pupil. The translation is in the exact words of one of the lower standard teachers and, being a typical example of that class, is allowed to stand as in the original.

"Subba Row writes giving thanks to say that he was protected for the last so many days just as a father would do. On your recommendation, the District Collector of Cocanada gave an appointment in the carpentry department of the workshop of Dowlaishwaram. They are paying Rs. 18 per month. I am safe both by the grace of Almighty and by your kindness. I will go there after the year for the purpose of seeing you and the teachers. I am doing my work to the satisfaction of my brother, my mother and the maistry under whom I work. I am praying the Almighty God day and night for life and prosperity of yourself and teachers. My best compliments to all the teachers."

He gives the following advice to all the boys :—

(1) "Pray God daily."

(2) "Obey to the teachers and maistries who are teaching you, and should not show your angry temper towards them."

(3) "You all should learn to work well."

(4) "If you know the work well, you will earn daily not less than 8 annas."

'Work and pray' is evidently the motto of this youth.

A few letters from ex-pupils are appended :

VENKATASWAMI NAIDU, ex-pupil No. 579, most respectfully addresses the Superintendent as follows : "By God's grace and by your blessings, I am getting on well here and I wish to be informed of your welfare and the welfare of the pupils and those under you.

I have not forgotten the date of your birth-day. I am quite sure that it will be in the memory of everyone of the

Reformatory pupils. For my part, I am able to remember it as the 6th June from the rejoicing and festive appearance the school puts on that day. I have only to pray that God be pleased to grant that the same day this year wears a merry aspect as ever before.

I have, however, one point about you which tends to make me sad when I think of you and that is the bachelor life which you have been leading till now. I pray that God may soon bring about your marriage.

The education that I have received at your hands, together with drill and gymnastics, ever remind me of the gratitude I owe you, while the good lessons that you have inculcated on various occasions have left a lasting impression on my mind.

My work here is rather heavy now and so I am unable to be present there for your birthday. I beg that you will kindly consider me as having been present for the occasion and may not feel angry with me for my absence.

I am ever praying that God may bless you with many happy returns of your birthday.

(Sd.) K.S. VENKATASWAMI NAIDU,
Carpenter Instructor,
Newington College Buildings, Teynampet, Madras.
5/6/1914.

Translation of the letter written by VELU, ex-pupil 741, to the Deputy Superintendent: "Revered and Dear Father,—It is with feelings of profound love and respect that I begin to write to you. I am doing well here and wish to know your welfare. Ever since I left the Reformatory, I had been thinking of your Birthday for which I had resolved to be present; yet my failure to realise what I had so eagerly wished for, grieves me most. In the first place, I am not able to get leave for going over there and even if I succeed in getting leave, the railway fare is high enough and I am not to get my pay for the day I absent myself. I therefore pray that you will kindly excuse my absence this time.

LETTERS

A word to my brethren of the school. In this world there is often a keen struggle or competition of life and the big fishes swallow the small. We have therefore got to be very careful as to how we should prepare ourselves to be able to fight the battle of life successfully. We should very carefully listen to our master's advice and take interest in the trade taught to us. We should entirely forget our old ways and associations and try to conduct ourselves nobly and well so as to do everything in our power to heighten the fame of the Reformatory without tarnishing it. I pray sincerely to God Almighty that He may turn you all from bad ways and temptations and bring credit to the Reformatory.

(Sd.) VELU, dated 5/6/1914.

GOPALAKRISHNAN NAIR (Gopal Nair), ex-pupil No. 872, respectfully writes to the Superintendent: Dear Father,—I was not able to write to you these days because I was some days laid up with fever and suffering from stomach-ache. I am eagerly waiting to hear from you. I can well remember your advice 'work hard' repeated three times at the time of parting and I am now going to Calicut where I promise to do my work satisfactorily and well as advised. Kindly send me my Technical Examination certificate.

I was not able to realize the difficulties of worldly life when I was there, which I have since begun to feel after leaving the Reformatory. I hope all the Reformatory pupils are doing well. A few words to them: "Brethren, some of you are disobedient. Disobedience will, after all, bring you to ruin. A few others amongst you are haughty and self-willed. This bad trait in you is sure to harm you. You should know that we are all the children of one father and as such we should all be of one mind and try to love one another. I hope bad boys have already left the Reformatory by the close of the 6th June. I therefore wish that you all be of one mind and strongly united. Take this as coming from one of your own friends. GOPAUL NAIR."

CASTE

MUSTHAN and THAYYAN, ex-pupils Nos. 900 and 993, respectfully write to their father the Superintendent as follows: Kind and dear father,—We left Chingleput and arrived here at Madura on the 2nd instant, and we both have been doing well ever since. The "DHORAI" here was glad to see us. On the 3rd instant we played hockey with the Madura Reserve and gained a goal over them. We can never forget the valuable lessons of advice you were pleased to give us when we left the Reformatory, and we always pray that you may live long and be happy. I (Thayyan) play bugle and drum and Mustan blows bugle. We request that our compliments be paid to our schoolmates. Praying for an early reply.

Caste is observed in the school only so far as eating and drinking are concerned. The boys are arranged in different rows according to their caste, and there is a clear separation between the meat-eaters and the vegetarians, the smell of the meat being an abomination to the latter. The highest caste, the Brahmans, are provided with a separate kitchen and cook their own food, if there are less than four boys, otherwise they are provided with a cook. Accidentally a boy of one caste happens to touch the eating plate of another belonging to a different caste. In such a case, the offending party pays for the new dish. With all this scrupulosity, a boy does not hesitate to use spit tobacco when he finds it lying on the road-side. In their games and at their work, no caste is observed. They mix freely and feel for each other. On one occasion, what struck me forcibly was the universal grief into which the pupils were thrown when a boy of the lowest class (the sweeper-class) died, and his body was being carried away to be burnt.

All the cooks are caste-men, and are selected more for their muscular strength than for their knowledge of the culinary art, for the mixing of ragi flour in the preparation of puddings demands no skill, although it makes no slight demand on their strength.

A Black Brahman is a contradiction in terms, for it points to a mixture of Dravidian blood in his veins which ought to warrant his expulsion from the caste. There can be no doubt that at the present time the Brahman as a race in Southern India is far from being of fine descent owing to the fact that Sudras lived in concubinage with the Brahman, and also to the growing tendency of the lower caste to raise themselves one degree higher than their forbears in the social scale. Some non-Brahmans adopt the *Gotras* or tribal names of their Brahminical preceptors, and thus easily pass the line of demarcation. Others again, like the Sudras, who do not profess to have been descended from the Aryan Rishis, select certain animals or trees as totems, each being held sacred by a particular clan, and for the purpose of creating an excuse for social distinction without which there could be no pride of birth, marriage is prohibited in the same clan.

No wonder therefore if our boys, carried away by this whirlpool of social distinctions, begin to wear most formidable looking caste-marks and affix to their names the titles of a higher caste shortly after they leave the school. An Indian Christian of the Panchama class easily glides into the status of a Pillai and a criminal class boy becomes a Mudaliar or attaches himself to some sub-division of the Vellala. But to demonstrate how feebly the bonds of caste shackle a juvenile when material advantages are in prospect, a Brahman boy on admission represented that his father was a Brahman and that his mother was a Sudra when the fact was that both his parents belonged to the Brahman class. The apparent reason was that he was keeping in view the flesh pots of the school, and when his parents discovered what he had done they were surprised and advised the boy to stick to his caste, but the other Brahman boys refused to allow him to join their mess till he went through the ceremony of purification which was never performed.

When an old boy visits the school he is the hero of the hour. Caste marks are scrupulously applied to his forehead and these attract attention. He arms himself with an umbrella—always a sign of respectability—and wears bangles or a pair of ear-rings or some other form of ornament. The Panchama boy, especially if he has been trained in the Band, gets easily converted to the Roman Catholic faith, though ignorant of its tenets, to masquerade and is very gratified at the dignity of bearing the name of a Saint. Next in order comes the Indian Christian of the Panchama class who adds a Pillai or Mudaliar to his name, thus creating an anomaly in a Christian community where all are supposed to be equal. These so-called caste Christians are so jealous of their social standing that they insist upon first ministrations by the Priest, otherwise there is a row in the church, and, strange to say, the system is tolerated by priests even to the extent of having separate entrances to the church, and separate burial grounds for caste Christians.

The Vanians, the Pallis and Vellalas next in social scale, with their numerous sub-divisions, offer a wide field for the transfer of their inherited status to one on a higher plane. Juvenal states that it is a thin partition that separates us all from death, four fingers' breadth or seven if the plank be wide, and similarly it is a narrow line that divides one caste from another. Is it therefore any matter for surprise if members of a lower stratum yield to a temptation fraught with such little or no risk of detection? The Oddas of the North call themselves Telegas and the Koravas of the South, Mudaliars; thus the higher castes gradually swell in numbers. The name also of the individual is changed into one appropriate to the caste. The termination *gadu* in a name indicates inferiority of class and therefore Venkatigadu becomes Venkatasan Naidu. In this way the change becomes complete in a very quiet and effective manner. If, in higher circles of Western life, there is the tendency to try and get into a higher social grade, one cannot blame our school boys for possessing the common instincts of humanity which in the struggle of life secure the most favourable conditions for one's welfare and happiness.

The evolution of man proceeds apace at all times in all climes and in every direction—physical, intellectual and spiritual, and the levelling-up process is not to be decried if it gives an individual a chance to fight the battle of life more successfully. Is it any wonder therefore that our boys who are branded in the eyes of most of their fellow countrymen with the taint of having passed through a Reformatory, and are handicapped in a peculiar way in the race of life, should look to caste-marks to come to their assistance to make good in overcoming the obstacles that lie in their course. With everybody's hand against him from the employers to the policeman, he seeks refuge in a circle of respectability that would ensure his safety from at least some degree of molestation. The remarks apply particularly to a class of boys who have the ambition to get on in the world. As outcastes, they realize the uphill work of obtaining a respectable position, and therefore it is pardonable for them to add to their names a term that connotes in the eyes of their fellow creatures, a higher plane of social existence.

The lad who becomes a Weaving Instructor or Carpenter Maistry or Gymnastic Instructor or teacher, controls others under him and it is so easy to cast up to one's face one's former antecedents and thus to lower one in the eyes of the world. It is a blessing that a door is left open for those who wish to move in a higher circle in order to keep clear of the prejudices that cling to one, and drag him down for a whole life time. Caste is only after all a convention and, except in the very highest, when it is a very real and exclusive thing to be opened only by a golden key. It carries with it no monopoly of brain or pride of birth and caste does good in recognising the desire for a levelling up, if a lad chooses to force himself into a position that injures nobody and is, on the other hand, advantageous to himself. It is a question of choice to be backed up by appearances, and therefore if we do not directly encourage our boys to assume higher dignity in the classification of human beings, we at all events, appreciate the motive that leads to their adoption of higher caste marks and names.

It is different in the case of a Hindu who assumes a manner of living that is an offence to his neighbours. It is reported in the North of India that a Hindu of the sweeper caste once set up a bazaar in the role of a Bania and that caste people patronized him in the purchase of such stuff as ghee, dal, oil and condiments, till one day it transpired that an old friend or relative of his recognised him in the bazaar and exclaimed " Ah, my brother, where have you been this long time "; then when the heart had been tapped there flowed out affectionately words having a common interest to them both to the surprise and disgust of those customers who were present at the scene. Needless to say that the untouchable sweeper Bania was mauled and illtreated for presuming to sell eatables to caste people. No motive of offence however can be laid to the charge of our boys. They simply compensate themselves for the stigma that wrongly attaches to the epithet " Reformatory " by the equipment of a higher caste mark in order to get square with an unsympathetic and caste-ridden world.

CHAPTER XXIII

CONDUCT AND OCCUPATION OF PAST PUPILS

THE number of pupils favourably reported on works out on an average from 65 to 75 per cent., the pupils not reported on, who have emigrated or could not be traced, a good proportion of whom no doubt are doing well, being excluded. The percentage of good reports compares favourably with the average percentage of good reports in the Reformatories in Great Britain and Ireland. Among the boys who cannot be traced, a large number belong to the Dasiri, Korava, Villi, and Yenadi castes. These are wandering gangs, and at present reformatory training seems to be useless in their case, notwithstanding the efforts made by the school to start them in life with some kind of work. As regards well-behaved pupils, who benefit by the training given them in the school, some of them obtain employment as school-masters, gymnastic instructors (one Inspector of Schools remarked that the best gymnastic instructor he came across was an ex-pupil of this school), peons, and process-servers.

A large number enlisted in the Army, and as buglers in the police, jail and salt departments. Several are maistries or foremen and among a few may be counted a railway sub-inspector, a field surveyor, a village munsiff, and some clerks. The rest are generally labourers in the trades taught them or in trades akin to them.

A propos of the Reddi caste, of one boy who was trained as a carpenter, the Magistrate wrote that he would do better as a teacher than a candidate from the plains, many of whom do harm to education (in the proper sense) by inculcating notions of caste pretensions, pollution, and other unhealthy ideas from which the Koyas and Reddis are still to a large extent exempt. The subsequent record of the boy relates that he leads the semi-savage life of his kinsmen, the hill Reddis, and that "hunting and kadu-cultivation" are his occupation. The Magistrate adds that, as he was sent to the Reformatory School for having killed another boy, a crime which does not imply vicious surroundings or bad associates, there is little likelihood of his falling into a life of crime.

The instructors in some of the important weaving schools of the Presidency are ex-pupils of this institution. One boy actually tried to patent a loom which would weave, shape and put together pieces of garments, thus doing away with tailors! A few of our boys are reported on (by the lower Revenue officials) as earning their livelihood by begging, and in the same sentence their conduct is reported to be satisfactory, which is rather a contradiction in terms from an English point of view.

Some pupils of the artizan class go wrong because they cannot understand starting on low wages and sticking to their work till they rise. They go from pillar to post and do not settle down to any regular work. I give below statistics to show the percentages of boys who follow agriculture and other trades, as well as those who are well-behaved and earn a livelihood in other ways. The figures are comparative, and relate to the seven reformatories in India and Burma.

In the first column, the percentage of well-behaved boys is given. In the second column, the percentage of pupils who follow agriculture of those taught that industry in the school, and in the third column, the percentage of those who follow other trades taught them at the school are given.

Statistics relating to after-conduct of released boys for the three years previous to 1908.

Yeravda Reformatory	65.2	29.3	17.8
Insein do.	52.2	9.6	14.8
Jubbulpore do.	61.0	27.2	32.3

Chunar Reformatory . .	54.06	42.3	20.1
Alipore do. . .	64.6	52.9	19.4
Chingleput do. . .	65.5	....	19.1
Hazaribagh do. . .	70.8	60.3	21.9

It will be seen from this table that the percentage of well-behaved boys is higher in the Hazaribagh Reformatory than in the other reformatories, and taking all things equal, the cause is probably due to the fact that it is essentially an agricultural school, and that boys after their discharge are less likely to fall into temptation as agricultural coolies than as artizans. The industrial population is more or less located in towns where the conditions are not favourable. From statistics covering over twenty years, it has been noted that 75 per cent. of the boys who relapse belong to large towns.

Mr W. S. Hadaway, Principal of the School of Arts, sends some interesting notes in reference to a short article that appeared in the *Madras Times*:—

So far as the training given in jails goes towards helping the discharged inmate to practise a trade afterwards, I cannot say, but I should think that a great reason for its general failure, *if* such is the case, was because of too short a period of training, or of material too stiff to mould. Our poor benighted Presidency can, however, boast of a reformatory school the inmates of which practise the trade taught to them, on their release, to a very remarkable degree. I can speak from actual experience of six or seven carpenters and one metal worker, out of whom only one has "reverted." One of the carpenters, who proved himself a very able and energetic workman, first got a good position after a short time here, as a teacher of carpentry in a school in the mofussil; he stopped there but a short time and soon bettered himself with a similar position, which he still holds, in Madras. Of another lot of two woodworkers, one was a restless spirit, somewhat easily influenced, and he gave up the strenuous work of a sawyer, though he has not reverted to any evil ways. The other is as steady and straightforward a lad as one could wish to see, good and trustworthy at his work. A fourth old boy from the same school, after working here for a few years has joined an artificers' corps and is now working well as a carpenter in Mesopotamia. Another boy is doing excellent work here as a carpenter, and still another as a metal worker. It is, I think, a fairly severe test for lads out of a reformatory school to come to work in a city the size of Madras, and in a school in which there are many holidays when they are left entirely to themselves. There is a very real *esprit de corps* among these boys, and one fresh from the school can nearly always find an old boy of the same trade who will look after him temporarily. As to any spirit of humiliation concerned with the place where they learned their trade, the contrary is noticeable; and so far as it would affect them among others of the same trade, I have enough faith in the artizan community to believe that such a consideration is beneath them—at any rate, beneath the notice of real men of skill. It is only of my own experience, and that a mild one, that I can speak with certainty, but I think I am right in saying that about forty per cent. of the old boys of the Chingleput Reformatory benefit by the training they receive there, permanently.

The Editor on this remarks: "It is a matter of much satisfaction that the Reformatory School at Chingleput is a particularly well-managed institution, which is a credit not only to the management, but also to the Presidency. Mr Hadaway's figures are a striking evidence of this, in face of the official report from Bombay that out of 139 lads discharged from the Yarowda Reformatory School only eight are employed in the trades learned in the institution."

The "after care" of boys discharged from a reformatory is a matter of no less importance than the manner of their training during detention in the school. Much of the good work done by a period spent in a school of detention is often rendered nugatory by the lack of proper supervision over a lad soon after his discharge. It is all very well bringing up a lad under proper discipline, equipping him with bodily health and a trade in hand, but all the good is undone if he leaves the school to find himself again in evil surroundings only too familiar to him before his advent. He must therefore be protected by some strong and friendly hand till he begins to adapt himself to an ordered state of society.

Reformatory treatment is only the beginning of the work which has to be continued for some time after a boy has passed through the outer world if the best results are to be obtained. It is too much to expect of a boy who is accustomed to be looked after and to have everything done for him, and who is hedged in by rules and regulations for years, to keep straight when he is suddenly thrown into the world with no guiding hand or discipline of any kind. It is difficult for a youngster who is more or less negatively good to suddenly develop positive virtues without friendly supervision for a year or two after discharge. But no organised effort exists for this purpose. As there are only a few reformatory schools, each school follows its own method of keeping in touch with the boys.

In one province, two Deputy Inspectors of Schools are set apart as whole-time officers to trace and report on the conduct of boys. They remain at headquarters for ten days in the month—a period far too short to forge any link between them and the inmates, so that when these leave the school the personal influence of the Deputy Inspector cannot be of any account. A better plan would be to send out a couple of the regular teachers, who have gained the respect of the pupils, to do the work of looking after the boys. Every year fresh masters should be deputed in turn after the pupils have become known to them before they leave the school. In another province, the Deputy Inspectors of Schools, in addition to their own duties in supervising ordinary schools, are expected to send a half-yearly report on the conduct and occupation of reformatory boys discharged in their respective districts. This means that the village schoolmaster has ultimately to look after the work.

The circumstances of English and Indian boys, it must

be remarked, are as wide as the poles. In England, voluntary effort plays a great part in human work on behalf of children in tracing them after they have passed through an institution. In the case of the Borstal Institution, for boys between 16 and 22, an association exists to look after discharged pupils. In every large town throughout the country there is a small committee composed of not necessarily a clergyman or a professional philanthropist, but of workers taken from all classes, some of them even in firms and shops. These people provide for the future of the released youth by providing him with clothes, securing him employment, arranging for his place of abode, and placing him under the kindly supervision of a local representative of the association. Every youth on his release remains for a period, varying according to his conduct, under the control of those who undertake his "after care," during which time he must satisfy the association that he is doing his best to live honestly, that he is not keeping bad company, and that he keeps steady at work. Should he fail in any of these particulars, he may be arrested and sent back to Borstal or to an ordinary prison. The agents of the association have access to the young fellows while they are under detention, and any provision they make is with the approval of the youth and with the concurrence of the Borstal association.

In India it is impossible to hope much in the direction of extensive philanthropic charitable work to help released youths, the only body inclined to do the work at present being the Salvation Army; not that charity does not exist in this country; nay, it abounds everywhere, but it takes such curious forms that it needs education to direct it into new channels.

The caste system militates to some extent against organised effort, and under existing circumstances the best plan seems to be to continue to discharge a boy before a Magistrate, asking him to exercise a friendly supervision over him, or, if a voluntary association exists in the place, to hand him over to the local representative, who should enlist the sympathy of the Magistrate or the influential men of the district to help the boy to find employment, while all future inquiries relating to him should be made through educational officers. If a voluntary association is composed of business men, or men with some influence, to whom a boy may be handed over, well and good, otherwise nothing practical will be done by men who join a body with no real love for social service. In certain cases where the home surroundings are bad, the Superintendent should have power to send a boy direct to an employer fitted to take charge of him—the term employer covering the profession of the Army, so eminently suited for our lads. In this way it would be impossible to lose sight of any lad or deny him the help he requires in making a start in life.

The following points in the English system are noteworthy :—

1. Superintendents keep up correspondence with old boys. This is encouraged as much as possible. Letters show that there is a positive affection existing between Superintendents and boys. The Chief Superintendent writes: "The letters which I have had the privilege of reading speak volumes for silent, unnoticed and devoted work done in the schools."

2. In the Somerset Industrial School the C.E. Men's Society, Bath, have made themselves responsible for the after care of the boys. Twenty-three are under supervision. A member looks after a boy or two.

3. In London the Charity Organisation Society and the Children's Aid Society render the required help.

4. The St Vincent De Paul Society look after R.C. boys, and splendid work is done by them for the St Joseph's Industrial School, Manchester.

5. The object of all societies is to find a real friend for each boy in the locality where he is placed.

6. Where the Superintendent has a personal knowledge of home surroundings, a boy is allowed to go home before his time.

Following on these lines an effort should be made in India to enlist the services of one of the noted bodies.

(*a*) Non-official members of the District Board.
(*b*) Do. do. Municipalities.
(*c*) Do. do. Unions.
(*d*) Prominent official members who have earned a name for their marked sympathy and local influence would be willing to unofficially help.
(*e*) The Salvation Army.
(*f*) The particular Mission Society working in the locality.
(*g*) Ladies who have done similar work before, *e.g.*, Miss Reed of Cuddalore and Mrs Taylor of Salem. Each district may have its Reed or Taylor.

CHAPTER XXIV

JUVENILE CRIMINALS

A HISTORY of some noteworthy examples of juvenile criminals may have some interest.

SWAMINATHAN was a Roman Catholic Indian Christian of doubtful parentage. He was a Brahman by birth, sold as an orphan by his mother to a reverend Father, when he became a Christian. At 8 years of age he seems to have developed a disposition to wander and steal. He seems to be devoid of all sense of morality, but curiously enough he is at times pious. He is very artful in his ways, and knows how to ingratiate himself into the good graces of those with whom he is thrown. He is very obliging by nature, but his tendency to steal is ineradicable. He is a boy of poor physique, but intelligent. His school offences are (1) disobeying the Sergeant; (2) stealing a piece of cloth; (3) entering a garden and cutting flowers. I am tempted to refer to a little incident connected with this lad. The Superintendent of the Museum at Madras was once kind enough to send a few pigeons as pets for the boys. Swaminathan, who knew English best, was asked to write and thank him for his kindness. The second sentence of his letter was: "We pray God He will make you more honest." The letter of course was not sent, but Mr Thurston, I think, would have enjoyed its contents most.

Boys sent for counterfeiting coin come from the Bijapur District in the Bombay Presidency. These chapper bands leave their homes after the rains, about September or October, to practice their calling. Laying aside their ordinary Muhammadan dress, they assume the dress and appearance of fakirs, and unaccompanied by their women, wander from village to village, begging as they travel, women and simple country folk being their victims. This is the way they palm off their counterfeit coins. The false coins are kept in pockets in their waist cloths or *langotis*. They offer copper for a silver piece, and this, by sleight of hand, they change for a counterfeit silver coin which they return as bad, thus getting back their copper coins.

Their stock-in-trade consists of earth for making moulds, stone for polishing coined rupees, filings of pewter or lead, a file for milling, tongs and pincers, gum for joining the halves of the moulds, a melting ladle, and a die for making false rupees. The father of one of the boys sent here was discovered with an intestinal cavity for a storage capacity of 100 rupees. I believe the cavity is formed and gradually enlarged by means of pebbles placed in the lower bowel, the pebbles gradually being increased in size. This fact was discovered by the man sitting uncomfortably.

KRISHNAIYAR was a Brahman of Tinnevelly. He was guilty of a series of thefts of three watches and three time-pieces. He entered a house for alms, and when the occupant went inside to fetch him something he disappeared with a watch or time-piece lying on the table. The boy is intelligent and gave an intelligent story of his chequered career in Ceylon, where he had been sold to a coffee planter. That gentleman took pity on him and sent him back to India.

SHAIK DADA, a Muhammadan by birth, with Mongolian type of features, aged 9, both parents alive: convicted of theft by an old offender. His record in the school is a bad one. He was licensed out to a firm of tailors, and within a month he was sent back for having stolen a 10-rupee note from the pocket of the proprietor. A few months after, he was caught stealing two pieces of new cloth. He is able to assume the most innocent exterior when suspected of wrong-doing. Flat-footed, repulsive in features and in gait, he has contaminated several boys by his indecent acts and thieving propensities. Such a boy is incapable of reformation. He even tried to bring the maistry into trouble by removing the shuttle of a sewing-machine and throwing it over the boundary wall.

JUVENILE MURDERERS

All persons who have had anything to do with criminology may be roughly classed under two heads. The one group holds the criminal responsible, the other not. This divergence of opinion was brought out clearly in a recent trial. The case of a juvenile murderer came before Mr Justice Piggott and Mr Justice Walsh at the Allahabad High Court. A boy of fourteen, convicted of the murder of a girl of seven for the sake of her ornaments, appealed against the sentence of transportation for life passed upon him by the Sessions Judge. Mr Justice Piggott was for confirmation of the sentence, as he considered that the alternative order for detention in a reformatory school would be an unduly lenient one, inasmuch as such detention would come to a close with the accused attaining the age of seventeen, or less than four years from the date of his conviction. Mr Justice Walsh refused to confirm the sentence, and considered that the boy should be sent to a reformatory school, if the system of reformatory schools in this country was worthy of public confidence at all. He said that detention in such an institution for three or four years ought to be a sufficient preventive of any future recurrence of that kind of crime on the part of the accused. As the Judges differed, the case was referred to a third Judge, who agreed with the latter. The difference of opinion held by two such eminent Judges, simply stated, amounted to this. While the one held that the accused was a fully responsible agent and deserving of punishment suitable to the crime, the other considered him to be morally deficient, incapable of distinguishing the gravity of the offence, and prescribed moral training as a cure for future bad conduct. The same division marks the opinion of all persons who have given the subject a thought. Metaphysicians have gone deeply into the principles regulating human conduct, but as my object is to help the practical people who have to decide whether a youthful offender is or is not a fit subject for a reformatory, and those who have the care of their training in such institutions, the examination of a few leading cases, with the principles involved, may prove of profit, while not without interest to the general reader.

JUVENILE MURDERERS

CASE No. 1.—Juvenile murderers may be divided into three classes. Those who commit the crime for robbery; secondly, those who do it in a spirit of revenge; and the third class is the criminal imbecile who suffers from a "kink" in the brain. A period in the reformatory for the first class will, doubtless, do good, but the lad aged about 15 who murders in a spirit of revenge should certainly be transported, and the place for the third set of boys ought to be in a school for the mentally deficient where the children are treated in the open air and on the lines of the Montessori system. A Nair boy between 14 and 15 took it into his head to murder another about a year younger than himself with whom he was on freindly terms, in the following peculiar circumstances. The mother of the boy was separated from her husband and was to a small extent maintained by the leading members of the family. There had been disputes between the boy and the man as to the cultivation of a paddy field belonging to the latter.

One Sunday just after dawn the Nair boy and the deceased went off to plough the paddy field, the former calling for the deceased. A tenant and two young serfs of the owner, under orders given to them the previous evening, followed shortly afterwards to help to plough the field. They found the accused ploughing one plot and the deceased sitting on a ridge watching him, but when they started to plough the boy asked them to desist. They refused, as they had orders to plough the field. At this the Nair boy said: "If so, do you plough; I am leaving," and, having unyoked his bulls, he led them off the field, followed by the deceased. He made straight for his house and brought a knife about 20 ins. long and 2 ins. wide. The boys told the mother of the deceased that they were going to bathe the bullocks, but they returned to the field. Near the ridge the aggressor asked his companion to pick up a bark rope that lay there, and when he stooped to pick up the rope he struck him on the back of the neck which killed him on the spot, and then went on hacking at him for a short time. The accused then ran away, wandered about for several days, and at last, while begging for food from a stranger, he told him who he was and that he wished to give himself up as he had killed a boy. When he appeared before the Sub-Magistrate he gave a full account of what had happened up to the time of his ploughing the field, and how he had run off from home because two or three persons and his own grandmother had at various times and various places said he had killed the boy.

The Judge was of opinion that the motive for the crime seemed to be that the accused got tired of having nothing to live on and of not being allowed to cultivate even the field near his own home, and so he took the sudden resolution of killing the deceased in order to get the head of the family into trouble. The boy was found guilty of murder and sentenced to transportation for life, but being between 14 and 15 years of age the sentence was commuted to one of detention for five years in the reformatory.

Now the question arises, was he responsible for his act and did he know that he was doing wrong? As far as the deceased was concerned, he had done nothing to cause resentment in the mind of the murderer; in fact, he was his friend and neighbour, although of a lower caste, and on the morning when the deed was committed the young criminal called for his neighbour and took him along with him. Why, then, did the boy kill him in such a brutal manner? His confession, after two years of stay in the school, was that the deceased was asked by the three others who began to plough the land in opposition, to cut the nose-string of the bullocks attached to his plough. The deceased did it, and the Nair resented a lower caste boy presuming to offend him in this way at the instigation of the others, and, therefore, went for him.

This confession was made with more than one outbreak of smiles and with no apparent sign of regret or sorrow for his past act. The fact that he admitted the murder, when really there was no satisfactory motive, was sufficient evidence that the boy was not normal. When he left his house in the morning he had no more thought of killing the boy than of running away from home, and as soon as he committed the deed he made himself scarce, for there was the instinct of fear lest he should be captured by the police. Then again he did not feel at ease till he confessed to a man from whom he begged food that he ran away from home and that he wished to give himself up as it was said that he had committed the murder. Not only was there no reasonable motive, but the brutality of the deed convinces one that the boy was an imbecile, for having struck his companion and severed his spinal cord, which resulted in instant death, he kept hacking at him, inflicting numerous wounds.

The Judge believed that the motive might be discovered in the condition of the lad as he got tired of having nothing to live on, but, as a matter of fact, he had at the time sufficient, and there is no evidence that he was starving. His father, it was true, was not living with his mother, but he was always ready to help the boy, and the garden attached to the house was certainly a means of livelihood to fall back upon. There is no doubt that he resented being told that he was not to plough the field, but the wrong for which he claimed to have desired revenge was not committed by the boy he murdered. There was no motive, and the act was done on a sudden impulse while he was in a morose, depressed, unsettled mood. He had a heavy knife in his hand and his friend's neck was in a very tantalising position. The suggestion came to him to slash and kill and he could not resist it. The youth, therefore, must be regarded as mentally unbalanced. Later medical evidence confirmed this, for he had a very strange formation of the bony framework of the chest.

His expression was peculiar and the shape of his head abnormal, and there was lack of symmetry, the right cheek being fuller than the left, and the right ear, in addition to being peculiar in shape, was much larger than the left. The Medical Officer was of opinion that he was to be regarded as dangerous and should be sent to a lunatic asylum for life. On this report the boy was sent to the asylum, but was returned after a year as he had been continuously free from insanity. The first day after his return the boy felt the contrast of the treatment in the reformatory and the asylum, and he in a very crude manner pretended to be mad by mounting to the top of a tree and refusing to come down.

After being threatened he descended with fear and trembling, and a few sharp cuts brought him to his senses. Is the reformatory, one may well ask, a suitable place for such a lad? The surroundings there certainly afforded the minimum chance of his exercising any homicidal tendencies, but it was doubtful whether the boy's mentality could be depended on to lead one to hope that he would not commit a similar crime again? Our ignorance in regard to this type of feeblemindedness is so great that we are apt to take a wrong view of the case, but experts are now beginning to make clear important points which are often misunderstood and which will inevitably result in a change in criminal procedure.

CASE No. 2.—A District Magistrate hesitated to send to the school a lad of 15 years who was concerned in a murder case; for, though the prisoner took no active part in the crime, and was present under the advice and support of an older person, the crime in which he was concerned was a particularly horrible deed. An old woman of 60 was done to death at night. There was evidence to show that a previous attempt to secure poison for her death was made. A month before the crime this prisoner went to one of the prosecuting witnesses, with the first accused in the case, who was the person most deeply interested in the death of the woman, and attempted to buy aconite. The Magistrate doubted if such a youth was a proper person to be an inmate of a reformatory school, and he therefore declined to make a direction under Sec. 10 of Act, 1897, for his detention in the reformatory school.

The Magistrate was probably right in his conclusion. There was no overt act, no criminal tendency was established, but only moral weakness at most.

CASE No. 3.—A typical case is that of a child of 11 who unable to resist a sudden temptation, commits murder with intent to rob. The father, accompanied by his son, went to a neighbouring village to transact business. The little boy was left alone in the village for a while when the father was busy, and having met a child of 4 or 5 wearing gold ear-rings, the temptation came to him to become possessor of the ornaments. With a knife he cut off the lobes of both ears, causing the child to scream out. The noise attracted a passer-by, who saw the accused in a pit covering up the child with earth, while it was practically unconscious and breathing hard.

The boy admitted the deed, and in school confessed to having done it because he wanted money for the purpose of gambling, a habit contracted with the full knowledge of his mother, who at times even encouraged him with pice, knowing what it was intended for.

CASE No. 4.—This illustrates the little value placed on human life by some classes. A boy aged 13 years committed murder because he wanted money to buy sweets. He and his companion, aged 8, went to school and left to return as usual for their mid-day meal. When they arrived near a well the accused, according to his own statement, pushed the boy into it, and when the little fellow swam to the steps, he got down, held his head and cut his throat, and removed his ear-rings. There was no evidence of premeditation, only that the accused thought his offence was no worse than giving his companion a pinch.

CASE No. 5.—A youth of 12 was tried for murder in the Tanjore District. The evidence showed that the accused was plucking mangoes from a tree when the deceased came up to him and asked for some. The accused promised to give him fruit if deceased would give in return some "murukku," or rice cakes, which he had with him. The deceased agreed, took the mangoes, but gave him only half the "murukku." This the accused refused, and demanded the return of the mangoes. The deceased declined to take back the "murukku," which accused, a Valluva (superior class of Pariah) had touched, and tried to run off with the mangoes. Accused followed and tried to wrest them from him, but did not succeed. Thereupon the accused threw stones at him, one of which struck the latter on the forehead and knocked him senseless. The accused then dragged him to the pond and dropped him into it, in order that dogs or jackals might not tear the body and wayfarers might not notice it.

The accused himself says that he never dreamt of the fatal result. The fight was sudden and the accused was hit in a sensitive part of his body and felt excruciating pain. Evidently he lost his head and hit out blindly three times, as admitted by him, causing, doubtless, the fatal termination to the scuffle.

The case against the accused was for an offence under Section 334, I.P.C., for voluntarily causing hurt under grave and sudden provocation. The accused, moreover, admitted taking the money and cloths found on the person of the deceased after he had died, appropriating the same dishonestly, thus making himself further liable under Section 404, I.P.C.

He was found guilty and sentenced to undergo rigorous imprisonment (1) for one month for the offence under Section 334, I.P.C., and (2) for eleven months for the offence under Section 404, I.P.C., *i.e.*, in all one year's rigorous imprisonment.

CASE NO. 6.—KUPPU PANDARAM, a boy of 11, with another aged 14, were committed for the murder of another 10 years old, by pressing his head under water, and misappropriating the jewellery on him, consisting of bracelets, ear-rings and a wrist cord. They did it for the purpose of obtaining money for gambling and drink. This is a case of progressive crime from the lack of home influence and healthy surroundings.

CASE NO. 7.—PORUSU DOMB, aged 13, killed a little girl by striking her on the head with an axe, theft being the motive, as he wanted money to buy something extra to eat as he was not fed sufficiently by his parents. Murder was a superfluity; theft would have sufficed. The boy's mental calibre could not have made any advance since the time of his aboriginal ancestry.

CASE NO. 8.—JANGAM DODDAYYA, of Bellary, murdered a small boy aged 6, the son of a Reddy, by strangling him with a wrist cord. He said that he had killed the boy for his jewels (some silver beads and three gold ear-rings). The accused at the preliminary inquiry before the Sub-Magistrate said: "It is true I killed: God put it into my head." The gist of his later confession was that he enticed the boy away on the pretext that he would get him some margosa fruit, and then stripped him of his jewels. Siva Reddy cried, abused him, and said he would tell his parents. The accused thereupon pulled the child down, took off his wrist cord and tied it tightly round his neck. Siva Reddy stood up for a moment and then fell down. The accused covered the child's head with mud, absconded with the jewels in his pocket and secreted them. The District Surgeon certified that the accused was quite normal in intelligence but in very poor health physically. He was anæmic and suffering from some disease of the knee joints, but his physical state was apparently not sufficiently bad to have affected him mentally. His primary intention was not murder but theft, and the murder was a result of a sudden impulse arising from the fear of detection.

CASE NO. 9.—The trial of KANDASWAMI CHETTY, a juvenile murderer, was one of those cases which should never have been dealt with under the Reformatory Act. His father married two sisters, but loved the younger more than the elder. Kandaswami, the son of the elder woman, resented his father's treatment of his mother, and whether it was at her instigation or not, with a heavy stone he crushed the head of the child of the younger sister while it was asleep. Kandaswami was a well-developed lad and was certainly not under 15. The result of his base deed was three years' detention in the Reformatory. The period of detention in all ordinary cases is here, on the average, for five years, but Kandaswami, who in a spirit of revenge killed his half brother, is sent, under the existing rules, for only three years. The letter of the law was enforced, but the spirit of the Act was evaded. The boy himself felt that if this were all, he was too lightly dealt with, for when he was told that he had to remain in the school for three years, he asked the question: "And what becomes of me afterwards?" meaning thereby to inquire whether transportation to the Andamans was in store for him afterwards. The boy certainly behaved well during his stay in the school —in fact the juvenile murderer is as a rule well behaved— and will probably continue to behave well in after life.

But will the treatment meted out to him prove a sufficient deterrent in regard to himself or to others. It cannot be said that the boy did not know what he was doing, although he was blinded at the moment when anger was aroused in him. He was of a sufficient age to understand that he would get into trouble for his act, and he himself was surprised to find he did not get his deserts when, instead of transportation, he received in lieu of it three years in a reformatory. The law, therefore, was not vindicated in his case, and justice remained unsatisfied. This was clearly a case in which the sentence should have been retributive rather than reformative.

Case No. 10.—Sivaramayya, a Brahman boy, aged about 12½ years, is an instance of a minor committing murder at the instigation of an adult brother for the sake of property. The boy was adopted by the deceased Ramayya's brother, Subbiah, who died four or five months before Ramayya was poisoned. The brother of Sivaramayya, being a disreputable character, was not allowed to enter the house of Ramayya. He therefore plotted his death in order that his younger brother might become the sole owner of the property, knowing that then he would step in to look after the lands during the minority of his brother. For this purpose some aconite was supplied to his brother, who put it into the evening meal which was cooked and served by him to Ramayya that day, there being no one else in the house. When Ramayya began to suffer from the effects of the poison, he suspected at once that Sivaramayya had poisoned him at the instigation of his brother, and made mention of his suspicions to the village Kurnam and others who came to see him.

Meantime Sivaramayya, apparently to divert suspicion, pretended that he himself had been bitten by a snake, and actually induced the Kurnam to fetch a snake-charmer, who however, found no trace of any snake bite on him. Sivaramayya was coaxed to state the kind of substance he had mixed in the food as it would help them to save Ramayya by prescribing the proper antidotes. This was before the police arrived. Before the Committing Magistrate the accused denied he had made any confession, but the High Court found no reason to doubt his guilt. He was only about 12 years of age, but his conduct in pretending that he was bitten by a snake indicated a guilty knowledge on his part, and instead of transportation for life he was sent to the school. The boy never admitted the murder, but charged a nephew of the deceased with having administered the poison, as he resented the loss of the property which, but for the adoption, would have come into his possession. No attempt was made to support this accusation by evidence, and it was dismissed as having no foundation. The boy by his behaviour in the school, gained the respect of his fellows to such an extent that they voted him the good conduct medal. This was rather due to the fact that, being a Brahmin, he was astute enough to keep up appearances, and was ashamed to admit the dastardly deed. He had ingratiating manners, which would account for his adoption, but at the same time there were indications in his character which made one feel that he was not altogether trustworthy. There was no fear, however, that his future would ever be marred by a similar act, for his training in the reformatory must have opened his eyes to the heinousness of his offence.

Case. No. 11.—Palaniandi Kudumban was charged with stabbing in the back his mother's maternal uncle, Kaluvan, under the following circumstances. Kaluvan asked the accused's uncle why his nephew had beaten his boy. Abuse followed, and the principals caught hold of each other's top-knots. In the course of the disturbance the accused ran to his house, which was close at hand, and returned with the knife with which he stabbed Kaluvan in the back while he was stooping in the struggle. The only trivial justification for the accused's act was that there was a quarrel some two days before the murder happened between Palaniandi and the boy of the deceased, and Palaniandi was beaten by Kaluvan. He seemed to have then made up his mind to have his revenge, and when the scuffle between Kaluvan and the accused's uncle took place, the boy saw his chance, ran to the house, fetched the weapon and deliberately used it with vicious determination to cause death.

He belonged to the criminal tribe of Pallars, and his act was perhaps a recrudescence of the blood-feud feeling of the past which suddenly made its appearance in the boy.

CASE NO. 12.—KARUPPAN. This boy was sent here at the age of 12, charged with the murder of a little girl 2½ years of age, for the sake of her ornaments, worth from two to four rupees. His statement proved that he was aware that his action was a punishable offence, for he appears to have decoyed the girl to the vicinity of a well, where he deprived her of her paltry jewels and then pushed her in. He hid the jewels in a prickly pear bush and then, presumably to avoid being questioned, he went off to his aunt's garden which was some little distance away. He is a Vellala by caste, of the Coimbatore district, and a shepherd by occupation. His school offences were—:(1) Striking his class monitor; (2) entering the kitchen and stealing boiled dal; (3) disrespect to the Jemadar. He was rather a quick-tempered boy.

CASE NO. 13.—YEDLA DALIGADU, a Kapu of Chicacole. His first conviction was at the age of 11. Three boys went out together to cut grass and to play. As one of them had not returned for his midday meal, the father went to look for him, and found he was unable to speak, being badly cut about the neck and lower part of the skull. Two gold ear-rings which he had been wearing were gone. The other two were pointed out by the injured child as having cut him with a hoe. Trephining had to be resorted to, but he died the same evening. The accused admitted having taken the ear-rings and beaten the boy with a hoe and spade, because he said he would tell his father. There were six gaping, incised wounds on the back of the child's head. In spite of their youth, both the accused (the name of the other being Latchigadu, aged 12) are precocious urchins, so says the Court, and were perfectly self-possessed, answering questions with the utmost readiness. Whatever the immediate cause of the quarrel may have been, it was clear that they meant to cause the child such severe bodily injury as was very likely to cause his death, and the only difference in their favour on account of their youth was in

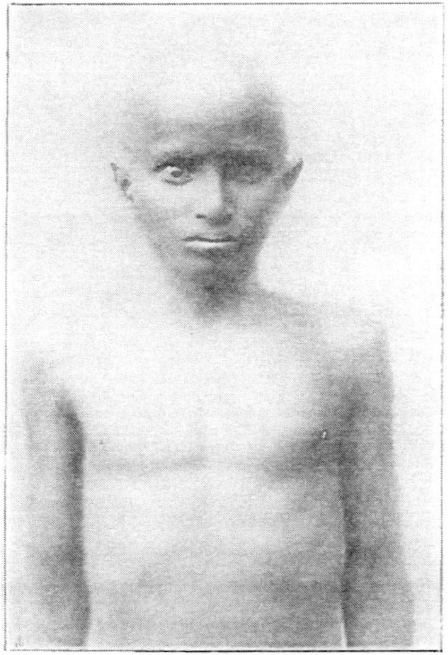

A Juvenile Convicted of Murder

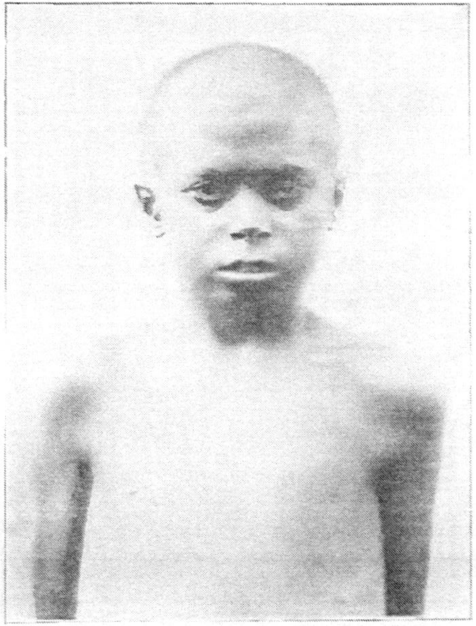

A Juvenile who Killed his own Nephew

He has the face of a sloth (page 393)

the Judge not inferring (as in the case of an adult) that they *knew* that they were likely to cause his death.

CASE No. 14.—SELLAPPEN, a Goundan, aged 14 years, has a mother living. He was charged with having killed his own nephew, a child of three. Both the assessors found the accused not guilty. They believed that the accused threw a stone at a blood-sucker and that the stone accidentally hit the deceased. The evidence of a prosecution witness showed that the accused was the only person present when the deceased was murdered. The story of the blood-sucker would not explain the three injuries on the deceased. Nor would it explain the disappearance of the silver waist-cord. The Judge did not consider it proved that the accused intended to kill the deceased. It would not have been necessary to do so to steal the waist-cord. All he intended to do probably was to stun the child, and frighten it so much that it would not dare complain. The accused must, however, have known that he was likely to cause the death of the child when he struck him hard blows with a stone or other blunt instrument.

CASE No. 15.—MANICKAM PILLAI, a Vellala, aged 13, with parents living: he looked after goats. He was convicted of murder. Accused admitted that he went with the deceased to catch young parrots, and that eventually they went to a spot where they bathed, after deceased had removed his waist-cord. He said that they tried who could stay longest under water; that deceased held him under whilst he counted 30; that he then held deceased under till he counted 15; that bubbles then came up; that he lifted deceased, found that he was dead, left him there, and ran away. The assessors found accused guilty of murder, and with their finding the Judge concurred. "It is impossible," he added, "to believe the whole story told by accused. There probably is some truth in it, but that a little boy of five would take off his waist-cord before entering water about two feet deep cannot be believed. The dead boy was about three feet in height, according to the civil apothecary, so that he could not have been drowned in two feet of water unless he had been held down. It appeared that what happened was this. When accused and deceased got to the pond, accused, finding that they were alone, decided to rob deceased. So he suggested that they should see who could remain longest under water. He ducked first. When deceased ducked, he held him down until he was drowned. He then removed his waist-cord and ear-ornaments, which could be easily removed, went and hid them, and then coolly went off to play. He is evidently a hardened young ruffian. The civil apothecary thinks he is about 12, but it is clear that he has attained sufficient maturity of understanding to know that he was doing wrong and what the consequence of his conduct would be." He was found guilty of murder, but, in the cirumstances, sentenced to transportation for life, in lieu of which he was sent for five years to the reformatory. In school, he was a kleptomaniac and stole a towel, a knife, and a bunch of keys belonging to the maistry, on different occasions. He was also strongly suspected of using a false key to a master's table drawer.

Since the school was founded in 1888 there have been 19 admissions of pupils who committed murder, and 12 of those who committed culpable homicide not amounting to murder. Ganjam and Coimbatore have contributed 4 each to this list; Vizagapatam, 3; and Bellary, North Arcot and Madura, 2 each; every caste being represented, from the Brahman to the Domb, with ages ranging from 15 to 11 years.

CHAPTER XXV

THE CRIMINAL CLASSES

In Southern India there are no criminal classes of the "Jack Shepherd" type, and the so-called criminal classes are of the wandering type who formerly carried on trade but who, with the advent of railways, lost their job and took to thieving. The chief criminal classes admitted to the school are briefly referred to below.

The desire for other men's goods is a weakness of human nature, and to wander over the face of the earth is "a life that all would like to lead." These two characteristics reign supreme in the Gipsy, who having no home of his own, finds one somewhere near the forest in a temporary hut or in the outskirts of a town. The Indian Gipsy, or Korava, has all the "idiosyncracies" of his fraternity in other parts of the globe, but the juvenile members of the branch are interesting from a psychological point of view and well worth a study. They are quiet and timid, pleasant in features and possess intelligent looks. They will never rob, but steal. Even now they ostensibly carry on a trade to help them in their marauding practices, picking up information to be turned to good account later on. Their chief occupations are the making of baskets, combs, date mats, and the selling of beads and curry leaves. Some of the men catch birds by liming twigs, and a few women go about and earn a livelihood by tattooing. There are others, who belong to the Kavalkaru or watchman classes of Koravas. Their duty is to protect the village against raids of robbers by giving the alarm, and they are paid for the work by the village officials, but these men need watching themselves. The fortune-telling wife in her wanderings tries to learn as much as she can about the family property of the local residents and observes closely the construction of houses as regards entrances. Although Tamil in origin, they have a slang of their own to help them in their professional thieving. The members of each sub-section thoroughly identify themselves with a gang, and completely subordinate themselves to the leader of it. To throw off suspicion, the property acquired is handed over to an individual fairly well to do, who disposes of all valuables in the shape of jewels and cloths. If a man belongs to a criminal gang, he is generally discovered by being asked whether he is *puthar*. The chief centres from which juveniles are received are Malur in Mysore, Vembakkam and Vellari Tangal in the Tiruvallur Taluk of Chingleput District, Ariankuppam in Pondicherry, Port Novo, Edayampatti in Trichinopoly, and in Palghat.

The Korava boys are among the best behaved. Offer prizes for cleanliness and they carry them off. A Korava youth at the time of which I write heads the list in the whole Presidency in drill and gymnastics. At football the best player in the art of passing is a Korava. In school not a few attain the position of monitors or assistant-monitors. What is the reason of it all? It can only be accounted for by the fact that from the age of five onwards they are schooled, disciplined and trained to their profession. A boy is placed in a basket and let down a well, to frighten him into saying "no," "no," "no," with a view to train him to give false evidence. A small boy about 9 years, on admission, states as a first lie that he belongs to the Mudaliar caste, and in order to get a "soft job" in workshop training, he gives out that his father is a tailor, and sticks to his statement until threatened with corporal punishment on receipt of correct information from the Magistrate. They are accustomed to look far ahead. They are taught by their elders to observe the motion of their eyes and movements of their hands in order to learn the cue for effective action. A rub along the right cheek would mean that the article was on the right side of the owner. A jerk of the hand would mean run away.

At the time of general festivals in religious centres like

Koravas
A Criminal Tribe of Basket-makers

Oddas
A Criminal Tribe of Roadmakers (page 306)

Conjeeveram, Chidambaram, Tiruvallur and Srirangam, a gang dress themselves like respectable men and make use of the boys for committing crimes, constantly changing their names as they go from place to place. Some of the feints practised by them to create an opportunity for stealing are to raise a cry that there is a snake on a tree. A crowd collects, and a rogue then gets a chance of picking pockets. Native females are in the habit of washing and drying their clothes outside. A rogue passing along remarks: "I have often told these women not to dry their clothes outside," to make people passing along believe that he is the owner. He then collects them under his arm and walks away. A boy who knows how to swim throws himself into a stream, and a cry is raised that a boy is drowning, to create a crowd, and in the confusion pocket-picking goes on.

With such training to strict obedience, it is no wonder that the juvenile falls into line in every department of work and excels in it. They can be reformed, therefore, but the pity of it is that as soon as they go back to their former criminal associates, their connection with their past good intentions and desire for work is snapped in a trice, and they take to thieving as a duck takes to water. The only solution lies in subsequent supervision by some responsible and philanthropic body.

A boy is usually discharged in the district to which he belongs, but it is not always so, for a cunning mother often comes to the school with the story that she has changed her residence, and asks that the boy be discharged in the place where she now resides. The request is made with the object of preventing the whereabouts of the boy being traced. Compulsory emigration is put forward as a possible remedy for these boys, as their previous training is generally undone by their criminal parents. The Government have wisely ruled that, in the case of a pupil of the criminal class, the Magistrate may dispose of him in such a way as to keep him apart from his former criminal associates, and without his parents' consent; but this is not always an easy matter. These boys can be turned to good account, provided always that they can be kept away from their people. They are amenable to discipline, well behaved and pleasant in features. The usual report, however, we obtain about these boys after their discharge is that their "whereabouts cannot be traced," especially those from the N. Arcot and Kurnool Districts.

It has been truly said that one half of the world does not know how the other half lives, and the straits to which some castes are reduced to earn a livelihood is amazing. The patriarchal system is still the custom in some communities, and several families, more or less connected by family ties, move about the country doing the kind of work to which the caste belongs. Interesting details of the life of a Villi have been culled from the inmates of the reformatory.

The settlement of a Villi generally consists of about 12 houses, and these families, under the pretext of honest labour, offer their services to a rich Mudaliar or other influential landowner of the village to construct thatched roofs or do other odd jobs of a miscellaneous description.

The youthful members of the family render valuable help in seeking for the wherewithal to keep body and soul together. They are first-rate hands at collecting honey in the forest. The bees are smoked out by means of a few twigs covered with margosa or neem leaves, and when these are set fire to a stifling smoke issues, to the discomfort of the bees. Sometimes the hives are not easily accessible, for they are situated on a high rock—the youth then lets himself down over the precipice by means of a rope. Yams or sweet roots, hares, winged ants, field rats, bandicoots, jungle cats, and squirrels, form the delectable items of their bill of fare.

The so-called yam, which is boiled and eaten, is the bulbous root of a thorny creeper. The serious work of catching a hare is converted into a mild pastime at hare-sticking, but with lack of true sportsmanship, for a long bamboo, pointed wtih an iron prick, is hurled headlong at the animal while in the act of dodging. This method is very successful, and also remunerative, for the quarry fetches from 5 to 7 annas a piece at the Toddy Bazaar, where it is converted into an appetising dish served with coarse hoppers (rice dumplings) and washed down with arrack.

The working members of a family sometimes resort to netting hares in a manner that hardly appeals to modern ideas of sport. A net is put across the path generally taken by the unsuspecting rodent, and stones are thrown into the bushy undergrowth to startle them out of their hiding-place. This they do; they make a dash and rush into the nets, when they are clubbed to death.

In the months of August and September, just before the monsoon sets in, the Villi is at another occupation. Winged ants, the precursor of the wet weather, make their appearance. The neuter or working members of the ant family build their barns underground, with an exit and an entrance to make it easy to go out and in. For the purpose of driving out the lazy winged ones, the Villi closes up the entrance and digs a pit about 2 feet long and 1½ feet broad near the exit, and at the mouth some powdered broiled seeds, obtained from the forest, are scattered about at 4 a.m. The ants crawl out at the smell of food and fall into the pit. They are then gathered in a cloth and divested of their wings with a few good shakes. A savoury dish is soon concocted from a mixture of the broiled ants, curry powder and broiled cholum, and dainty morsels are taken round for sale and readily purchased by the lower meat-eating classes. If the ants are slow in leaving their cosy corner, recourse is had to a burning torch, and attracted by the light they swarm out and fall into the pit.

The catching of rats is quite an art with the Villis. At harvest time they watch the fields carefully for any marks of fresh mud, which is the outward sign of an underground nest. They dig at the spot and discover little heaps of paddy which the field rat has stored up for its future use. This is collected, and the quantity obtained thus is not to be despised.

As a rat burrows in a direction almost parallel to the ground, the earth is examined below laterally by means of a crowbar, and four or five individuals are ready with sticks to belabour the animal as soon as it makes its appearance. The flesh of the field rat, which lives exclusively on grain, is considered to be a great delicacy, and of all meats the Villi prefers that of the rat, as he says it is most savoury. Perhaps there is some truth in this, for the field rat is a good eater, living on grain and roots, and is not to be classed with a sub-division of the family that delights to feed in drains on offal. On the continent, puppy dogs are bred for the table on the same principle at Genoa.

No abstruse knowledge of the culinary art is required to prepare a tasty and succulent dish out of this carnivorous animal turned vegetarian. The Villi roasts it over a fire, removes the hair and viscera, and drops it whole into the curry gravy. When they go through villages singing and collecting money and paddy from the people, the chief theme of the Villis' song is the rat.

The Villi is a fairly light-fingered gent. He goes through paddy fields at night when the harvest is ready and steals the ears of grain. At the time of a big fair he gets ready for a dacoity a gang numbering at least twenty, and if this number is insufficient, pariahs are enlisted for the job. The implements used are only knives and sticks, the former is intended for sheep and the latter to be laid on human beings. Their one redeeming point is that they do not break into houses, perhaps because it is too risky a business on account of the village policemen, whom they dread, and when they scent the approach of these guardians of the peace to their village, they hide their sticks, paddy, and mutton, in manure pits.

One juvenile confessed that he had been in a gang four or five times in the month. The biggest haul he remembers was made from a man who, having sold his bullocks for Rs. 200, was returning home alone during the day along a lonely road. At another time he was caught with a gang of thirteen, while in a forest, the surrounding villages offering tempting grounds for depredations on the paddy fields. Previous to this, they had stolen bags of ground nuts, for which offence the police were on their track. They had their females with them at the time, and as there was a dispute about the division into shares of certain jewels and money among the males, the females quarrelled and a disruption took place in the gang. They had no time to get away and were easily apprehended. The juveniles are taken on a thieving expedition only when the coast is clear, but they sometimes from a spirit of adventure launch out on their own account, steal a sheep, skin it in the forest, and sell the skin and meat. The father on learning of it remonstrates with his son in some such terms as these: "It is enough that I am a thief, but if my son should be caught and sent to jail, who would look after the family."

The goddess Kanniamma is the chief deity among the Villi, and they worship her. Under a lonely hut is placed a pot and a fashioned miniature car decorated with margosa flowers and leaves, and a lime is placed on the top, these being her symbols. On a festival day a trident is fixed in the ground and five pots are arranged, one on top of the other, containing rice and water, and fire is placed underneath till the bottom pot boils. A fowl, sheep or goat is sacrificed with gram and fried rice, coconut is broken, and camphor lit when the females dance with the spirit of the goddess possessing them, giving answer if the puja is satisfactory, upon which liquor and food are distributed to the women and men, and the latter foretell future events.

The soothsayer's aid is frequently resorted to, and the whole performance is attended with plenty of mysticism. A man beats a drum and sings, a woman behind him repeats the song, while in front is the fortune-teller with the symbols of the goddess in view. His eyes are uplifted, his head shakes for five minutes, with the mouth shut, and great drops of perspiration fall. He utters a mystic song, meaningless to the crowd, and swallows seven pieces of burning camphor, one after the other. He now rises and walks through fire, being armed with the protection of the goddess and inspired with wisdom: he sits down and answers questions to soothe the troubled minds of his favoured brethren. The lot of the Villi, therefore, is reckoned to be a not unenviable one. He is either soothsaying, hare-sticking, rat-catching, or seeking his fortune by other equally remunerative ventures.

Donga Woddars.—These people, of the criminal class, who were originally Telugus, are now to be found as settlers in the districts of South Arcot, Madura, Tinnevelly, Coimbatore, Trichinopoly, Cuddapah, Anantapur and Bellary, and they travel far and wide to Trivandrum, Cochin, the Nilgiris, Palghat, Calicut and Bangalore. They are divided into two great exogamous classes—the earth diggers (Mannu) and the stone workers (Kallu). The septs or sub-divisions of these are classed according to household names, such as Gumpa (basket), Panta (harvest), Avula (cows), Peetla (seats), Banala (fireworks), and Pasupuletti (turmeric). Intermarriages take place between these various sections; but the Mannu Odda will not eat, drink, or intermarry with the Kallu Odda because the women of the former wear their cloth over the left shoulder, while the women of the latter wear their cloth like the Bandla (bandy) Oddars, over the right shoulder.

The Oddas as a class are addicted to drink, and whole families indulge in it; in fact, they have taken to thieving as their hereditary profession for purposes of drink. If a fine is inflicted on any member of a community for wrong-doing, the money is set apart for merriment and is spent in drink for the benefit of the whole gang. If they cannot obtain work, they will steal for drink, and those who have no fixed abode go about in gangs to fairs and festivals to commit thefts in broad daylight. This particular caste is known as Pachipas. Some do not find it even necessary to teach their children to steal, for these pick up their knowledge from grown-up youths, and the parents encourage them when they do steal and show their appreciation by taking charge of the stolen articles. In several instances the parent is known to beat his child if he does not steal and carry out instructions.

One boy admitted having stolen a gold-wire necklace with a few gold coins on it, which he sold for Rs. 30 to a goldsmith who had the reputation of buying stolen articles. This money was handed over to his mother, who buried it for some future special occasion; he did not give it to his father, as he knew he would spend it in drink. He confessed to having drunk country liquor with other boy friends almost every day, and to having removed any ill effects by indulging in a bath. Another boy admitted that his father gave him liquor to encourage him to steal, and he liked the taste of it. In a crowd little boys are carried on the shoulders by their elders, watching for an opportunity to edge close up to a female wearing jewels, and with the aid of a small knife the coveted article is cut away. When boys cut open a bag containing grain they take the precaution of covering the bag with a bed-sheet and hiding under it. If a boy is caught the father makes himself scarce, taking care to trace a line on the ground by which his son could follow him up, even for two miles.

Pasupuletti Subbadu, one of the pupils of the school, stated that he belonged to the class of agricultural coolies. He grazed 10 or 12 goats, and he was once beaten for losing a kid that was carried away by a jackal; at times he would steal at the instigation of his father and mother. He had a cousin in the school who was in jail once for six months in a murder case, over a land dispute between the headman of the village and his family, when two of his uncles were killed with a hatchet. The headman of the village, for the purpose of a counter charge, poisoned one of his gang and put the guilt on the Oddas. (The land in dispute was given by his grandmother, without his father's knowledge, to the headman, a Reddi.) He confessed that he went to a marriage house to rob, and took some jewels and hid them. The next day he tried to steal another jewel, when he was caught, and to get off he affirmed that he belonged to the bridal party; but the bride having disowned him, they tore his coat in pieces, tied his hands with the shreds, poured kesosene oil on and set fire to it, burning his fingers. He fell senseless, and when he awoke the marriage people put him in a bandy and took him to the hospital about six miles away. The village munsiff who saw him on the way collected Rs. 10 from the people in fault, and gave the amount to the hospital assistant to look after him properly. He was there for four days, when he ran away to his home because he thought they were going to cut off his hands, but not before he dug out the jewels and secreted them on his person. Arriving at his house, a goldsmith, who knew something of dressing, healed his hands, but only at the expense of the use of his fingers. Then again he robbed (his father instigating him) at a festival at Pushpagiri (Cuddapah) about two days' journey from his house, his father following. He purloined two silk female cloths from two Komte females bathing at the river Pennar, when he was caught and sent to the school. This poor lad, for want of his fingers, was put to light garden work.

In order to obtain information from householders the Odda females sell fuel, bodices, and bags made of cloth. A crowbar is used to make a hole in the wall to effect an entrance, and very silently is the operation performed.

The Oddas in their settlements live in thatched huts, beehive or conical. They eat bandicoots, squirrels and field rats, but a boy declared that he would not eat squirrels again because he now knows it to be a sin. These people are Vaishnavites and wear the "Y" mark; they will not touch leather. They worship a number of local deities. Ankamma is a favourite with one sub-division. They prepare an idol of copper, and each family keeps one in the house to be propitiated on marriage and other ceremonial days. She is also represented under a tree with four bricks standing together and one placed before it, with turmeric and red powder (sign of a "she" god) daubed over the bricks. Cooked rice and flour are offered to her and a goat or sheep sacrificed, to be afterwards taken home and cooked. Some worship Venkatesa Perumal of Tirupati. He is made of brass and kept in the house. On five Saturdays in September they bring him out and offer to him grain, ghee, coconut and vegetable, but never meat or liquor. One boy remembers his head being shaved at the age of five, the mother offering the hair to the god. Others worship Munuswami as a household deity. They represent him by daubing a "Y" mark with a red centre over bricks placed in position near a well, and offer flowers, boiled rice, grain, jaggery, camphor, coconut, limes and liquor. They sacrifice also a fowl and partake of the offerings. Others, again, worship Sunkalamma as their chief deity. They represent her in an effigy of boiled rice with eyes and nose. On the top of her ghee is poured, which runs into a hollow and is ignited. Coconut, grain, etc., are offered and a fowl is killed, the fowl and the rice god being partaken of after the sacrifice. Some few worship Subbamma and Ulagamma. They represent the deity in mud and place it on a platform with a roof over it. They sacrifice a goat, cook the meat, and offer it with boiled rice to the god. On the following day a fowl is killed and rice cooked.

Mariamma and Peddanna (the cholera god) are the minor deities of some householders. The former is represented in wood and placed in a temple. They sacrifice to it a black goat once a year, oftener if they have money. Mariamma is represented also in clay, and sheep and fowl are offered to her. Karuppannan, another local deity introduced by Tamil criminal tribes, is represented by a copper Chembu or pot called *Ganga*, because they pour water from it. They place the vessel bottom upwards and cover it with betel leaves representing eyes, whiskers and the mouth. They sacrifice a fowl and sheep, and after cooking them, the liver and head being cooked separately, they offer them all, a bottle of toddy or arrack being poured as a libation. They have no special priest, and about 30 or 40 people congregate at a sacrifice.

The monkey god, the most trusted servant of Rama, is a favourite with some families under the name of Sanjeevi Rayan, because he is the ideal servant faithful unto death, humble and resourceful. An outline of the god is engraved on a silver plate which is kept in a box, and when required it is cleaned and exposed on a prepared ground decorated with flowers, with offerings of coconut and camphor. Rice flour and water are mixed into balls and over them ghee is poured and lighted. As Hanumanthadu is a "civilised god," neither sheep nor fowl is sacrificed to him, nor do the people eat or drink before him, but they let loose their tongues and ears under his shadow.

The Donga Dasari are also known as Guda Dasaris, the word Guda in Telugu meaning a secret. Their chief centres are Gollakuppam (Chittoor), Motupalli (Kurnool), where they are known as Pachiapas or Kattrias. There is a gang at Rajamundry and its surrounding villages, and also in Nellore, Bellary and Kumbum. They travel over Bangalore, Kolar, Salem, Trichinopoly, Tirupattur, Pondicherry, Tiruttani. Ten or fifteen houses make up a gang, who pay regular visits to fairs and festivals from March till September, dressed sometimes as Balijas or Telegas, while the old folk remain at home. At these festivals they erect a stall for the sale of beads, rings, red powder, turmeric and looking-glass boxes to make a show of their honesty. In their wanderings they obtain information by pretending to beg, and at night, arming themselves with a crowbar 1½ feet in length, a knife and some solid bamboo sticks, the information is put to practical use; with a curved knife they easily scoop out bricks from a wall. Picking pockets is the usual avocation of the youngsters of this class. The boys steal bundles hanging over the shoulders of people by deftly untieing them and passing them along quickly. They also accompany their elders when they go into the fields to steal grain, and make away with fowls by enticing them away with paddy. A famous dodge is to collect a crowd by means of a dance, and then to rob those interested in the play. A boy goes through various antics while the cymbals are beaten by a player with a lamp in front of him, who at the same time accompanies himself by singing to another man in the crowd in a sing-song Dasari language, in which the word Dasari occurs in every other line. They usually secrete their wealth at night under the oven in a corner of the hut.

The Yerukalas (the name meaning fortune-tellers) belong to the same class as the Koravas, but are Telugus by birth, and did originally belong to the Ceded Districts. They are also known as Korachas in the North Arcot and Chittoor Districts. But these castes will not intermarry. The Koravas use a turmeric thread as a *Tali* in marriage, while the Yerukala wear black beads tied to the neck, sometimes with a bottu (ornament) sometimes without, when the turmeric thread holds the bottu; in fact, both are used.

As a class, livelihood is chiefly stealing. The females always stay at home, and the men while wandering about occupy chatrams, wearing garments of respectability. A gang attacks carts and travellers with solid bamboo sticks, committing dacoities and house-breaking 100 miles away from their homes, travelling by rail, not in a body, but separately, after having settled upon the spot for their depredations. The property stolen is despatched in charge of a man quickly by rail to their houses. As a rule they are away for three to four months.

CHAPTER XXVI

CRIMINAL CHARACTERISTICS

Boys of a criminal character, I have observed, are so weak-willed that they easily and readily listen to bad advice, especially when it comes from one who offers to give them excitement in the assertion of what they imagine to be their rights, but it is just as easy to get them to see the reason for any change introduced. They are also very clannish, and a wrong committed against one of their own is bound to create a strong feeling which may have a regrettable termination. In football, an insulting word from the other side, particularly with reference to their criminal past, has resulted in stone-throwing, and I remember a case where a peon was set upon in my presence when one of the boys was ill-treated by him. Of course, the peon brought this upon himself. Easily excited, they are also easily brought under discipline, and by firmness and kindness the majority of the boys are led to respect authority. But if a suspicion of harshness and injustice is aroused in them, rioting and frequent occurrences of impertinence and insubordination result, and to no small extent the menials are responsible for these outbursts of feeling.

It has been very interesting during the past fifteen years trying to discover whether the boys who come to us with criminal tendencies exhibit any marked traits of character to distinguish them from the normal pupil. Though the opportunities for observation are unlimited, it is not easy to classify acts in the absence of a knowledge of the motives, opportunities, temptations and inducements involved.

The following incident that took place on the football ground brings out more prominently than others a number

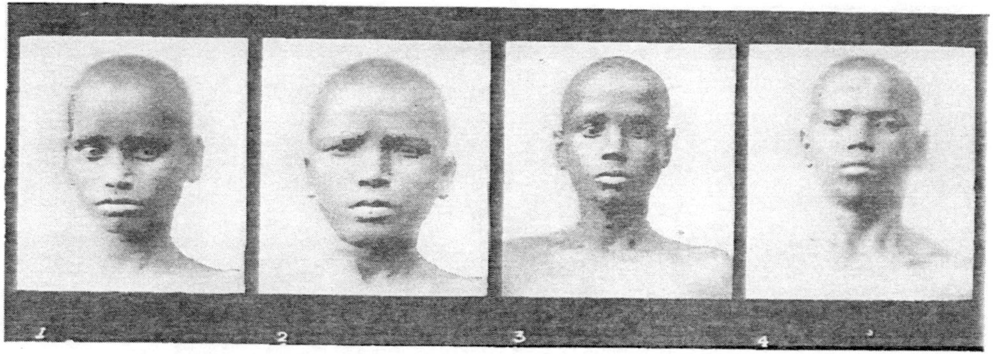

Juveniles with Thieving Propensities in School

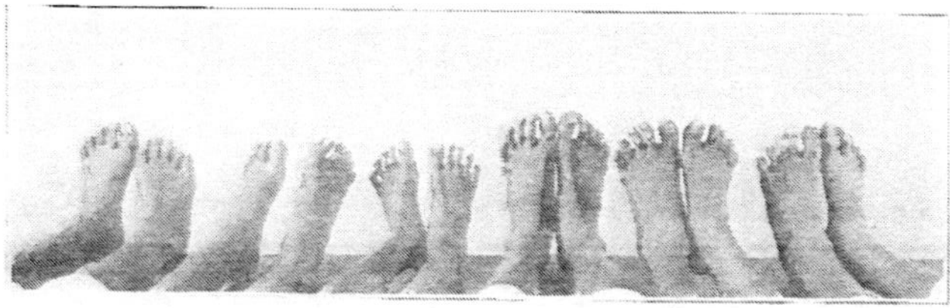

This plate exhibits some types of feet among juvenile criminals. One chief characteristic is their flat-footedness. Notice that the space between the great toe and the second toe is wide, and that the space also between the several toes is abnormal. The pair of feet, third from the right, is prehensile in character and closely resemble those of a monkey (page 318)

of characteristics common to juveniles, chief among them being the spirit of clannishness. At the time of this occurrence, the school drill-sergeant was both young and inexperienced. As he was in charge of the games he was allowed the assistance of a form master and the son of the Headmaster. The master on one occasion hustled and played roughly in the game, but when the boys followed suit and hacked him, he at once tried to stand on his dignity, and openly remarked with resentment that the boys were wanting in respect and did not know how to behave towards a master. These remarks were casually brought to my notice by the Headmaster's son, but they fell on deaf ears as I attached no importance to them. The next day the team conspired together to play a slow game on account of the remarks let fall by the master on the previous day, and carried their proposition into action. I discovered on my arrival at the playing field that the game was going slow, and shouted to the sergeant to quicken the pace of the game. Thinking no more of it, I proceeded home. Shortly after, to my surprise, I found the team at the entrance of my house with distressed faces, and one or two even with visible tears, which startled me into an inquiry. Then followed the doleful tale of a violent outburst of temper on the part of the sergeant, who smacked them openly and in public for wilful neglect of orders on the field. I had some difficulty in reconciling the parties, but knowing that the master was to blame for all this trouble, the sergeant and the captain of the team were soon induced to make it up and shake hands, although it took a few hours for the school to settle down to a friendly feeling towards their games master. On the following day their pent-up feelings against the master took a novel form of retaliation. The master anticipated trouble, and was standing uneasily at the wicket-gate leading to the field. The team captain came up to him, and with a cynical reference to the previous day's occurrence placed a garland of flowers round his neck, while as he moved on the school lost all control of themselves, cheered him along, and the boys exuberantly enjoyed "ragging" him. The master, unnerved at the odds against him, began to pose as a martyr. He even went so far as to take off his coat and subject himself to any indignity that might be imposed upon him—in short, he was prepared to make complete reparation. The school instantly became abashed and the turmoil ceased, for they merely felt that some reprisal was necessary to rehabilitate the status of the monitors, most of whom composed the football team, in the eyes of the school! They felt that they had been lowered in the eyes of everybody by being publicly caned, while the master looked on with supreme indifference, bordering on encouragement, tantamount to an invitation to the sergeant to use the cane on a team who were imbued with higher ideals of sport perhaps than the master himself.

The boys certainly did take the law into their own hands, but the master really courted disaster and was too ashamed of his part in the matter to officially bring the culprits to book. The Headmaster's son was also supposed to have looked on with approval when the caning was inflicted, but as they could do nothing to him, they revenged themselves on the Headmaster by refusing to fetch water for his domestic use. This impertinence was soon put a stop to when the ringleaders were punished.

Gratitude, I am sorry to say, is a quality not too often found in a juvenile criminal. A preliminary step necessary to all reformation is that a boy should be removed from his evil surroundings to a safe asylum. But whatever advantages a school may offer, they can never compensate a boy for the loss of his home and liberty. Everything that he receives, therefore, is looked upon as a matter of course, and of right rather than one of privilege. Individual love and care is responded to certainly, but the more this is shown the less it is viewed as anything strange, and the little ingrate, when he leaves the school, attaches himself once more to his old parents and expects favours to be shown him all through life because of his previous connection with the school. In some very few cases, even blackmail is resorted to to extort help. An officer once wrote to me to say that a boy would not search for employment, nor would he bestir himself to secure work, on the ground that as a reformatory pupil he expected everything should be done for him, even after discharge.

Gratitude, of course, does exist, but it differs in its degree of spontaneity from that of the normal boy. The same remark applies to the feeling of ambition. Efforts are made to raise a boy in a certain walk of life, but these are thwarted almost at every step when sustained effort is called for. As one boy put it: "God won't put into me good thoughts unless I see your face," thereby acknowledging the absence of any high ideal. On the other hand, selfishness, vanity, curiosity and sensitiveness to a fancied wrong done to them all exist in an active state. All the rewards, therefore, in the school, like good conduct marks, are with a view to stimulate the strong instinct of self interest that appeals most to the juvenile, and if this be not sufficient to put down delinquencies, recourse is had to corporal punishment, which on the whole has a salutary effect. It is found, strange as it may read, that the youthful murderer or the one guilty of a cruel assault, is the very one least able to bear physical pain.

Vanity is a mental quality that can easily be appealed to in the classroom, but it has its limits, lest arrogance, insubordination and obstinacy should breed out of it. As for curiosity, it is of the lower kind that is in search of excitement, disorder and the like, which soon forms a storm-centre, attracting a crowd; but of the higher mental quality that leads to observation, discovery and judgment there is a total absence, at least so long as the boy is in the school. When he leaves, his character may and does develop, with the aid of the glimpses of conscience kindled in him, but in school he acts as though he were incapable of appreciation of what is being done for him in the matter of food, clothing and education, while there is in him the sensitiveness to imaginary wrongs and so-called acts of injustice. The fact that one boy is treated unlike another on account of his different temperament, or one is selected for a position of trust, for although he may not have passed all his examinations, yet possesses the necessary qualities for the exercise of authority, or that a third boy is punished for insubordination to a supervising officer who perhaps is to blame for his want of tact or for aggressiveness, but whose action has to be supported for the sake of discipline, are acts which are misunderstood; but these are all causes which militate against gratitude, reverence and remorse, being stimulated as feelings that are so successfully appealed to in normal children. The environment and the surroundings are, it is true, such as to secure freedom from wayside temptations, but the absence of parental love, of home attractions, of freedom of person can never make a sub-normal boy respond sufficiently to activities organised for his benefit. It is only when he comes into contact with the cold, cruel world that he begins to appreciate what he has lost, and begins to discover the meaning of the word gratitude.

Insubordination is not altogether a common offence, but occasionally it does give rise to serious trouble. A boy does not like to be spoken to roughly. He imagines that some ill-feeling lurks within the mind of the master, and this makes him feel that he is watched with the object of "being run to earth." An offence should be inquired into, and visited with punishment with no anger or temper visible, and in a calm, judicial attitude, the reasons for the punishment being conclusively explained to the boy. In order that he may feel that there is no personal element in the matter, he is made to salute the officer immediately the punishment is meted out to him. If a boy is assured of your sympathy and just treatment, he takes the punishment he deserves; otherwise he resents it.

The number of offences varies with the circumstances and time of the year. Generally, after a long vacation, like the Christmas holidays, the boys get out of hand and the number of offences increases. And yet perhaps there is wisdom in allowing the pupils a fortnight's holiday, for even if there be a tendency to revert to old habits of life, it reveals the direction of these tendencies. It is a valuable aid in the development of character in the hands of the authorities, who should take due advantage of it and adopt a treatment necessary for each individual case.

Then, again, punishments increase in the hot weather, when a boy's mood and temper are not of the best. Insubordination is then likely to show itself, as well as wrangling and fighting. The hot weather synchronises with the fruit season, such as the mango and coconut, and it helps to swell the number of offences, the temptation to knock down fruit when no one is about being too great for a certain section of boys. And the offence should not be treated as a boyish prank, for, however venial it may be viewed in the case of ordinary children, it must be viewed in a different light, when a boy of the criminal class is concerned.

In the sister institution at Trivandrum an impending riot was averted by the tact of the Superintendent, who wrote to me asking for advice and, wisely, acted on it.

The practice of tattooing, or puncturing the skin according to certain patterns, and afterwards rendering them permanent by means of colouring matter rubbed into the incisions, is common among savage and primitive tribes, and as an art it has become highly developed among the Burmans, Maories and the Japanese. The original object of tattooing was probably to attract the opposite sex, but certain tribes practise it, giving to it a religious significance to avert evil influences.

That the criminal classes should carry on the practice is what one would expect. On examining the juveniles sent to the school, it was found that 47.3 per cent. were tattooed, a percentage which is non-existent in an ordinary school, and may be considered high. All the Madrassis were found tattooed; almost all the Vellalas, who are a respectable class; all the Padayachees, all the Panchamas, Koravars, Idaiyans, and Shanars, and, excepting the Idaiyans, these belong either to the lowest or to the criminal class. The motive is various in the several castes. The Vellalas and the Idaiyans, who form the highest castes among the Tamil-speaking non-Brahman castes, tattoo their bodies either for the sake of beautifying their persons, or to protect themselves from diseases. The Shanars also believe that tattoo-marks will ward away such diseases as small-pox. The Madrassis and the Panchamas adopt the practice perhaps because it is considered fashionable. Some of the Panchamas were found to be tattooed to keep green the remembrance of their friends. A few of the Koravars confessed to having tattooed themselves in order to hide their marks of identification in case they found themselves once again in the presence of a Magistrate. With such a variety of causes, further investigation is required before one can accept the theory that tattooing reveals a tendency to vice in the character of an individual. The balance of opinion is, I think, on the side of instinct.

The so-called criminal classes are not criminals in the sense of being degenerates as regards physical or mental, and I would even add moral qualities, but only in the sense of having adopted thieving as a profession. To look at, they do not exhibit a criminal type of face, but on the contrary are pleasant in features, possessing intelligence, and a sense of discipline which has been perverted into professional habits of thieving. This state of things has been brought about by an upheaval in the social condition of India, and made emphatic by the advent of British rule. Others were expropriated from their ancestral possessions through causes which were more or less natural. These tribes have proved such pests to society that Government have been forced to gradually curtail their liberty by the establishment of settlements where they are registered and located, the services of the Salvation Army and other missionary bodies being enlisted to bring about a change in the habits of these unfortunate people. A Criminal Tribes' Act was passed in the year 1911, and the local Government, in exercise of the powers conferred on it, have framed rules by which every member of a criminal tribe becomes registered in the village in which he intends to reside, the headman of the village being notified of the fact, as well as of any subsequent intention to change his residence. Moreover, the movement of certain tribes have been confined within certain limits, *e.g.*, the Donga Yerukalas are limited in their movements to the Godaveri, Nellore, Guntur and Kurnool Districts, according to the leadership and gang to which they belong.

The Criminal Tribes' Act deals in a more effective manner

in regard to the prevention of crime than the use of the security sections of the Criminal Procedure Code or prosecutions under Sections 400 and 401, I.P.C., under which an individual is liable to punishment for belonging to a gang of dacoits or thieves, methods resorted to in the past, but found insufficient to check the evil. The police were practically powerless to prevent criminal gangs leaving their residences during the dark, moonless fortnights, although well aware that these absences were for the purpose of committing crime. The working up of a case under the security sections, moreover, involved much delay, and the villagers were averse from giving evidence, as they knew it would lay them open to reprisals. The Criminal Tribes' Act of recent origin affords an efficacious method of not only preventing members of criminal gangs from committing crime, but also admits, in special cases, of the restriction of a criminal tribe to a particular settlement, thereby removing the source of annoyance of such members as are settling down to an honest life.

Criminal settlements have already been formed in the Districts of Nellore, Guntur, South Arcot, Chittoor and Madras, and they are working well. The following tribes or gangs have been notified by Government to be criminal in this Presidency :—Donga Dasaris, known under the various names of Peddeti Gollas, or Kathiras, in the Nellore District, Donga Dasaris in Kurnool and Guntur Districts, Pachapas in Godaveri and Kistna Districts; Dongo Yerukalas, the Nawalipetta, or Voyalpad Korachas, the Veppur Pariahs; the Donga Oddars, the Thogamalai Koravas, or Kepmaris; the Rudrapad Korachas (Bellary); the Salem-nad and Attur-nad Koravas; Vengamur Pariahs (Chittoor), Velliyankuppam Padayachis (S. Arcot); Morakalakurichi Maravars (Tinnevelly), Vadavarpatti Koravas (Ramnad and Tinnevelly, certain Velayur gangs in Coimbatore District, Dommaras (Nellore), certain Kallar gangs in Madura.

When it is found expedient to restrict the movement of a criminal tribe, the Government takes care to be satisfied that the means by which it is proposed that each criminal tribe shall earn its living are adequate, before permission can be granted to register a gang. Every encouragement is given to the establishment of industrial, agricultural and reformatory settlements and even schools, the latter being intended for children who may be separated and removed from their parents. The course of providing for the education of the children of criminal tribes in criminal settlements has more in its favour than the system of sending those convicted to a reformatory school, as their admission keeps out boys of a more promising type and of a non-criminal tribe caste. The criminal caste boy can be reformed, but labour is lost in the system of after disposal, when a lad is allowed to rejoin his relatives, which is what happens at present.

The industrial home for children established by the Salvation Army at Perambur (Madras) is one of the schools recognised by Government for the reception of children of criminal tribes. The police are never employed to escort children to the school, but a member of the school staff is deputed to take charge of them and lead them to the school. No legal means exist for compelling such transfers, and if the child possesses a parent or guardian, the consent in writing of that person is obtained. Another measure for the amelioration of the condition of the criminal is the establishment of prisoners' homes at Guntur and Madras, which are intended for the reception of conditionally released prisoners, whether belonging to criminal tribes or not. There is no objection to transferring before the expiry of their term of sentence members of a criminal tribe from the home to the settlement established for the tribe.

It will thus be seen that of late years great activity has been shown in the reforming and humanising treatment of crime, and so far as this Presidency is concerned, the name of Sir Harold Stuart will always be connected with these recent improvements.

Of the convicts sentenced to imprisonment, a little over 5 per cent. are committed to jail for failure to furnish security, and this number would be even larger if it were not for the fact that the worst characters are generally able to find people, who are benefited by their career, to stand security for them. But with the advent of the criminal settlements, the habitual prefers to go into one of those rather than into a prison, when the security sections of the Indian Penal Code are explained to him and in time; the cost to Government for the support of this class ought, therefore, to show a decrease. The development of the reformatory element in prison administration, moreover, is to be seen in the provision for class separation, the Salem Central Jail being specially set aside for the confinement of habituals admitted to the jails in the Tamil-speaking districts; while the Tanjore Jail is reserved for adolescents, treated on the Borstal system.

Previous to the step being taken of starting settlements, the duty of managing the criminal tribes formed part of the work of the police, who tried to solve the problem by harrying these people till they moved off to some other territory; and this policy on the part of police officers eminently suited the purpose of these wandering tribes, and made matters worse. A special officer was therefore found necessary to supervise the work of restricting the movements of tribes by registering every man, woman and child, and compelling them to live in settlements where the work of reformation, education and teaching them trades and industries may be proceeded with. The work has been by no means easy, and many difficulties had to be overcome with infinite tact and discretion. One gang transported to a settlement refused to settle down or do any work until they had consumed all the stock of alligator flesh which they had brought with them. Another gang which refused to work was brought to its senses by the manager separating the women and children from their husbands. The women, of course, carried away their pots and pans with them, and the men soon came to their senses when they found that if one did not work neither should he eat, and they begged to be allowed to join their wives, promising to go out to work.

The following interesting story of an official who refused to change his watchman (a member of a criminal tribe) when he changed his residence, illustrates the adroitness and skill of many of these criminal tribesmen. Having disregarded an anonymous letter asking him to change his watchman, he woke up one morning to find the pictures from his drawing-room swinging from the branches of the tree under which he had been sleeping. Inside, his furniture was turned upside down and his bureau stood wide open, and while no money had been taken, his book of postage stamps had been neatly disposed round the edge of his lawn, with a pebble on each stamp so that it might not be blown away. The official, of course, soon changed his watchman.

On another occasion, when a regiment was passing through a station, 100 special watchmen, in addition to the usual sentry, were placed on guard by the police. During the night, though there was a brilliant moon, all the valuable regimental dogs were stolen. Loud were the complaints of the officers, and the police were sent for, but not a trace of the dogs could be found. The Indian Police Inspector mounted his horse and galloped to the nearest camp of the criminal tribesmen, and sure enough the missing dogs were there. Afraid that the dogs might be destroyed, he dismounted at a distance from the camp and sent for their leaders. "You have blackened my face; you have covered me with shame. The regiment were my guests and friends, and you have stolen their dogs!" he exclaimed; and their reply was: "Sahib, we did not know they were your guests, we are very sorry; we will return the dogs."

If a police officer happens to be over smart in his work, revenge is taken upon him, followed by some such note: "Sahib, you are a clever Police Officer. You have suppressed crime with a strong hand. Now tell me what has become of your two horses and who has stolen them."

The following report, which was written at the request of Government, may be of use to those in charge of, or who are about to start criminal settlements:—

1. I accompanied the Inspector of Schools, Bangalore Circle, and inspected the Salvation Army Tata Silk Farm at Bangalore, where the boys of the Salvation Army Industrial School, Madras, are at present undergoing training, 30 of these being on the farm at Closepet.

2. It will be necessary to state very briefly the history of the movement

for the amelioration of the so-called criminal classes. Under the Criminal Tribes' Act certain settlements have been established for the purpose of restricting the movements of criminal tribes or gangs who are habitually addicted to the commission of grave crime. The object of Government I take it is to fix these people to the soil by giving them not waste land but good land which will bring them a good return. At the same time the young criminal is to be taken in hand and Industrial schools are to be established for their reception for training them to earn a livelihood with the object of getting them to settle down in the larger industrial and agricultural settlements. The school at Perambur will be one such institution. The average period of detention will be 5 years and no boy will ordinarily be allowed to remain after his 18th year.

3. At our visit to the school at Bangalore, we found the settlement industry taught there to be sericulture, under the following heads:—

(a) Growing silk-worms.
(b) Reeling silk.
(c) Weaving silk.

The boys work under superintendence and the time-table in force allows for 6½ hours of industrial work and 3 hours for general instruction arranged thus:—

7.30 A.M. to 12 NOON	... ...	Industries.
12 NOON to 1 P.M.	... ...	Mid-day meal.
1 P.M. to 4 P.M.	... ...	Education.
4 P.M. to 6 P.M.	... ...	Industries.

(No work on Saturday afternoon when games are played, and Sunday when moral and religious instruction is given).

This course of instruction would be satisfactory with just a little organisation. In regard to general education, we think that an hour less general education a day might do, and games take their place between 3 and 4 p.m., as there seems to be insufficient provision for games. Also the teaching seems to suffer from want of direction and experience.

Under INDUSTRIES provision should be made for teaching the boys the twisting of silk as the course should be a complete one. In addition Carpentry may find a place in the curriculum since it would be of use to them in making or repairing apparatus. We were told that a Drawing Master is shortly to be employed.

Besides the cultivation of the mulberry plant, each boy is allowed a small plot of ground for the growing of vegetables. This part of the work requires to be organised. There should be a correlation of school work with industrial training and with their environment. The vegetables on the garden and their value at market prices, the cost of seeds, manure, etc., must be real arithmetic to the child.

4. The question is will a boy be able to earn a livelihood after going through a course of instruction outlined above? If the Salvation Army is able to find work for their ex-pupils on their settlements well and good, but if the boy is to find work in Bangalore, I am afraid there is little prospect at present. No doubt there is money in the silk industry, proved by the fact that till lately out of 4000 weavers, half employed cotton and the other half silk, but now the silk weavers number 3000. There is a future therefore for raw silk and woven silk. But the boys turned out of the Salvation Army Farm and more particularly those of the criminal tribes will never be able to find work in the homes of these weavers unless they belong to the weaving class and these latter also as soon as they become Christians will be treated as outcastes. Their prospects, however, would improve with the introduction of small factories. So much for the boy who is recruited from Bangalore and its suburbs. With the criminal boy, the orphan and destitute are mixed up and no difference is being made in their treatment or training. This we think is perfectly correct for it will tend to raise or create self-respect in the so-called criminal boy.

5. I am inclined to think, however, that the Salvation Army is on a wrong track when it tries to run the silk industry in places ill-adapted for it. In Bangalore and Closepet the tender leaf of the mulberry is available right through the year in both of which places the industry is successful as silk-worm rearing is possible. But with regard to other places in Southern India the geological distribution of sericulture is not taken into consideration and the same thing is also being tried at Madanapalli, which is only 2000 feet in height and where the mulberry is an annual and the univoltine race of silk-worms can alone be hatched. It is true that cocoons may be obtained from other places to keep the industry going. This would mean that the boys would have to confine themselves mainly to silk reeling, a delicate industry intended for women or girls and in itself is hardly a sufficient hand and eye training for boys. It would require to be supplemented by manual training of some sort, carpentry being the best in this case.

The same course of training would also be out of place in Madras or Perambur and I am of opinion that agriculture should form the main industry of the place and the boys be trained in agricultural pursuits. With this object in view the time-table may be arranged thus:—

7 A.M. to 11 A.M.	Agriculture.
11 A.M. to 12 NOON	Mid-day meal.
12 NOON to 2.30 P.M.	General Education
2.30 P.M. to 5 P.M.	Gardening, Carpentry, Blacksmithy or Masonry.
5 P.M. to 5.30 P.M.	Games or Drill.

The whole morning should be devoted to the growing of such crops as rice, ragi, cholum, cumbu, etc., and in the afternoon each should attend to his own garden plot for the purpose of raising vegetables. For this purpose a portion of the land should be divided off into garden plots.

In the afternoon selected boys may be taught Carpentry or Blacksmith's work and if there are any Woddar boys, Masonry may be added. It is difficult to make criminal boys follow any other trade but what their forefathers have done and after being trained it is almost impossible to separate them from their people. They always find their way back to the old settlement. If therefore the parents are to be fixed to the soil, the children should have an industrial training in agriculture—in the raising of field crops and garden crops and in such necessary industries as Blacksmithy or Masonry or Carpentry, which are involved in the maintenance of a settlement, and everything done in the school should function in as large a measure as possible in the education and training of its inmates as future dwellers of a settlement.

The Erukala Industrial Settlement of the American Baptist Telugu Mission was organised in 1912 with 25 families, totalling 100 people. Fibre work was the chief industry, but as it proved difficult to find profitable work enough for all the people, efforts were made to increase the number engaged in agriculture. A second settlement was founded in 1916 at Allur, and a third settlement in 1917 at Bitragunta.

As the purpose of the settlement is the reformation and reclamation of criminal tribes, moral and religious training, with adequate discipline, long continued, offer the only solution. But it is a case of "preaching to a procession," for the numbers are yearly increasing, more than double in 12 months, and thereby totally swamping with the new additions the work of the previous months.

In the settlement at Allur intended for the well-behaved, there are no police. At Bitragunta, where the records are good, 4 special constables, chosen from among the people, preserve order, and at Kavali, 2 head constables of the regular police and 18 special constables, chosen from among the settlers themselves, look after the settlement day and night. The nature of the administration, therefore, depends on the grade of the settlement. There are three classes on each settlement:—The old men and women who cannot work; the lazy and degenerate, who won't work; and the "will works." These latter are composed of the incompetents, the unskilled workmen, and those who are good workmen and are trying to be better men and women.

Difficulties there are in arranging the groups of workmen. One is that there is a surplus of women whose husbands are absconders or serving sentences in jails. Another is that as soon as a workman proves himself competent and trustworthy, he is transferred to the higher grade of settlement to make good on his own land, and there is the necessity of attempting to carry out public contracts with the poorest workers. The Public Works Department place a number of contracts in the hands of the manager, who, as far as possible, pays for work on the contract basis. Chits are made out to each worker, which are redeemable for provisions at the settlement store-room, to eliminate any temptation on the part of the staff in the way of commission. A fixed deposit of one sixty-fourth of his weekly wage is retained to the credit of each worker, and three sixty-fourths for the purchase of clothing. Each worker purchases his own tools on the instalment plan.

As regards education, each boy and girl between 6 and 12 years of age is required to be in school, and a night school is provided for the young men who work during the day and who have a desire for education.

As regards discipline, no walls are built to secure physical restraint, for that would not develop strength of character, but certain limits are laid down, and any transgression beyond is punished under the Criminal Tribes' Act, and if the offender is incorrigible, he is transferred to a different type of settlement.

In the matter of religion, a roll-call is held every morning at which the word of God is read, followed by a brief exposition, after which prayer is offered, and all who wish join in repeating the Lord's Prayer.

It is interesting to review the contribution that the Chingleput Reformatory is making in this movement. In spite of the heavy handicap, I venture to say that the progress made in their reformation has not been unsatisfactory. The following results relate to the criminal classes alone.

From 1888-1911, in 24 years, 110 boys were discharged, trained to earn an honest living—31, or about 29 per cent., relapsed; hardly 2 per cent. followed the trade taught them;

the whereabouts of 52, or 48 per cent., were not known; and 19 followed a trade other than that taught in the school.

From 1912-1918, in 8 years, 88 boys were discharged. Of these, 10, or 11 per cent., relapsed; 18, or 20 per cent., followed their trade; 21 followed other trades; and the whereabouts of 30, or 37 per cent., were not known. There has been, therefore, a distinct advance in the results obtained, and the trades most in favour were gardening, blacksmith and masons' work. Government service, carrying with it a badge of office, fair pay, permanent service and a pension, was the height of their ambition. Many aspired to the post of taluq peon, process server, masalchi (lamp-lighter) successfully.

I wonder how many people outside India know that in this country of diverse nations, tongues and religions, whole communities live by crime—that this method of earning a livelihood is taught to their children as a profession, by example as well as precept. These "criminal classes," as they are termed by the Indian Government in all official documents, have flourished for centuries in Southern India, where my sphere of work exists. Thoughtful administrators and legislators have long recognised that they require special treatment. Much has been done in the past to stamp out the more serious forms of crime, but it is only in recent years that the preventive method has produced, in some places, the most satisfactory results. Large tracts of land have been given by Government near industrial centres, hundreds of families have been induced to settle there, regular occupation has been found for them, and the new generation have few object-lessons in the old methods. The Salvation Army has come to the rescue in some districts to help in the work of regeneration. It is needless to add that many parts still remain untouched.

CHAPTER XXVII

INCORRIGIBLE SONS

"I HAVE a wayward son who is a source of a world of trouble to me" is the plaintive notes of the opening lines of a letter addressed to me by the Headmaster of a Government High School, a University graduate in the Nizam's dominions, and it is typical of a number of letters received from time to time from respectable parents for the admission of their sons into the school. The letter adds that the "son requires to be kept under a very strict check, for which, I am of opinion, your institution is the best." The request is made for his admission, agreeable to the monthly charges being paid.

The absence of reformatories in Native States (Travancore proving the exception) causes helpless parents to turn to this institution for succour in their anxiety. Nothing can be sadder than the sight of a parent harassed by a son who has grown up without discipline. In one case a respectable Brahman writes on behalf of a Brahman lady in Mysore, who has an unruly, misconducted and troublesome son, a veritable thorn in her side. She tried to put him to some industrial training, but he was said to be altogether untractable. She was therefore anxious to send him to this institution, in the hope that judicious treatment, wholesome restraint, and firm handling would bring the boy round.

Another Brahman writes from Rajahmandry to say that he comes from a well-to-do family and has a son given to evil ways. He is prepared to pay the cost for the up-keep of his boy if his admission can be sanctioned.

One, Krishna Row, from Madras, writes that he has a

son of stone-hearted conscience, who disappears from home for days together, and he thinks that in the interests of the boy, as well as of the family, he should be taken under our charge.

A letter was also received from the manager of a European firm, stating that a pensioned havildar (non-commissioned officer) in his employ has a very bad son, 12 years of age, who is giving him a lot of trouble. The boy bolted from his house with Rs. 2, which he stole from his father's coat pocket, and suddenly turned up after an absence of ten months, feeling a hero while recounting to his mother the various places he went to in the north of India, with a nonchalance unbecoming a minor. Since returning he has given no end of trouble, and cannot be tamed. The manager states that he would like to help the old man in this matter, as he is really a good fellow.

The only test of the result of reformatory work is the number who are re-convicted after discharge. For this purpose, a history of ex-pupils is maintained for three years. In reply to a reference from the Government of India, the Madras Government decided to continue the plan of asking revenue officials to exercise a friendly supervision over discharged pupils and to report to the school authorities, half yearly, on their conduct and occupation, rather than the plan adopted by the other Provincial Governments of granting small stipends to discharged pupils as a means whereby the school may keep in touch with them. This latter method will probably have the effect of placing a premium on laziness.

When a pupil leaves the institution, he does so with a desire, more or less, to lead an honest life. The first few weeks are the most critical portion of his reformed life, and if he does not get a fair start within that period, he is likely to get into idle habits which will ultimately land him in trouble. There is also the want, due to overwork, of close and friendly supervision over ex-pupils on the part of the subordinate revenue officials, and the half-yearly reports in such cases are "whereabouts not known."

Then, again, the home life of the boy may be bad, and he finds himself once again surrounded by evil associates, and he falls a prey to them. If reformatory work is to have any success, the youth must be frequently visited during the dangerous period following his release, and not lost sight of until he is able to look after himself. It is noteworthy that even with this want of proper surveillance, only 15 per cent. are re-convicted on the average taken for the last twenty years, and it is certain that this percentage can be reduced by proper supervision and control over juveniles discharged. Hence my plea for compulsory enlistment, or the establishment of an institution where discharged pupils will be under control and at the same time live amidst ordinary social surroundings, or a non-official philanthropic body, such as the Brahmo Somaj, the Anjuman, or the Salvation Army, to advise and help the released boy, or approved Probation Officers.

Since the school was opened, over 1500 boys have been discharged, and, taking the average, about 14 per cent. of these relapsed into crime. A number of these were Madras boys, who come to the school full of the vice of city life, and who go back to their old surroundings to fall into evil habits again. Madras boys require a separate corrective institution, where strict discipline and hard manual work are the conditions, with a suitable staff to cope with difficulties. On discharge, they should be sent elsewhere than to their old homes; for the weak point in the whole system is the want of proper supervision after release. A technical institute to provide work for these boys will perhaps partly solve the difficulty.

Some of our pupils were sent to jail because they could not give security for good behaviour.

I give a typical case. A boy living in one of the taluqs around Bangalore was found in company with another boy "suspiciously loitering" about, and, being unable to give a satisfactory account of themselves, they were arrested by the police, who informed the Magistrate that the boy's father and uncle were members of a criminal gang, and that the boy, as well as his relations, stood on the register of suspected persons. The boy was asked to execute a bond for Rs. 50, with two sureties, for his good behaviour for a period of six months, and because he was unable to furnish the requisite security he was ordered to be rigorously imprisoned for six months.

In the first place, the boy's name should never have found a place in the register of suspected persons. Then, if his relatives belonged to a criminal gang, how could he possibly furnish security of any value. The Government expect that the boy should be kept away from his criminal associates and be given a fair start in life. This boy is described as being found by the police "suspiciously loitering" about. What the expression exactly means I cannot tell; but I imagine that the police, finding his name on the K.D. list, hauled him up before the tribunal as a suitable subject for trial. This is the way to manufacture criminals and undo the work of reformation. I may state that this youth, soon after his discharge from the school, was placed under the surveillance of the police, who called for certain information about the offence he committed *prior* to his admission into the school. The Director of Public Instruction was referred to in the matter, and his orders were that the information should not be furnished, as it was contrary to the orders of Government. Notwithstanding the correspondence, the unfortunate boy was tried and convicted. This is one of several cases, and has reference specially to boys of the criminal classes.

Requisitions are also frequently received from the Police Department, contrary to the standing orders of the Inspector General of Police, regarding present pupils in the school. A roll, headed "roll of a bad character," is sent, and certain columns requiring information about the age, caste, residence, offences, etc., are required to be filled up, evidently with a view to place such pupils on the K.D. list. In the face, therefore, of the unsympathetic attitude taken up by the lower ranks of police officials, and of the enormous difficulties and temptations in the way of making a start in life, it is very gratifying to be able to state that only 15 per cent. are re-convicted. It is gratifying to think that all these objectionable features of the treatment received by our boys in the past will be removed with the advent of the Madras Children Bill.

How to produce the best results from reformatory schools has always been the aim of the Educational Department, and a great deal of controversy raged on the question of the location, concentration, and distribution of such institutions. A central reformatory in the Madras Presidency has much to commend itself—an ideal climate, model buildings, a strong literary and technical staff, a saving of cost, labour and supervision, are both attractive and sound. This view, however, is not wholly in the interests of its inmates.

The opposers of the central scheme state that where the distance from the homes of the pupils is great and the climate is different, the removal to a central reformatory in the Madras Presidency is open to grave objection: such a removal will practically be adding transportation to imprisonment. As no one wishes to retard the remaking of these unfortunates, there is a great deal of force in this objection; a blending of the two sets of views, therefore, seems to approach nearest to the happy mean, and the establishment of reformatories at different centres, having one in each of the great divisions into which the Presidency naturally falls with regard to language, is desirable. In addition to the one in Chingleput, there should be a school in the south, one or two in the west coast and two in northern districts. The reasons are two-fold. In India the people are much attached to their homes, and are averse from sending their chiildren to any distant district. They are still strongly imbued with the spirit of the ancient family system prevailing among the Hindus, where the sons, even after marriage, live with their wives in their father's house, so that the brood never disperses. Parents and relatives would therefore feel it a grievance if their children were sent from one end of the Presidency to the other. The second reason is that there are four distinct dialects spoken in the Presidency, not to mention Hindustani. In the Chingleput school the teaching of three languages is a difficult matter, and necessitates the employment of a double set of teachers who work on a shift system. As the moral training of the boys is always a matter of much concern, the individual attention each one requires is only possible to be given in a school limited to about a hundred boys, any larger number militating against individual attention. This is a further reason why the Chingleput school should be split up, the Telugu boys being removed to the north and Malayalees to the west, while another Tamil school in the south would solve the difficulty raised by the social, moral and language problems.

There is need, therefore, for more reformatories in the Presidency, particularly as juvenile crime is bound to rise with the advent of Western institutions, not on account of any inherent defect in these; but in the transition period, before the attainment of self government is reached, ideals are built upon quicksands—they lack cohesion and stability, and they are pressed into the service of thinly disguised obscurantism and reaction, while human passions run riot and new temptations concomitant with a new type of civilisation arise, giving a chance to the young cockerels to sharpen their spurs and crow with greater energy. Juveniles then are at a loose end and easily get out of hand. To mention only one source of future danger, the cinema is bound to fire the imagination of youth unless properly controlled, for the Indian boy, whose blood has been watered by generations of servitude and enervating tasks will find himself spinning up when a social or political upheaval takes place. Here would be a chance for young India to run wild, and as youth becomes more difficult to control, reformatories alone remain to deal with the problem. This, also, is to be remembered, that, however advanced the state of education may be, as things progress, we shall always have our youthful pirate kings. In the recent riots at Lahore and other parts of the Punjab, the action taken by boys in looting, burning and violence, under some organised leaders who kept well in the background, was painfully brought into prominence.

For the purpose of comparison, a short description of other systems for the reclamation of juveniles is given Among them, the "George Junior Republic" takes foremost place. This institution arose from the Freeville Fresh Air Camp, which was intended, more or less, for the purpose of giving fresh air and health to the boys and girls of New York; and when it was discovered that they were claiming charity as a right, Mr George informed his young company that in order to get the most fun out of life they should do some hard work, and he proposed that they should construct a model piece of roadway in front of the Fresh Air cottage, and the boys were taught to work for their clothing, and that there was nothing for them without labour. It was on these foundations that the future integrity and stability of the Republic were securely laid.

It was next discovered that the young men and women were not particularly strong in respect to the rights of other people, and they did not allow an opportunity to pass without breaking some of the regulations, and to see these boys punished was the circus feature of the day. It was then decided that the boys and girls themselves should dispose of all cases, and corporal punishment was commuted into extra labour, *e.g.*, picking up stones. The system of trial by jury was fairly started, and a further step was taken when the boys worked, not only for their clothing, but also for their food, and they received pay for their work in "token money," which represented a medium of exchange. The idea of a junior republic, with boys and girls as citizens, with powers of Government, Legislative, Executive and Judiciary, was unfolded to Mr George. The junior republic, when I visited it, resembled a little village with a number of cottages, each cottage being in charge of a house-mother, who looks after a dozen youths. There are no large buildings used as dormitories, no big shop in which everything is done. There are many modern "homey" looking dwelling-houses and several commodious shops, a beautiful chapel, a fine school-house, a splendidly equipped hospital, and a large and very conveniently arranged barn. Four cottages are devoted to the use of the girls and six cottages devoted to the use of the boys, and the girls and boys are given every opportunity to cultivate the social side of their lives. There are no "regulations" governing this question. It is worked out quite as naturally as in the world at large.

They pay for their food and clothing out of their earnings,

and the village is governed by the boys. They elect a president, a vice-president, and form laws. A police force, judges to try criminal and civil cases, a jail, bank, post office, all enter into the scheme. The president appoints the judges. The vice-president is the chairman of the board of officers, who have charge of the police, prison, and health affairs. The board is formed by the vice-president, the secretary (who has custody of all official documents) and the treasurer (who is the custodian of the public funds). The district attorney is elected by the citizens, and all offices are held for one year. There are simple offences and indictable offences, the latter being tried by a jury.

A person charged with a crime is given his choice of being tried by judge or jury consisting of four. If the prisoner is found guilty, he is sent to the school jail, and the sentence may be anything between a day and a year. If the prisoner behaves well he can get out on parole. Prisoners are let out on bail. The fact that boys order the locking up, because they cannot trust one of their own, takes all the romance out of wrongdoing. Outside, a boy becomes popular with his kind, because he is a terror. There are three classes of citizens, and the second class is responsible for the third. The president can grant twenty-four hours' leave of absence, and anything beyond must be sanctioned by the superintendent. The superintendent has power to place any boy in the fraternity for an indefinite period. The scheme, no doubt, is on the whole good, and ought to flourish on American soil, but to a visitor there comes the impression that a little too much liberty is given to the citizen. It is true that the superintendent exercises certain powers, but they are more or less undefined. When a boy can be locked up for a year—a period long enough to make him get accustomed to his surroundings, the punishment becomes a farce. Water cannot rise above its level, and taking into consideration the class and standing of the boys, the republic can never attain a high ideal by self-government, and all its institutions, unless carefully supervised by outside authority, will be coloured by the character of the citizens themselves. This seems to me to be the great drawback of the scheme. Still, it is better to err in the direction of giving the boys liberty of action than in restraining their freedom, as is done in the State Reformatory School at Elmira.

The Elmira Reformatory is nothing less than a junior jail, where military discipline is strictly enforced. Two-thirds of the prisoners committed are from the city of New York. There is great disparity of ages, which range from 16 to 30. All the incorrigibles are sent here who have been found unfit for other institutions, and an indefinite sentence is passed, and in accordance with its provisions it is possible for an inmate to be released within one year of his admission. As soon as a lad earns his discharge, by a certain number of good marks, he is let out on parole for six months; and if he behaves himself during that period he is absolutely released. About 75 per cent. are thus discharged on parole. The inmates are divided into three grades, and the various grades are distinguished by difference in clothing or collar device. The ration of the first grade admits of a somewhat greater variety than the other two.

The inmates are divided into three grades. Each youth upon admission is placed in the second grade, from which by making a good record he may rise to the first grade, or by failure to do this may drop to the third. Six months of good record in the second grade ensures promotion to the first, and a like six months in the first grade entitles the prisoner to consideration by the board of managers for parole.

The inmates' daily routine. During the morning hours, until about 10 o'clock, a large number of the prisoners are occupied in cleaning up the place, while others, including all new arrivals, are being drilled in military exercises. There is also a class in physical culture of the weaklings. A little after ten, general military exercises begin, and occupy the remainder of the morning. The prisoners dine at noon. The first part of the afternoon is devoted to the trades' school, where session lasts till about half past three. From there they pass on to the school of letters and receive instruction till 5 o'clock. After half an hour for supper, the prisoners retire to their rooms to rest, read or study, until their bedtime at half past nine.

The military organisation is a characteristic of the school. A citizen termed "colonel" commands what is known as the reformatory regiment, of which all the prisoners are members. The regiment is divided into four battalions of four companies each, and a citizen major is in command of each battalion and a citizen captain is in charge of each company. All officers below the rank of captain are inmates. The rank and file wear summer uniforms of khaki and winter uniforms of heavy cloth, the coats of black and the trousers grey. During military exercises, all the citizen officers carry swords. The regimental brass band is under the direction of a citizen instructor.

To teach the inmates the value of self-support, wages are given for work, and food and clothing are paid from it. For bad work, and misconduct, they are punished by fines, which are worked off by confinement, a day representing a fine of thirty-five cents. The third grade is really a reformatory within a reformatory, and thirty days of perfect demeanour entitles a third grade man to promotion, which means restoration to the general life and activity of the institution. Few remain over a month, as even the most hardened men try to get out of this humdrum place.

Corporal punishment is abolished. The objection to it was not so much that harm was done to the individual who suffered it, but that the rest of the population, never in a state of very stable equilibrium, were stirred up by it and kept in a state of unrest, rendering the development of relations of confidence and regard between them and officers of the institution difficult or impossible.

In its place the grade system was adopted, and the lowest grade contains the dregs of the population. The work given to the third-grade man is either scrubbing the floor, or darning socks all day, one inmate sitting behind another in a row. All the inmates are locked up separately in cells. To my thinking, very little reformatory work is done in this institution, which is for all practical purposes a junior jail.

I visited the Society for the Prevention of Cruelty to Children, and found it doing excellent work. The State recognises its good work, and contributes five thousand dollars a month towards its expenses. If the police charge a child below the age of sixteen, they are expected to telephone at once to the Society and inform them of the case, who, after obtaining full particulars, watch the proceedings. All children are housed by the Society till the case is disposed of by the probation judge. In the museum attached to the institution I found as exhibits, dirty feeding-bottles in cases of baby-farming, gambling boards, pistols, knives, thongs used by parents on their children, and a variety of other articles.

Probation courts did not impress me to any great extent. I sat next to the judge—who, by the way, is one of the ordinary circuit judges—and watched several cases for two hours. The court-room was crowded, and the judge sat on a raised daïs, in his magisterial robes. The child prisoner is brought up before him on a charge, say, of playing tip-cat in the streets. He is warned by the judge, and leaves the court feeling degraded for having played a game which every schoolboy indulges in. The irony of the proceeding was brought home to me when, on leaving the court, I found several boys playing the game just outside the precincts of the court. When all the paraphernalia of a court of justice is observed in a children's court, the good which such an institution has for its object is lost. The police, also, should exercise discrimination in the cases they bring up.

In one case a boy, for throwing stones, was fined one dollar; another, for using filthy language in a car was fined four dollars; a third, for using a revolver which went off and hurt another boy, was sent to a reformatory; a fourth, for going to the docks during the summer vacation and persisting in bathing, was put on parole till school reopened. Assault, setting fire to a cart, stabbing a boy in the thigh, and robbing dollars were the other cases tried in my presence.

The Catholic Protectory is a reformatory for Catholic boys. It numbers over two thousand inmates, a number too large to permit of it doing very much good. I noticed that the bond between master and pupil was of the feeblest kind. If a boy behaved well, he was sent back to his home and put on parole. He could be recalled, however, at any time for misconduct. The Lincolndale Agricultural School, which is a branch, is doing better work. There are dormitories for twenty-five and fifty boys, and small tables are arranged in the dining-room for them to sit at during their meals. A sitting-room is also provided for the boys. The pupils being small in number, are under better control. The dairy is a model one from point of construction and sanitation. Corn is grown on the farm, also potatoes. A fair crop of hay is always harvested, and alfalfa grass is also grown.

Every boy has a vegetable plot of his own to cultivate, and in addition contributes to the work in the general garden. The object of the school is to turn out trained dairymen, gardeners and agriculturists.

The Orphan Asylum Society. The building and grounds are located on the left bank of the Hudson. The buildings comprise eleven cottages, an administration and school building, hospital, laundry and stable. A crib, 50 by 150 feet, along the river front, affords an excellent opportunity for bathing and swimming. The ideal which the managers strive to realise is—first, a complete and natural home; and second, a complete school. The Orphanage plant, the material equipment of the home and all the necessary industries and interests involved in its maintenance are made to function in as large a measure as possible in the education and training of its wards. Gardening, poultry raising, tree planting, the stable, the apiary, the piggery, rabbitry and duck-pond, the orchard and meadow, the kitchen, sewing-room, laundry, supply store, all contribute to the correlation of school-work and home experience, which vitalises and makes concrete the usual dull abstract work of general instruction. The earning, saving, spending and giving of money, of which the children have experience, involve constant moral responsibility.

I had a talk with Professor Boas, the American anthropologist, and he affirmed that crime was not hereditary, but that certain pathological conditions of the mind were so, and these may produce a criminal, and he became one for want of self-control.

"The Children's Village" is a reformatory on the cottage system. About twenty children are housed in a cottage, and are looked after by a married couple. For good conduct the inmates receive one cent. a day. There is no corporal punshment, and solitary confinement takes its place. This I consider a defect. A boy must earn four and a half dollars before he can be discharged, and this amount represents a period of eighteen months, which is the minimum period of detention.

"The Parental School" is similar in character, except that it is intended for truant boys, who can be detained only for six months. They must be under sixteen years of age, and are committed by the superintendent of the city schools. The boys wear a uniform, and to deprive a boy of his uniform is considered one form of punishment. Detention in a room for two or more weeks takes the place of corporal punishment. The school has a good band, and I witnessed the ceremony of lowering the flag, which takes place daily at sunset. The boys are drawn up in a square, salute as the flag is lowered, and sing their National Anthem.

"The House of Refuge" was the first reformatory. Juveniles are sent to the school as a last resort, before recourse is had to detention in the State reformatory at Elmira. It is usual to assign boys when they first enter the institution to some of the domestic departments. After four of five months in such departments, they are given the opportunity to take up industrial work. The fourth division is the solitary confinement division for boys who misbehave themselves. They toe the line, and do extension motion silently the whole day. All cases are tried by disciplinarians called "colonels," who are also instructors of military drill. The boys are in uniform. All boys are discharged at twenty-one. After seventy-eight weeks of good behaviour a boy is discharged on parole, and it is possible for a lad to be discharged in fifteen and a half months, which I consider too short a period for a training which will fit him to earn a livelihood, or even for any effective teaching.

The committee consider each month the cases of all boys eligible for parole. Notice in writing is previously sent to the boys' parents, who are asked to appear personally before the committee. The parole is granted if he is provided with a proper home and suitable employment. After the release of a boy on parole, the parole officers keep in touch with him, and the boy submits a monthly report, endorsed by his parents or employers, to the superintendent. All boys on parole are encouraged to consult the superintendent at any time upon any matter affecting their welfare.

Among other institutions, I visited a Boys' Hostel and a Boys' Club. In the former, a clean bed and good, wholesome food may be obtained for a nominal charge. The payment of one cent. entitles a boy to admission to the club, and on the ground floor provision is made for a few games. As soon as the superintendent notices a group of big boys among the children, he questions them as to whether they would like to form a club among themselves. These boys pay ten cents a month, and enjoy greater privileges, and in like manner the biggest boys form a club, and billiards, theatricals, etc., are added to the list of amusements.

The establishment of "The Little Commonwealth" in Dorchester, England, on a farm given rent free by the Earl of Sandwich, points to a recognition of the success of what are called "the junior republics" established for young delinquents in America. While the latter set out to reproduce as far as possible the democratic system in use in the outside world of their own land, the Commonwealth adopts a more direct and primitive method of government by the whole group, as is found in the history of village communities where the virtues and faults of each member are familiar to the group.

To get rid of the ill effects of institutional care, cottage homes are established. But the Commonwealth families are real families. Children of different ages and both sexes live in a relationship involving the normal responsibilities of the older for the younger.

As self government presupposes self respect, and self respect cannot be attained without self support, the citizen has the same problems of securing employment as in the outside world.

The relation between the citizen government and the committee are as follows :—The committee provides fully equipped houses and lets them out, and the proprietorship of the various departments employing citizen labour are in their hands under the executive control of the Superintendent, and are conducted strictly as business enterprises. The citizens have nothing to do with the administration of the same except as employees.

Some authority is always necessary in human society, and in the Commonwealth that authority is vested in public opinion, which expresses itself at the meetings, judicial and legislative, of the whole group of citizens, including as equal units the Superintendent and the staff. The undoubted disapproval of the wrong-doer by public sentiment is in itself the chief punishment of the violator of the law. Not only does the community conduct its affairs without a jail, but each citizen is made so responsible to the laws that there is no necessity for maintaining public supervision, as every citizen is a peace officer. In the court of justice, his honour the Judge is one of the boys (or girls) selected by popular election every six months. He enjoys no special privileges, but is merely the person appointed by the citizens to preside and to pass sentence—with the proviso that if his sentence outrages the sense of the community, it may be set aside.

Boys and girls live together, but the boys sleep on the one side of the house and the girls on the other, and therefore the sex problem disappears, for the girls keep the boys very much in their place. The idea is that if you minimise the romance and mystery of sex by allowing intimate social and economic relationship on a basis of full social and economic quality, personal defects are uncovered and the usual sexual ideal is shattered.

The Commonwealth has developed indications that the genius of delinquent children in destruction of social welfare is proof of the existence of a corresponding genius for constructive purposes, and that this perversion may be redirected into its proper course by means of environment that will awaken the social consciousness and stimulate the natural virtues.

Whatever has been accomplished in the direction of prosocial ability in the institution is the product of the inmates' own nature, and not the result of some personal influence exerted from without.

GLOSSARY OF INDIAN TERMS AND WORDS

Anna	An Indian coin worth one penny.
Baddha Sahib	Great master.
Bandy	Cart.
Chappati	A small cake.
Chapper	Wandering.
Chit	A note.
Choultry	A rest house.
Conjee	Gruel.
Dhal, or Dal	Lentils.
Dhobi	Washerman.
Dorai, or Dorey	Europeans.
Gingalli	An oil seed.
Goparum	Facade.
Jagir	Freehold estate.
Jutka	Two-wheeled pony cart.
K.D.	An old offender.
Kala-azar	A deadly fever.
Kolatam	An Indian dance.
Kulam	A tank.
Kutcheri	Courthouse.
Maistry	Foreman.
Mammoti	A hand spade.
Mandapam	Hall.
Mirasidar	Hereditary landholder.
Monsoon	The rainy season.
Naicks	Princes.
Namam	Caste mark on the forehead.
Pagoda	A coin worth about six shillings.
Palanquin	A sedan couch.
Panchama	The fifth caste.
Peon	Office attendant.
Pial	Verandah.
Pice	A coin worth one halfpenny.
Plantain	The banana.
Puja	Sacrifice.
Puthar	A test word.
Ragi	Edible grain resembling mustard seed.
Salaam	A salutation.
Shastras	Indian sacred books.
Shikari	Indian sportsman.
Taluq	A subdivision of a district.
Tiffin	Lunch.
Totem	Emblem of a clan.

INDEX

INDEX

INDEX

INDEX